Rejoice In
CHRIST

DAILY INSPIRATION FROM THE BOOK OF MORMON

Rejoice In CHRIST

DAILY INSPIRATION FROM THE BOOK OF MORMON

ED J. PINEGAR & RICHARD J. ALLEN

Covenant Communications, Inc.

Cover image: *Shepherd's Lane* and *You Are Not Forgotten* by Jon McNaughton ©
McNaughton Fine Art Co. For print information go to www.mcnaughtonart.com

Cover design copyrighted 2007 by Covenant Communications, Inc.
Cover designed by: Christina Ashby

Published by Covenant Communications, Inc.
American Fork, Utah

Printed in Canada
First Printing: October 2007

13 12 11 10 09 08 07   10 9 8 7 6 5 4 3 2 1

ISBN 10: 1-59811-454-9
ISBN 13: 978-1-59811-454-6

Preface

We are commanded to live by God's words: "And I now give unto you a commandment to beware concerning yourselves, to give diligent heed to the words of eternal life. For you shall live by every word that proceedeth forth from the mouth of God" (D&C 84:43–44).

The love of God is shown through His Son Jesus Christ, who is in fact "The Word" (Revelation 19:13; see also John 1:1). The actual words we receive from our Savior were and are given that we may, through obedience, gain eternal life through Christ's Atonement (see 2 Nephi 25:23, 25). His words become our Liahona for life (see Alma 37:38–44). We should liken His words to our lives (see 1 Nephi 19:23) and nourish them with faith, diligence, and patience (see Alma 32:40–43). As we heed them, we will be pointed in a straight course to eternal life (see Alma 37:44).

The word of God is given through revelation by the power of the Holy Ghost (see 2 Nephi 32:3; D&C 68:3–7) to His servants the prophets (see Amos 3:7; D&C 43:2).

As we search the scriptures or listen to our living prophets, we should seek to understand their words and put them into practice in our lives, allowing them to sink into our souls and change us. This becomes the essence of scripture study and of learning from our leaders: We must take the word of God into our souls. Then, by yielding our hearts unto God, we will become sanctified. This process of purification is part of the mighty change—being born again—that causes us to become the sons and daughters of God (see Mosiah 5:7; 27:25).

In this little book of daily inspiration, you will find on each page

- ฿ A scripture with an identifiable principle or practice,
- ฿ A quote from a General Authority or noteworthy person that magnifies or brings a better understanding to the process of applying the principle or practice to our daily living, and
- ฿ A list of ideas for Daily Living—either for personal application or further study.

We hope you will feel the Spirit of this work and find joy in living the word of God.

The Authors

JANUARY
❦

Rejoice, O my heart, and cry unto the
Lord, and say: O Lord, I will praise
thee forever; yea, my soul will rejoice
in thee, my God, and the rock of my
salvation.

—2 NEPHI 4:30

ANOTHER TESTAMENT OF JESUS CHRIST

Which is to show unto the remnant of the House of Israel what great things the Lord hath done for their fathers; . . . to the convincing of the Jew and Gentile that JESUS is the CHRIST, the ETERNAL GOD, manifesting himself unto all nations.
FROM MORONI'S TITLE PAGE TO THE BOOK OF MORMON

I told the brethren that the Book of Mormon was the most correct of any book on earth, and the keystone of our religion, and a man would get nearer to God by abiding by its precepts, than by any other book.

(Joseph Smith, *History of The Church of Jesus Christ of Latter-day Saints,* 4:461)

Note: Of the 6607 verses in the Book of Mormon, 3925 refer to the Savior—a reference every 1.7 verses.

Daily Living

LEARN TO LOVE THE BOOK OF MORMON AND THE WORD OF GOD.

- ଚ As you read and study the Book of Mormon, recognize and remember that salvation is only through and because of the Savior Jesus Christ and His Atonement (see 2 Ne. 9).

- ଚ Remember that life eternal is to know Heavenly Father and Jesus Christ (see John 17:3), and we come to know them and get closer to Them through the Book of Mormon.

- ଚ Plan to study of the Book of Mormon daily—only five pages a day and you can read the Book of Mormon three times a year.

PARENTING

*Therefore I was taught somewhat in all the learning
of my father.*
1 NEPHI 1:1

Fathers and mothers are needed who will rise and stand upon their
feet to make of their homes sanctuaries in which children will grow
in a spirit of obedience, industry, and fidelity to tested standards of
conduct. If our society is coming apart at the seams, it is because the
tailor and the seamstress in the home are not producing the kind of
stitching that will hold under stress. In the name of giving advan-
tages, we have too often bartered away the real opportunities of our
children.

(Gordon B. Hinckley, *Be Thou an Example*
[Salt Lake City: Deseret Book, 1981], 18)

Daily Living
QUESTIONS OF CONSCIENCE FOR PARENTS

- ಲ Do you counsel together as husband and wife in regard to your
  marriage and family?

- ಲ Do you have a plan to teach your children?

- ಲ Is family home evening a major priority?

- ಲ Do you know the special needs of each individual child?

- ಲ Do you organize every needful thing—scripture time, family
  prayer, family counsel, individual family visits with the children?

- ಲ Simply remember that your greatest work and success will be in
  the home!

THE LORD PROVIDES

I know that the Lord giveth no commandments unto the children of men, save he shall prepare a way for them that they may accomplish the thing which he commandeth them.

1 NEPHI 3:7

We all have confidence that when we have fully prepared ourselves, the Lord will provide a way for us to take the gospel to those lands now closed to our missionaries. President Spencer W. Kimball has said, "Somehow, brethren, I feel that when we have done all in our power that the Lord will find a way to open doors. That is my faith." We all share this faith.

(Ezra Taft Benson, *The Teachings of Ezra Taft Benson*
[Salt Lake City: Bookcraft, 1988], 185)

Daily Living

REMEMBER THAT THE LORD IS IN CHARGE

- ஐ Trust in the Lord—Proverb 3:5–6

- ஐ Your strength is in the Lord—Alma 26:12

- ஐ All things are possible with the Lord—Mark 9:23

- ஐ As you keep the commandments you will be nourished and strengthened by the Lord and He will provide means whereby you accomplish all things—1 Nephi 17:3

BE LED BY THE SPIRIT

*And I was led by the Spirit, not knowing beforehand the things
which I should do.*
1 NEPHI 4:6

Nephi went forth determined to do the Lord's will, even though he
did not know exactly how to do it. Right after that, the Lord began
to reveal to Nephi almost exactly what should be done. And, finally,
he was able to obtain the plates. . . .

You are in the same position as Nephi was. As you go forward in
faith, the Lord will reveal his will to you so that you will know what
you should do. I have been greatly moved to see the amount of revelation that the Lord has poured out upon the members of his
church about how to do his work and solve their problems, just as
Nephi had revelation poured out upon him.

(Gene R. Cook, *Living by the Power of Faith*
[Salt Lake City: Deseret Book, 1985], 51)

Daily Living
SEEK TO LIVE BY THE SPIRIT.

- ಳ Pray for the Spirit—3 Nephi 19:9

- ಳ Faith: Increased faith brings the Spirit—1 Nephi 10:17

- ಳ Love: The Spirit bestowed upon those who love the Lord—
D&C 76:116

- ಳ Obedience: By keeping the commandments you can always
have the Spirit to be with you—D&C 20:77

THE PROPHETS' WORDS

*For the fulness of mine intent is that I may persuade men to
come unto . . . God . . . and be saved. . . .
[I write] the things which are pleasing unto God and unto
those who are not of the world.*
1 NEPHI 6:4–5

John, who bore testimony of Jesus, did so for one reason and one
reason only: he was seeking to persuade men to believe in Christ, to
come unto him, to accept him as the Son of God, and to be saved
by obedience to the laws and ordinances of his gospel.

(Bruce R. McConkie, *The Mortal Messiah:
From Bethlehem to Calvary* [Salt Lake City:
Deseret Book, 1979–1981], 1:438)

Daily Living

HEARKEN TO THE WORDS OF THE LIVING PROPHETS.

- ❧ Remember the word of God comes to you through the
  prophets of God.

- ❧ The word of God tells us all things to do—2 Nephi 32:3

- ❧ You must live by every word that proceedeth from the mouth
  of God—D&C 84:43–46

- ❧ You are blessed when you heed the words of the prophets—
  3 Nephi 12:2; 28:34–35

PRAY FOR STRENGTH

*O Lord, according to my faith which is in thee . . . give me
strength that I may burst these bands. . . .
When I had said these words, behold, the bands were loosed
from off my hands and feet.*
1 Nephi 7:17–18

Let us pray for health and strength and wisdom. Pray for faith to
carry on when our strength seems insufficient, and the answer is
delayed. Let our prayers go out as well as upward. We must work as
well as pray. Let us pray for peace and concord, in our hearts, our
homes, and country. . . . Prayer will rid our hearts of hatred; it will
chasten our ambitions; until with love of God and neighbors we
shall keep his two commandments. Let us pray.

(Hugh B. Brown, *Eternal Quest* [Salt Lake City:
Bookcraft, 1956], 81)

Daily Living

Increase your strength through prayer.

- Pray with faith—Mosiah 27:14
- Pray for forgiveness—Enos 1:4
- Pray to know the truth—Alma 5:46
- Pray to overcome temptation—3 Nephi 18:18
- Pray and fast to be strong in humility and firm in your faith—Helaman 3:35
- Pray to have charity—Moroni 7:47–48

HAPPINESS

*And it came to pass that I beheld a tree, whose fruit was
desirable to make one happy.*
1 NEPHI 8:10

Whence come the glorious feelings that you have when you feel the
best? Do they come from the outside? Do external circumstances
produce real happiness of the kind that I describe? Doubtless, they
contribute to happiness; but the purest joy . . . proceeds from within. A man must carry the principles of happiness and the love of
God in his own breast, or he will not be happy. It is not true enjoy-
ment when it comes from any other source. . . . Deity is within us,
and its development brings happiness and joy inexpressible.

(George Q. Cannon, *Gospel Truth: Discourses and Writings
of President George Q. Cannon,* sel. Jerreld L. Newquist
[Salt Lake City: Deseret Book, 1987], 78)

Daily Living
THE PURSUIT OF HAPPINESS

- ✌ You should repent and seek to live after the manner of happiness—Alma 27:18

- ✌ You can only be happy as you partake of the love of God and
come unto Christ—1 Nephi 8:10; 4 Nephi 1:15–16

- ✌ When you keep the commandments you can be happy—
Mosiah 2:41

- ✌ Happiness is not in position, possession, station, or title. It's in
living the gospel.

- ✌ If you value the things of the world you will always have trouble
being satisfied.

OUR FALLEN STATE

Wherefore, all mankind were in a lost and in a fallen state, and ever would be save they should rely on this Redeemer.
1 NEPHI 10:6

Man cannot be induced to reach up and acquire the goodness of God unless he realizes that in mortality he is in a fallen state and that he must rely upon Christ for mercy, truth, and power.

(Hyrum L. Andrus, *Principles of Perfection* [Salt Lake City: Bookcraft, 1970], 108)

Man must learn to rely upon Christ, for it is only in and through Christ that he can come unto the Father and be glorified. By experiencing the effects of mortal weakness and corruption in his flesh, man learns to rely upon Christ in order that he might receive of His grace and power unto redemption.

(Hyrum L. Andrus, *Doctrinal Commentary on the Pearl of Great Price* [Salt Lake City: Deseret Book, 1967], 248)

Daily Living

MORTALS CAN BECOME SAINTS THROUGH THE ATONEMENT.

- ᔥ Faithfully repent and apply the Atonement to your life—Alma 22:14; 34:15–17

- ᔥ Yield to the enticings of the Holy Spirit—Mosiah 3:19

- ᔥ Mortality is a time to prepare to meet God—Alma 34:32

PONDER

I had desired to know the things that my father had seen, and
believing that the Lord was able to make them known unto me,
as I sat pondering in mine heart I was caught away in the
Spirit of the Lord.
1 NEPHI 11:1

President [Joseph F.] Smith said, "As I pondered over these things
which are written [1 Peter 3–4], the eyes of my understanding were
opened, and the Spirit of the Lord rested upon me, and I saw the
hosts of the dead, both small and great" (D&C 138:11).

Such experiences are patterns that show us there is understanding
and new knowledge to be gained when we search, pray, ponder,
and . . . hear the voice of the Lord through his Spirit. In this way
we come to know not only the doctrines of the gospel and the will
of the Lord.

(Larry C. Porter and Susan Easton Black, eds., *The Prophet*
Joseph: Essays on the Life and Mission of Joseph Smith [Salt
Lake City: Deseret Book, 1988], 183)

Daily Living

TAKE TIME TO MEDITATE AND PONDER ON THE THINGS OF THE LORD.

- ༄ Take time to meditate and ponder on your eternal roles as children of God.

- ༄ Meditate and ponder on your values, standards, and goals in life.

- ༄ Meditate and ponder on the teachings of our Savior and prophets—3 Nephi 17:3

- ༄ Meditate and ponder on the goodness of God—Moroni 10:3

PRAY FOR UNDERSTANDING

If ye will not harden your hearts, and ask me in faith, believing that ye shall receive, with diligence in keeping my commandments, surely these things shall be made known unto you.
1 NEPHI 15:11

We have also inherited the Book of Mormon. If we live according to the principles taught in this inspired record, we will find happiness, strength, and exaltation. It was written for our day and for our problems. It addresses the challenges we face in today's world and will give us additional power to combat the adversary only if we will study and pray to understand its teachings and live by them.

(Joseph B. Wirthlin, *Finding Peace in Our Lives*
[Salt Lake City: Deseret Book, 1995], 140)

Daily Living
PRAY TO UNDERSTAND THE THINGS OF GOD.

- ℘ Pray to trust in the Lord and lean not to your own understanding—Proverb 3:5–6

- ℘ Pray for the Spirit through which you can understand the things of God—D&C 76:12

- ℘ Pray to nurture the word which will enlighten your understanding—Alma 32:28

- ℘ As you understand the things of God you will want to keep the law—Psalm 119:34

HEARKEN TO THE WORD OF GOD

Whoso would hearken unto the word of God, and would hold fast unto it, they would never perish; neither could the temptations and the fiery darts of the adversary overpower them unto blindness, to lead them away to destruction.

1 NEPHI 15:24

There is a power in the book which will begin to flow into your lives the moment you begin a serious study of the book. You will find greater power to resist temptation. You will find the power to avoid deception. You will find the power to stay on the strait and narrow path. The scriptures are called "the words of life" (D&C 84:85), and nowhere is that more true than it is of the Book of Mormon. When you begin to hunger and thirst after those words, you will find life in greater and greater abundance.

(Ezra Taft Benson, "The Book of Mormon—Keystone of Our Religion," *Ensign,* November 1986, 5)

Daily Living

HEED THE WORD OF GOD AND YOU WILL BE STRENGTHENED AND PROTECTED.

- ○ The word of God has the power to change souls—Alma 31:5
- ○ The word of God will tell you all things to do—2 Nephi 32:3
- ○ The word of God will lead you on the strait and narrow course—Helaman 3:29
- ○ Exhort all to heed the word of God—1 Nephi 15:25
- ○ Make a plan to search the scriptures and apply them to your life.

RECEIVE DIRECTION FROM THE LORD

And it came to pass that I, Nephi, beheld the pointers which were in the ball, that they did work according to the faith and diligence and heed which we did give unto them.
1 NEPHI 16:28

Now, the Lord has revealed unto us in these modern scriptures as well as in the scriptures that were given in ancient times, the necessary articles and covenants by which we may be guided and directed in church government and understand the truth of the gospel. Through the faith, diligence and heed we give to these instructions, we may know that the Lord and Savior of this world is indeed our Redeemer and the Son of God. We may know this provided our studies and faithfulness are guided by prayer, for in this same commandment, the Lord declared that we should pray always. "Wherefore," said he, "be faithful, praying always, having your lamps trimmed and burning, and oil with you."

(Joseph F. Smith Jr., Conference Report, October 1918, 54)

Daily Living

RECEIVE DIRECTION FROM THE LORD THROUGH HIS WORD AND BY THE SPIRIT.

- Counsel with the Lord and he will direct you—Alma 37:37
- Give heed to the word which will point you in a straight course—Alma 37:44
- The Spirit will show you all things to do—2 Nephi 32:5
- The Spirit will lead you if you're worthy—1 Nephi 4:6
- The Lord will lead you through your afflictions—2 Nephi 4:20

POWER OF THE HOLY GHOST

The things which he spake by the power of the Holy Ghost,
which power he received by faith on the Son of God.
1 NEPHI 10:17

This spiritual confirmation by the power of the Holy Ghost is given on the Lord's conditions to anyone who is willing to ask in faith, believing that an answer can come by that power. It starts by listening to the voice of the Lord, His servants, His prophets and apostles, and it continues by giving heed to their words. Spiritual knowledge of the Restoration is a matter of faith.

(Charles Didier, "Man's Search for Divine Truth,"
Ensign, November 2005, 49)

Daily Living

SEEK THE GIFT AND POWER OF THE HOLY GHOST IN YOUR LIFE.

- ଔ Be born of God and be filled with the Holy Ghost—Alma 36:24

- ଔ Be sanctified by the Holy Ghost—3 Nephi 27:20

- ଔ The Holy Ghost filleth you with hope and perfect love—Moroni 8:26

- ଔ Seek the gifts of the Spirit—Moroni 10:8–25; D&C 46:7–33

GOODNESS OF GOD

The commandments of God must be fulfilled. And if it so be that the children of men keep the commandments of God he doth nourish them, and strengthen them, and provide means whereby they can accomplish the thing which he has commanded them.

1 NEPHI 17:3

And if we will do His will and keep His commandments, He will provide for us; and we may yet learn, in the midst of all our reasoning and argument, that God has never yet desired us to live after the manner of the world. It is for us to keep His commandments and He will provide for His children. He will provide for His servants. Brethren and sisters, you will see the servants of God will have joy at heart; but the enemies of righteousness will have sorrow.

(Orson Hyde, in *Journal of Discourses* [London: Latter-day Saints' Book Depot, 1854–1886], 13:182)

Daily Living

BY KEEPING THE COMMANDMENTS THE LORD WILL BLESS AND PROSPER YOU.

- ಳಿ You can enjoy happiness by keeping the commandments—Mosiah 2:41

- ಳಿ You are blessed and prospered by keeping the commandments—Mosiah 2:22

- ಳಿ If you truly love the Lord you will keep the commandments—John 14:15

- ಳಿ The Lord will provide a way for you to keep the commandments—1 Nephi 3:7

- ಳಿ What commandments are you forgetting or failing to keep?

HARDENED HEARTS

Ye are swift to do iniquity but slow to remember the Lord your God. Ye have seen an angel, and he spake unto you; yea, ye have heard his voice from time to time; and he hath spoken unto you in a still small voice, but ye were past feeling, that ye could not feel his words.

1 NEPHI 17:45

When the Lord promises to soften hearts, it is indicative of his making them pliable and receptive to the message he intends them to receive (D&C 104:80–81; 105:27; 124:9). The righteous have soft and receptive hearts for things of the Spirit while the hearts of the wicked are hardened and are difficult to penetrate with spiritual truths and promptings.

(Hoyt W. Brewster Jr., *Doctrine and Covenants Encyclopedia* [Salt Lake City: Bookcraft, 1988], 539)

Daily Living

HOW CAN YOU KEEP OUR HEART SOFTENED AND EASILY ENTREATED?

- ଚଓ If you turn to the Lord He will soften your heart—1 Nephi 2:16

- ଚଓ Offer your sacrifice of a broken heart and contrite spirit—3 Nephi 9:20

- ଚଓ Experience the mighty change—Alma 5:14

- ଚଓ As you purify yourself and become the elect of God—D&C 29:7

LIKEN THE SCRIPTURES TO OUR LIVES

For I did liken all scriptures unto us, that it might be for our profit and learning.
1 NEPHI 19:23

How do we come to experience and believe that "the words of Christ . . . will tell [us] all things what [we] should do"? (2 Nephi 32:3.) Alma taught that [the words of Christ] had a "more power-ful effect upon the minds of the people than the sword or anything else." . . . If the "word" can have such a powerful effect in our lives, . . . how do we liken the scriptures to our lives and apply their messages to help us with our battles?

(Carolyn J. Rasmus, *In the Strength of the Lord I Can Do All Things* [Salt Lake City: Deseret Book, 1990], 18–19)

Daily Living

APPLY THE SCRIPTURES AND THE WORDS OF OUR PROPHETS TO OUR DAILY LIVES.

A method to apply the word of God might be stated in simple steps:

- Read the scriptures carefully.

- Ponder them as they relate to you.

- Write down each scripture reference and its main idea.

- Write a personal statement as to how you are going to live this scripture. Use "I will," "I must," "I shall," "I can." These first-person commitment statements will make the scriptures live in your life. This is the overall purpose of this book.

OPPOSITION IN ALL THINGS

For it must needs be, that there is an opposition in all things. If not so . . . righteousness could not be brought to pass, neither wickedness, neither holiness nor misery, neither good nor bad. Wherefore, all things must needs be a compound in one.

2 NEPHI 2:11

We are considering a basic perspective on all negative human experience, including adversity and inadequacy, miscalculations and carelessness, along with deliberate and willful transgression. All are part of opposition and mortality, and all can be the source of growth and development, depending upon our response to them.

(Bruce C. Hafen, *The Broken Heart: Applying the Atonement to Life's Experiences* [Salt Lake City: Deseret Book, 1989], 139)

Daily Living

LEARN TO OVERCOME OPPOSITION AND GROW FROM THESE EXPERIENCES.

- ৪০ You are free to choose good or evil; you are accountable—2 Nephi 2:27

- ৪০ You receive a witness after the trial of your faith—Ether 12:6

- ৪০ Recognize that you must be tempted as part of the test—D&C 29:39

- ৪০ Hold to the iron rod, the word of God—1 Nephi 15:24

- ৪০ Pray to overcome temptation—3 Nephi 18:18

- ৪০ Learn to be wise—Mormon 9:28

AGENCY AND CHOICE

Wherefore, the Lord God gave unto man that he should act for himself. Wherefore, man could not act for himself save it should be that he was enticed by the one or the other.

2 NEPHI 2:16

We can live our lives with "I should" and "I ought" rather than "I want," but that does not exemplify a use of agency. We are taught in the gospel of Jesus Christ that to achieve godhood and become like our Father and Mother in Heaven means to grow in righteousness to the point that our desires and actions have become aligned with Theirs, that we do what we do, not because we have to or because we are commanded to, but because we want to, because that is our choice! That ideal state cannot be reached without our exercising agency.

(Ida Smith, *As Women of Faith: Talks Selected from the BYU Women's Conferences* [Salt Lake City: Deseret Book, 1989], 214)

Daily Living

LEARN TO USE YOUR AGENCY AND MAKE RIGHTEOUS CHOICES.

   ❧   You are free to act for yourself—2 Nephi 10:23

   ❧   You are free to choose good or evil; you are accountable—2 Nephi 2:27

   ❧   Seek the will of the Father—Matthew 26:39

   ❧   Choose whom you will serve—Alma 30:8

   ❧   You have been given the way to judge—Moroni 7:15–17

   ❧   The Spirit will tell you all things to do—2 Nephi 32:5

MORTALITY, A TESTING TIME

*Their state became a state of probation, and their time was
lengthened, according to the commandments which the Lord
God gave unto the children of men. For he gave commandment
that all men must repent.*

2 NEPHI 2:21

Earth life is a unique time of testing. We are tested in mortality to determine the nature of our character. Our character is seen in the attitudes we develop, the thoughts we have, the priorities we establish, the words we utter, the habits we form, and the actions we perform. (See Alma 12:13–14; Rev. 3:21.) Life is a probationary period; we show whether we obey God and overcome evil, or we follow Satan and oppose righteousness. (See D&C 98:14–15.) The intent of our hearts is examined to see why we speak and act as we do. All of us are continually being so tested.

(Victor L. Ludlow, *Principles and Practices of the Restored
Gospel* [Salt Lake City: Deseret Book, 1992], 171–172)

Daily Living

TAKING THE TEST OF LIFE . . . PREPARE TO MEET GOD.

ဢ   You must prove yourself to God—Abraham 3:25

ဢ   This is the time to prepare to meet God—Alma 34:32

ဢ   You will be proved in all things—D&C 98:14

FREE TO CHOOSE

Wherefore, men are free according to the flesh. . . . And they are free to choose liberty and eternal life, through the great Mediator of all men, or to choose captivity and death, according to the captivity and power of the devil; for he seeketh that all men might be miserable like unto himself.
2 NEPHI 2:27

Free agency, or the privilege of choosing your course in life, has been given to every one of you as a divine right. You are "free to choose liberty and eternal life [by putting into practice in your lives the teachings of the Gospel] or to choose captivity and death according to the captivity and power of the devil" by your disregard of the laws of the Gospel and your failure to live according to Gospel standards.
(Harold B. Lee, *Decisions for Successful Living* [Salt Lake City: Deseret Book, 1973], 83)

Daily Living

MAKE RIGHTEOUS CHOICES . . . YOUR DECISIONS DETERMINE YOUR DESTINY.

- ᔉ You could not act save you were enticed—2 Nephi 2:16

- ᔉ If you yield to the devil you will make bad decisions—2 Nephi 26:10

- ᔉ Yield to the enticings of the Holy Spirit and become a saint—Mosiah 3:19

- ᔉ Study it out in your mind; ask the Lord for confirmation—D&C 9:7–9

- ᔉ You reap what you sow—Galatians 6:7

PSALM OF NEPHI . . . THE PLIGHT OF OUR EARTHLY EXISTENCE

O wretched man that I am! Yea, my heart sorroweth because
of my flesh; my soul grieveth because of mine iniquities. . . .
O Lord, wilt thou encircle me around in the robe of
thy righteousness! . . .
O Lord, I have trusted in thee, and I will trust in thee forever. . . .
Yea, I know that God will give liberally to him that asketh
2 NEPHI 4:17, 33–35

To trust in the Lord means to follow true principles and to leave the outcome in his hands. To trust in the arm of flesh is an attempt to manipulate the forces of life so as to get the outcome you desire, whether that is the Lord's desire or not. You do not always know what is best for you. God does. Trust in him. Have a believing attitude, regardless of what others might think or say. God is a God of truth and integrity . . . and he will never let you down.

(Stephen R. Covey, *Spiritual Roots of Human Relations,*
2nd ed. [Salt Lake City: Deseret Book, 1993], 303)

Daily Living
TRUST IN THE LORD IN ALL THINGS.

- ଚ Trust in the Lord forever—2 Nephi 4:34

- ଚ Trust in the Lord and ye shall be lifted up at the last day—Mosiah 23:22

- ଚ Trust in the Lord and ye shall receive mercy—Mosiah 29:20

- ଚ Trust in the Lord and He shall deliver us—Alma 61:13

- ଚ Trust in the Lord and he shall bless and prosper you—Helaman 12:1

ATONEMENT EMPOWERS THE RESURRECTION

Wherefore, it must needs be an infinite atonement—save it should be an infinite atonement this corruption could not put on incorruption.

2 NEPHI 9:7

The word Savior and the thought of the Atonement stir such feelings of gratitude and awe that I can hardly express them, but whenever we sing "I Stand All Amazed," it rekindles those feelings. I love that hymn but am so touched by the words that I can hardly sing it for tears:

> That he should extend his great love unto such as I,
> Sufficient to own, to redeem, and to justify.
> Oh, it is wonderful that he should care for me
> Enough to die for me!
> Oh, it is wonderful, wonderful to me!
> (*Hymns*, no. 193.)

(Elaine L. Jack, *Eye to Eye, Heart to Heart*
[Salt Lake City: Deseret Book, 1992], 24–25)

Daily Living

GRATITUDE FOR THE ATONEMENT OF JESUS CHRIST
WILL CAUSE YOU TO CHANGE.

❧ You can be redeemed from hell and encircled in His arms of love—2 Nephi 1:15

❧ He took upon Himself all your pains and afflictions and will succor you—Alma 7:11–12

❧ His atonement brought to pass the resurrection—Alma 42:23

❧ You will be saved by His grace after all you can do—2 Nephi 25:23

HEAVENLY FATHER'S PLAN

O how great the plan of our God! For on the other hand, the paradise of God must deliver up the spirits of the righteous, and the grave deliver up the body of the righteous; and the spirit and the body is restored to itself again.

2 NEPHI 9:13

Our Heavenly Father has given us a plan for our happiness. That plan is His gospel, and it is in His Church. God's authority and power are here. When you follow that plan, you will be happy, you will be successful, and you will be exalted in the celestial kingdom with all your worthy loved ones. (London England Area Conference, 19–20 June 1976)

(Ezra Taft Benson, *The Teachings of Ezra Taft Benson*
[Salt Lake City: Bookcraft, 1988], 27)

Daily Living

HEAVENLY FATHER'S PLAN WILL BRING YOU HAPPINESS AS YOU KEEP THE
COMMANDMENTS.

- ๙ Salvation will come to all who exercise faith unto repentance—Alma 34:15

- ๙ Through the grace of God you are saved—2 Nephi 10:24

- ๙ You can enjoy never-ending happiness by keeping the commandments—Mosiah 2:41

- ๙ You must pursue happiness through repentance—Alma 27:18

- ๙ You can be happy by coming unto Christ and receiving the love of God—1 Nephi 11:21–23

- ๙ The blessings of happiness come from the love of God—4 Nephi 1:15–16

KNOWLEDGE OF OUR PAST

*Wherefore, we shall have a perfect knowledge of all our guilt,
and our uncleanness, and our nakedness; and the righteous shall
have a perfect knowledge of . . . their righteousness, being
clothed with purity, yea, even with the robe of righteousness.*
2 NEPHI 9:14

They will have a perfect knowledge of their foibles and guilt in the
flesh; and the righteous will have a perfect knowledge of their enjoy-
ment, and their righteousness, being clothed with purity, even with
the robe of righteousness. Men, having become immortal, must now
appear before the judgment-seat of the Holy One of Israel to be
judged according to the holy judgment of God. Those who are
righteous shall be righteous still, but those who are filthy—the devil
and his angels—shall go away into the torment prepared for them,
which shall be likened unto a "lake of fire and brimstone" ([2 Ne.]
9:15, 16; cf. Alma 34:35; Alma 40:13, 14; D&C 76:36–38).

(Sidney B. Sperry, *Book of Mormon Compendium*
[Salt Lake City: Bookcraft, 1968], 169)

Daily Living

YOU WILL REMEMBER YOUR PAST, EITHER THE GUILT OF SIN OR THE JOY OF
RIGHTEOUSNESS.

- ༂ Memories of a just life will bless you now and in the future—
  Proverb 10:6–7

- ༂ The memory of sins prior to repentance can torment the soul—
  Alma 36:13–14

- ༂ Repentance brings memories of joy—Alma 36:17–19

- ༂ Repent and the Lord remembers your sins no more—D&C
  58:42–43

- ༂ A goal to consider: Make memories of joy through righteousness.

MERCY OF GOD

O the greatness of the mercy of our God, the Holy One of Israel!
For he delivereth his saints from that awful monster the devil,
and death, and hell, and that lake of fire and brimstone, which
is endless torment.

2 NEPHI 9:19

The sacrifice of the Father's firstborn in the spirit, His Only Begotten Son in the flesh, was the sacrifice of a Creator—God. The Atoner was the Lord God Omnipotent, who created this and other planets (see D&C 76:24; Moses 1:33; Mosiah 3:5). Therefore, unlike any sacrifice a mortal could have made, Christ's was an infinite atonement made possible, declared King Benjamin, by the infinite goodness and mercy of God and by His willingness to see His Son suffer and be slain (see Mosiah 4:6; 2 Nephi 9:7; Alma 34:10, 12; Mosiah 5:3).

(Neal A. Maxwell, *Men and Women of Christ*
[Salt Lake City: Bookcraft, 1991], 34)

Daily Living

CONTINUALLY RECOGNIZE THE GOODNESS AND MERCY OF GOD.

- ౭ Ponder the mercy and goodness of God—Moroni 10:3

- ౭ God's mercy and grace is paramount in the plan of happiness—Alma 42:15, 23

- ౭ Seek the knowledge of the goodness and mercy of God—1 Nephi 1:1; Mosiah 4:5, 6, 11

- ౭ The goodness of God prepares for you a way to escape death and hell—2 Nephi 9:10

- ౭ You should encourage all to partake of the goodness of God—Jacob 1:7

KNOWLEDGE OF GOD

*O how great the holiness of our God! For he knoweth all things,
and there is not anything save he knows it.*
2 NEPHI 9:20

An understanding that God knows all things, and that there is nothing which he does not know, is essentially necessary for man to have in order to exercise faith and gain salvation. As the Prophet said: "Without the knowledge of all things God would not be able to save any portion of his creatures; for it is by reason of the knowledge which he has of all things . . . that enables him to give that understanding to his creatures by which they are made partakers of eternal life; and if it were not for the idea existing in the minds of men that God had all knowledge it would be impossible for them to exercise faith in him" (*Lectures on Faith,* 44). Not only does the Father know all things, but so likewise does the Son, and the Holy Ghost.

(Bruce R. McConkie, *Mormon Doctrine*
[Salt Lake City: Bookcraft, 1966], 425)

Daily Living

SEEK TO KNOW GOD AND RECOGNIZE THAT HE KNOWS ALL THINGS.

- ಬ Life eternal is to know God and Jesus Christ—John 17:3

- ಬ Your faith, trust and love of God increases because He knows all things—1 Nephi 9:6; 2 Nephi 2:24; Words of Mormon 1:7; Alma 18:32; 26:35; Helaman 9:41; Moroni 7:22

- ಬ You can know the truth of all things by the power of the Holy Ghost—Moroni 10:5

SAVIOR'S PURPOSE

*And he cometh into the world that he may save all men if they
will hearken unto his voice; for behold he suffereth . . . the pains
of every living creature . . . that the resurrection might pass
upon all men, that all might stand before him at the great and
judgment day.*

2 NEPHI 9:21–22

We do not prosper ourselves; we do not, as the humanist affirms,
pull ourselves up by our own bootstraps. It is true that we must work
and labor and strive to do our best. . . . But whenever we obtain
blessings, . . . it is because God Almighty has elected to give us those
blessings. . . . Those who acknowledge his hand in all things (see
D&C 59:21), who in gratitude and humility offer "credit where it
is due," tend to avoid the perils of the prosperity cycle.

(Joseph Fielding McConkie and Robert L. Millet, *Doctrinal
Commentary on the Book of Mormon* [Salt Lake City:
Bookcraft, 1987–1992], 4:200–201)

Daily Living

RECOGNIZE THE BLESSING OF YOUR SAVIOR'S ATONEMENT AND MAKE IT
EFFICACIOUS IN YOUR LIVES.

- ಐ You are saved by grace after all you can do—2 Nephi 25:23

- ಐ You must suffer even as the Lord if you do not repent—D&C
  19:15–19

- ಐ You are reconciled to God through the Atonement of Christ—
  Jacob 4:11

- ಐ The Lord came to bring redemption of mankind—3 Nephi 9:21

- ಐ You can be perfected only through Jesus Christ—Moroni
  10:32–33

REPENT

And he commandeth all men that they must repent, and be baptized in his name, having perfect faith in the Holy One of Israel, or they cannot be saved in the kingdom of God. And if they will not repent and believe in his name . . . they must be damned.

2 NEPHI 9:23–24

As long as we believe that we totally earn forgiveness, we will still feel guilty, because we will sense intuitively that we do not have the power to make ourselves completely whole. The Lord's forgiveness is ultimately an act of grace—it comes as his gift, not as something we have a "right" to, even though we must repent as a condition of receiving it.

(Bruce C. Hafen and Marie K. Hafen, *The Belonging Heart: The Atonement and Relationships with God and Family* [Salt Lake City: Deseret Book, 1994], 84)

Daily Living

REPENT AND COME UNTO YOUR SAVIOR JESUS CHRIST.

- ෨ The message preached throughout the Book of Mormon is to repent—Mosiah 18:19–20; Alma 37:33; Helaman 6:4; 13:2; 3 Nephi 7:23; Moroni 3:3

- ෨ You are an enemy to God if you do not repent—Mosiah 2:38

- ෨ You must repent and forsake your sins—Mosiah 4:10

- ෨ You must repent in order to be saved—Alma 5:31

- ෨ You must repent and be born again and be baptized—Alma 7:14; 3 Nephi 23:5

TO BE LEARNED IS GOOD

O the vainness, and the frailties, and the foolishness of men!
When they are learned they think they are wise, and they hearken
not unto the counsel of God, for they set it aside, supposing they
know of themselves, wherefore, their wisdom is foolishness and it
profiteth them not. And they shall perish. But to be learned is
good if they hearken unto the counsels of God.

2 NEPHI 9:28–29

It will be necessary for the Saints to hearken to counsel . . . and lay aside every selfish principle, everything low and groveling; and stand forward in the cause of truth. . . . Like those who held up the hands of Moses, so let us hold up the hands of those who are appointed to direct the affairs of the Kingdom . . . and be instrumental in effecting the great work of the last days.

(Joseph Smith, *History of The Church of Jesus Christ of*
Latter-day Saints, 2nd ed. rev. [Salt Lake City: The Church
of Jesus Christ of Latter-day Saints, 1970–1976], 4:186)

Daily Living

REMEMBER, THE LEARNING OF MAN CANNOT SAVE YOU.

- ∞ Beware of pride from the learning of man—2 Nephi 9:42; 2 Nephi 26:20

- ∞ Learn wisdom in your youth—Alma 37:35

- ∞ Learn from the Lord Jesus Christ—D&C 19:23

- ∞ Seek learning by study and faith—D&C 88:118

- ∞ The knowledge you gain in this life will rise with you—D&C 130:18

- ∞ It is impossible to be saved in ignorance—D&C 131:6

RICHES AS TO THE THINGS OF THE WORLD

*But wo unto the rich, who are rich as to the things of the world.
For because they are rich they despise the poor, and they persecute
the meek, and their hearts are upon their treasures; wherefore,
their treasure is their god. And behold, their treasure shall perish
with them also.*
2 NEPHI 9:30

And so, I would like to leave with you this thought, this message,
that you will seek after the treasures of the Spirit, seek after the riches
of goodness and mercy and righteous living. Go always after those
things which are good. Follow along as you have been doing, seeking the finer cultural things of life. Discard the dross, cast it aside,
trample it underfoot; cherish always and guard that which is beau-
tiful in your lives.

(J. Reuben Clark Jr., *Behold the Lamb of God*
[Salt Lake City: Deseret Book, 1991], 338)

Daily Living

MAKE YOUR TREASURE THE THINGS OF GOD AND NOT THE WORLD.

- Seek the kingdom of God first—Jacob 2:18

- You can be prosperous and still remember those in need—Alma
  1:30

- Beware of riches because you can become prideful—Alma 4:6;
  Helaman 3:36

- Remember you can not take your earthly riches with you—
  Alma 39:14

- Lay up for yourselves treasures in heaven—3 Nephi 13:20

CARNALLY OR SPIRITUALLY MINDED

Remember, to be carnally-minded is death, and to be spiritually-minded is life eternal.

2 NEPHI 9:39

In all seriousness I believe it is, in fact, an awareness of the hereafter that provides the spiritual dimension for our lives today. As we learn to view our experiences in this life with the perspective of eternity, we tend to draw away from the things of the world. . . . When the reality of eternity presses upon our minds and we are guided by the Spirit, we begin to view life differently. The Apostle Paul expressed this thought: "We look not at the things which are seen, but at the things which are not seen: for the things which are seen are temporal; but the things which are not seen are eternal" (2 Corinthians 4:18).

(Ardeth Greene Kapp, *The Joy of the Journey* [Salt Lake City: Deseret Book, 1992], 83)

Daily Living

BE SPIRITUALLY MINDED FOR IT IS LIFE ETERNAL.

- ∞ Thoughts that lead to lust lead to sin—3 Nephi 12:27–30

- ∞ Know the things of God by the Spirit—Alma 36:4

- ∞ The word of God has a powerful effect upon your mind—Alma 31:5

- ∞ Keep your mind firm as to the things of God—Alma 57:25–27

- ∞ Hunger and thirst after righteousness—3 Nephi 12:6

- ∞ Always remember the Lord and you will have the Spirit to be with you—3 Nephi 18:7

FEBRUARY
❧

*Behold, my soul delighteth in proving
unto my people the truth of the
coming of Christ; for, for this end hath
the law of Moses been given; and all
things which have been given of God
from the beginning of the world, unto
man, are the typifying of him.*

—2 NEPHI 11:4

DON'T TAKE OFFENSE AT THE TRUTH

*I know that the words of truth are hard against all uncleanness;
but the righteous fear them not, for they love the truth and are
not shaken.*

2 NEPHI 9:40

To teach the young to love the truth above personal convenience is
the basis of it. They will be taught true courage, which becomes a
living and attractive virtue when it is regarded not as a willingness
to die manfully, but as the determination to live decently. They will
be taught honesty by habit and as a matter of course. . . . Such is the
power gained from loving the Lord, our God, and serving Him in
righteousness.

(Thomas S. Monson, *Be Your Best Self*
[Salt Lake City: Deseret Book, 1979], 97–98)

Daily Living

LOVE THE TRUTH AND THE WORD OF GOD.

- Truth (the Book of Mormon) shall spring forth out of the earth—Psalm 85:11

- The truth will make you free—John 8:32

- Christ is the way and the truth—John 14:6

- The guilty always take the truth to be hard—1 Nephi 16:2–3

- Glory in the truth—2 Nephi 33:6

- The Spirit will always speak the truth—Jacob 4:13

THE LORD IS THE GATEKEEPER

O then, my beloved brethren, come unto the Lord, the Holy One. Remember that his paths are righteous. Behold, the way for man is narrow, but it lieth in a straight course before him, and the keeper of the gate is the Holy One of Israel; and he employeth no servant there; and there is none other way save it be by the gate; for he cannot be deceived, for the Lord God is his name.

2 NEPHI 9:41

Each of us will be judged by the Lord when life on earth is completed. His judgment will be right; it will be merciful and just, and our eternal existence will be determined in accordance with our personal thoughts, deeds, and faith, and not by those of any other.

(Russell M. Nelson, *The Power within Us*
[Salt Lake City: Deseret Book, 1988], 132)

Daily Living
PREPARE TO MEET YOUR SAVIOR.

- ๏ You will stand before God to be judged—1 Nephi 15:33; 2 Nephi 9:15; Alma 5:15; 3 Nephi 26:4

- ๏ Alma felt the pain of coming into the presence of God and being judged of his deeds—Alma 36:12–15

- ๏ You will have a perfect knowledge of all your guilt or your righteousness—2 Nephi 9:14

- ๏ Moroni, like Jacob and many prophets, looked forward to the judgment—Moroni 10:34

- ๏ You will be judged according to your works—Alma 41:3

THE LORD DESPISETH PRIDE

And . . . the wise, and the learned, and they that are rich, who are puffed up because of their learning, and their wisdom, and their riches . . . and save they shall cast these things away, and consider themselves fools before God . . . he will not open unto them.

2 NEPHI 9:42

The Lord blesses the person of humility. In what ways? (1) He "shall lead thee by the hand, and give thee answer to thy prayers" (D&C 112:10). (2) The Lord's spirit enlightens the humble (Ibid., 136:33). (3) "Let him that is ignorant learn wisdom by humbling himself" (Ibid., v. 32). (4) The promise of seeing and knowing the Lord is made to the humble (Ibid., 67:10). (5) His arm of mercy is extended to the humble in freeing them of bondage (Mosiah 29:18–20).

(Roy W. Doxey, *The Doctrine and Covenants Speaks*
[Salt Lake City: Deseret Book, 1964], 2:336–337)

Daily Living

SEEK TO BE HUMBLE AND OVERCOME PRIDE.

- ❧ Are you sufficiently humble and stripped of pride?—Alma 5:27–28

- ❧ Pray and fast to be strong in humility—Helaman 3:35

- ❧ Pride is pulled down by the word of God—Alma 4:19

- ❧ Beware of learning and riches that can lead to pride—2 Nephi 28:15

- ❧ The reward for pride is destruction—2 Nephi 26:10

PREPARE FOR JUDGMENT DAY

Prepare your souls for that glorious day when justice shall be administered unto the righteous, even the day of judgment, that ye may not shrink with awful fear; that ye may not remember your awful guilt in perfectness, and be constrained to exclaim. . . . I know my guilt; I transgressed thy law . . . and the devil hath obtained me . . . I am a prey to his awful misery.

2 NEPHI 9:46

[The Lord] wants us to repent and prepare for judgment. Addressing both Gentile and Israelite, he says: "And for this cause I write unto you, that ye may know that ye must all stand before the judgment-seat of Christ . . . to be judged of your works. . . . And I would that I could persuade all . . . to repent and prepare to stand before the judgment-seat of Christ" (Mormon 3:20–22).

(Monte S. Nyman and Charles D. Tate Jr., eds., *Fourth Nephi through Moroni: From Zion to Destruction* [Provo, UT: Religious Studies Center, 1995], 96–97)

Daily Living

PREPARE FOR THE JUDGMENT DAY THROUGH REPENTANCE AND LIVING RIGHTEOUSLY.

ɞ Don't procrastinate the day of repentance—prepare to meet God—Alma 34:32–35

ɞ You will feel great sorrow for the past unless you repent—3 Nephi 8:24–25

ɞ Strip yourself of pride and envy in order to meet God—Alma 5:28–29

ɞ You will be judged by your works—3 Nephi 26:4

ɞ The righteous are favored of the Lord—1 Nephi 17:35

THINGS OF THE WORLD WILL PERISH

Wherefore, do not spend money for that which is of no worth, nor your labor for that which cannot satisfy. Hearken diligently unto me, and remember the words which I have spoken; and come unto the Holy One of Israel, and feast upon that which perisheth not, neither can be corrupted, and let your soul delight in fatness.

2 NEPHI 9:51

Our thirteenth article of faith states, "If there is anything virtuous, lovely, or of good report or praiseworthy, we seek after these things." Saints of God follow the admonition to come to Christ and "eat and drink of the bread and the waters of life freely" (Alma 5:34; John 4:14; 6:35, 51). We seek after that spiritual soil which produces good wholesome food. . . . We "feast upon that which perisheth not, neither can be corrupted," which is the "word of Christ" (2 Ne. 9:51; 31:20; 32:3).

(Hoyt W. Brewster Jr., *Doctrine and Covenants Encyclopedia* [Salt Lake City: Bookcraft, 1988], 217)

Daily Living

COME UNTO CHRIST AND FEAST UPON THINGS THAT PERISH NOT.

- ༂ Question of conscience: What do you treasure? Is it your God? 2 Nephi 9:30

- ༂ Lay up for yourself treasures in Heaven—Helaman 5:8; 3 Nephi 13:20

- ༂ The motive makes the difference—Moroni 7:6–8

- ༂ Feast upon the words of Christ—2 Nephi 32:3

REMEMBER THE WORDS OF GOD

*Behold, my beloved brethren, remember the words of your God;
pray unto him continually by day, and give thanks unto his holy
name by night. Let your hearts rejoice.*

2 NEPHI 9:52

The best way for children to learn how to pray and to know the
power of prayer is to see it in action in their own family. If they see
parents who humbly kneel and offer prayer, they will do likewise. If
they see parents who, when first confronted with a problem, turn
immediately to the Lord, so will the children. Our children ought to
see us daily give thanks to God in prayer. Again, if children see parents who are truly grateful, so will the children be.

(Gene R. Cook, *Raising Up a Family to the Lord*
[Salt Lake City: Deseret Book, 1993], 77–78)

Daily Living
PRAY ALWAYS WITH THANKSGIVING.

- ფ Constantly give thanks and praise to Heavenly Father for all
things—Mosiah 2:20

- ფ Live in thanksgiving daily—Alma 34:38

- ფ Counsel with the Lord in all things and let your heart be full of
thanksgiving—Alma 37:37

RECONCILE YOURSELVES TO GOD

Wherefore, my beloved brethren, reconcile yourselves to the will of God, and not to the will of the devil and the flesh; and remember, after ye are reconciled unto God, that it is only in and through the grace of God that ye are saved.

2 NEPHI 10:24

If we want to be good, faithful Latter-day Saints, we have got to be willing to submit to the will of God in all things. We must feel as was once exclaimed on a certain occasion by the ancient Israelites, "The Lord shall be our Judge, the Lord shall be our King, the Lord shall be our Ruler, and he shall rule over us." That is the way I figure up these things; and if this was not so I would not give anything for our religion, or our religious ideas. I do not think that any of us can regulate, manage or conduct any of these matters, unless God be with us. And I will tell you another thing, God will not be with us unless we are one.

(John Taylor, in *Journal of Discourses* [London: Latter-day Saints' Book Depot, 1854–1886], 18:282–283)

Daily Living

SEEK TO DO THE WILL OF GOD.

- In following Christ you too should suffer the will of the Father—3 Nephi 11:11

- Be willing to submit to all things—Mosiah 3:19

- Pray and work according to the will of God—Helaman 10:4–5

- By doing the will of God you will know the doctrine of God—John 7:17

DEPENDENCE UPON HEAVENLY FATHER AND SAVIOR

And my soul delighteth in proving unto my people that save
Christ should come all men must perish.
For if there be no Christ there be no God; and if there be no
God we are not. . . . But there is a God, and he is Christ, and
he cometh in the fulness of his own time.
2 NEPHI 11:6–7

The prayerful and humble man will always realize and feel that he is dependent upon the Lord for every blessing that he enjoys, and in praying to God he will not only pray for the light and the inspiration of His Holy Spirit to guide him, but he will feel to thank Him for the blessings that he receives, realizing that life, that health, that strength, and that all the intelligence which he possesses comes from God, who is the Author of his existence.

(Heber J. Grant, *Improvement Era,* December 1942, 779)

Daily Living

RECOGNIZE YOUR DEPENDENCE UPON GOD FOR ALL THINGS.

- ❧ The Lord is your strength—2 Nephi 22:2

- ❧ You are nothing without the Lord. In His strength you can do all things—Alma 26:12

- ❧ The Lord preserves you and lends you breath that you might live—Mosiah 2:21

- ❧ You are dependent on God for all things—Mosiah 4:19–21

- ❧ Acknowledge your unworthiness before God at all times—Alma 38:14

WORDS OF ISAIAH

Wherefore, they are of worth unto the children of men, and he that supposeth that they are not, unto them will I speak particularly, and confine the words unto mine own people; for I know that they shall be of great worth unto them in the last days; for in that day shall they understand them; wherefore, for their good have I written them.

2 NEPHI 25:8

[The Lord] command[ed] the Nephites to "search these [writings] diligently; for great are the words of Isaiah." He observed the remarkable breadth of Isaiah's declarations with the acknowledgment that in his examination of Israel's history and covenants, Isaiah touched on "all things concerning [the Lord's] people," the fulfillment of which either had been or yet would be (3 Ne. 23:1–2, footnote). That message must also go to the Gentiles, Christ said, a mission accomplished at least in part by the publication and distribution of the Book of Mormon.

(Jeffrey R. Holland, *Christ and the New Covenant:*
The Messianic Message of the Book of Mormon
[Salt Lake City: Deseret Book, 1997], 292)

Daily Living

SEEK TO UNDERSTAND THE WORDS OF ISAIAH, FOR THEY ARE GREAT.

- ෨ The Lord said that the words of Isaiah are great—3 Nephi 23:1
- ෨ Isaiah wrote words which are to be likened to your life—2 Nephi 6:4–5; 11:2, 8
- ෨ Isaiah's words will all be fulfilled—2 Nephi 25:1–7

THE GOODNESS AND MERCY OF CHRIST

And we talk of Christ, we rejoice in Christ, we preach of Christ,
we prophesy of Christ, and we write according to our prophecies,
that our children may know to what source they may look for a
remission of their sins.
2 NEPHI 25:26

We are Christians in the very best sense of that word. We believe in
Christ. We teach of Christ. We look to Christ. He is our Redeemer,
our Lord, and our Savior.

(Gordon B. Hinckley, *Teachings of Gordon B. Hinckley*
[Salt Lake City: Deseret Book, 1997], 280)

Daily Living
LOOK TO CHRIST FOR THE REMISSION OF SINS.

- ⅎ You enter the gate through repentance and baptism by taking the name of Jesus Christ upon you—2 Nephi 31:17

- ⅎ Your remission of sins comes through baptism—3 Nephi 1:23

- ⅎ The Atonement makes possible the forgiveness of sins—Mosiah 4:2–3

- ⅎ Always do good, especially blessing the poor and needy, to retain a remission of your sins—Mosiah 4:26

- ⅎ The remission of sins brings meekness and lowliness of heart—Moroni 8:26

CHRIST LAYS DOWN HIS LIFE FOR US

He doeth not anything save it be for the benefit of the world;
for he loveth the world, even that he layeth down his own life
that he may draw all men unto him. Wherefore, he commandeth
none that they shall not partake of his salvation.
2 NEPHI 26:24

The Savior spoke prophetically of that sacrifice and of the love that culminated in his redemptive sacrifice when he declared, "Greater love hath no man than this, that a man lay down his life for his friends" (John 15:13).

To all of us who would be his disciples, he has given the great commandment, "A new commandment I give unto you, That ye love one another; as I have loved you, that ye also love one another" (John 13:34).

(Gordon B. Hinckley, *Faith: The Essence of True Religion*
[Salt Lake City: Deseret Book, 1989], 48–49)

Daily Living

SHOW GRATITUDE BY LOVING OTHERS AS CHRIST HAS LOVED YOU.

- Seek to have charity for without it you are nothing—2 Nephi 26:30

- Teach your children to love and serve each other—Mosiah 4:15

- Love your enemies—3 Nephi 12:43–44

- Whatever you do to others you have done it unto Christ—Matthew 25:40

ALL ARE EQUAL IN THE SIGHT OF GOD

Hath he commanded any that they should not partake of his salvation? Behold I say unto you, Nay; but he hath given it free for all men; and he hath commanded his people that they should persuade all men to repentance.
2 NEPHI 26:27

[Jesus Christ] called and ordained twelve Apostles, and commanded them to . . . preach the Gospel to every creature, saying, "He that believeth and is baptized shall be saved; but he that believeth not shall be damned," or condemned. Thus placing it within the reach of every man to obtain the glory and exaltation referred to above, and leaving all men without excuse who would not obey the law and be subject to the conditions imposed.
(John Taylor, *Mediation and Atonement* [Salt Lake City: Deseret News, 1882], 180–181)

Daily Living

INVITE ALL TO COME UNTO CHRIST AND PARTAKE OF HIS GOODNESS.

- ✿ All are alike unto the Lord who wants all mankind to come unto Him—2 Nephi 26:33

- ✿ Come unto Christ and be perfected in Him—Moroni 10:32

- ✿ Seek to persuade all mankind to come unto Christ—1 Nephi 6:4; Jacob 1:7

- ✿ You come unto Christ as you hold to the iron rod and partake of the tree of life—1 Nephi 8:15–16, 24, 30; Alma 5:34–35

- ✿ Come unto Christ and enjoy the blessings of eternal life—3 Nephi 9:14, 21–22

THE LORD WORKS AMONG MEN ACCORDING TO THEIR FAITH

For behold, I am God; and I am a God of miracles; and I will show unto the world that I am the same yesterday, today, and forever; and I work not among the children of men save it be according to their faith.

2 NEPHI 27:23

The plan of salvation revealed in these latter days includes all that is needed for us to return to our Father in Heaven . . . but it unfolds gradually to each of us according to our diligence and faith in following the plan. Faith and salvation are linked together. As mortals we are in the process of ultimately gaining salvation. Faith possesses qualities that move us forward toward that ultimate goal.

(Larry E. Dahl and Charles D. Tate Jr., eds., *The Lectures on Faith in Historical Perspective* [Provo, UT: Religious Studies Center, 1990], 269)

Daily Living

INCREASE YOUR FAITH THAT THE LORD MIGHT USE YOU AS AN INSTRUMENT IN HIS HANDS.

- ๛ Faith increases by hearing the word of God—Rom. 10:17

- ๛ Faith is made firm in Christ through fasting and prayer—Helaman 3:35

- ๛ Through faith in Christ you can repent and be forgiven—Enos 1:5–8

- ๛ Salvation comes from faith in the Lord—Mosiah 3:9

- ๛ You are called according to your faith and good works—Alma 13:3

- ๛ By faith great things are done—Ether 12:6–20

GROWING LINE UPON LINE

I will give unto the children of men line upon line, precept upon precept, . . . and blessed are those who hearken unto my precepts, and lend an ear unto my counsel, for they shall learn wisdom; for unto him that receiveth I will give more; and from them that shall say, We have enough, from them shall be taken away even that which they have.

2 NEPHI 28:30

Challenges, obstacles, and stress are a natural part of life and personal development. But just as muscles need physical resistance to develop, meeting challenges straight on can actually become a positive character-building opportunity. . . . When challenges present themselves in our lives, we can either avoid them . . . or we can meet them head-on and try to overcome them.

. . . If we can master these hindrances, we will develop the technique and strength to overcome life's obstacles.

(Victor L. Ludlow, *Principles and Practices of the Restored Gospel* [Salt Lake City: Deseret Book, 1992], 338–339)

Daily Living

HEARKEN TO THE PRECEPTS AND COMMANDMENTS OF GOD.

- ❧ If you hearken to the word you will be protected—1 Nephi 15:24

- ❧ Seek counsel from the Lord—Jacob 4:10

- ❧ If you harden your heart you receive a lesser portion of the word—Alma 12:9–10

- ❧ Yield your heart to God and receive the blessings—Helaman 3:35

RECEIVE THE BLESSINGS OF THE HOLY GHOST

If ye shall follow the Son, with full purpose of heart, acting no hypocrisy and no deception before God, but with real intent, repenting of your sins, witnessing unto the Father that ye are willing to take upon you the name of Christ, by baptism . . . behold, then shall ye receive the Holy Ghost . . . and then can ye speak with the tongue of angels, and shout praises unto the Holy One of Israel.

2 Nephi 31:13

One may receive the ordinance of the laying on of hands for the gift of the Holy Ghost, but the responsibility clearly rests upon him to live in such a way that he will receive the blessings of the Holy Ghost in his life; for example, President Joseph F. Smith said: "The presentation or 'gift' of the Holy Ghost simply confers upon a man the right to receive at any time, when he is worthy of it and desires it, the power and light of truth of the Holy Ghost, although he may often be left to his own spirit and judgment."

(David H. Yarn, *The Gospel: God, Man, and Truth* [Salt Lake City: Deseret Book, 1979], 58)

Daily Living

THE HOLY GHOST BLESSES THOSE WHO HAVE FAITH, REPENT, AND ARE BAPTIZED.

- Sanctification comes by the power of the Holy Ghost—3 Nephi 27:20

- You can speak marvelous words by the power of the Holy Ghost—Helaman 5:45

- The Holy Ghost will fill you with hope and perfect love—Moroni 8:26

- Remember to use this gift that is within you—2 Timothy 1:6–7

ENDURE TO THE END

Wherefore, ye must press forward with a steadfastness in Christ, having a perfect brightness of hope, and a love of God and of all men. Wherefore, if ye shall press forward, feasting upon the word of Christ, and endure to the end, behold, thus saith the Father: Ye shall have eternal life.

2 NEPHI 31:20

By grace, the Savior accomplished His atoning sacrifice so that all mankind will attain immortality. By His grace, and by our faith in His atonement and repentance of our sins, we receive the strength to do the works necessary that we otherwise could not do by our own power. By His grace we receive an endowment of blessing and spiritual strength that may eventually lead us to eternal life if we endure to the end. By His grace we become more like His divine personality. Yes, it is "by grace that we are saved, after all we can do" (2 Nephi 25:23).

(Ezra Taft Benson, *The Teachings of Ezra Taft Benson*
[Salt Lake City: Bookcraft, 1988], 353–354)

Daily Living

PRESS FORWARD WITH FAITH, HOPE, AND THE LOVE OF GOD IN YOUR HEART.

- ༀ Failing to do your duty can bring sins upon your own head—Jacob 1:19

- ༀ Be steadfast and immovable, always abounding in good works—Mosiah 5:15

- ༀ Do your duty with unwearyingness—Helaman 10:5

- ༀ By enduring to the end you will be held guiltless—3 Nephi 27:16

FEAST UPON THE WORD

Angels speak by the power of the Holy Ghost; wherefore, they speak the words of Christ. Wherefore, I said unto you, feast upon the words of Christ; for behold, the words of Christ will tell you all things what ye should do.

2 NEPHI 32:3

In a world where the rightness and goodness of things have become obscured by evil-designing people, it is imperative that our children look to the scriptures for direction. If a parent truly loves a child, he or she will not rest until the child's hand has grasped firmly the "rod of iron" or "word of God" spoken of by the ancient prophet Lehi (1 Nephi 8:19; 11:25).

Do you want your children to know the purposes of God and the means by which those purposes will be realized? If so, get them into the scriptures.

(Carlos E. Asay, *Family Pecan Trees: Planting a Legacy of Faith at Home* [Salt Lake City: Deseret Book, 1992], 33)

Daily Living

SEARCH THE SCRIPTURES AND THE WORDS OF THE LIVING PROPHETS.

 • Give heed to the word of God—1 Nephi 15:25

 • Delight in and ponder the word of God—2 Nephi 4:15

 • Search the scriptures diligently—Mosiah 1:7

 • Lay hold to the word of God—Helaman 3:29

 • Wax strong in the knowledge of the truth—Alma 17:2

SEEK TO UNDERSTAND THE WORD OF GOD

Wherefore, now after I have spoken these words, if ye cannot understand them it will be because ye ask not . . . wherefore, ye are not brought into the light, but must perish in the dark.
2 NEPHI 32:4

The Lord has given us the charge to teach our children to search the scriptures; and he will prepare the way for us if we are willing to take the time, if we are willing to seek to understand the scriptures ourselves, if we are willing to ask for help, and if we are willing to see the exciting beauty of the word of God. . . . He will help us as Nephi said: "If God had commanded me to do all things I could do them. If he should command me that I should say unto this water, be thou earth, it should be earth; and if I should say it, it would be done" (1 Nephi 17:50).

(Ed J. Pinegar, *You, Your Family and the Scriptures*
[Salt Lake City: Deseret Book, 1975], xi–xii)

Daily Living
SEEK TO UNDERSTAND THE WORD OF GOD.

- ∞ Search diligently to understand the word of God—Alma 17:2
- ∞ Liken the scriptures to your daily life—1 Nephi 19:23
- ∞ Without the word of God you would dwindle in unbelief—Mosiah 1:5–7
- ∞ The scriptures will bring you life eternal (see John 17:3)—Alma 37:8
- ∞ Live by every word that proceedeth forth from the mouth of God—D&C 84:43–46

HOLY GHOST WILL SHOW YOU ALL THINGS TO DO

For behold, again I say unto you that if ye will enter in by the way, and receive the Holy Ghost, it will show unto you all things what ye should do.
2 NEPHI 32:5

May we through worship, meditation, communion, and reverence sense the reality of being able to have a close relationship with our Father in heaven. I bear you my testimony that it is real; that we can commune with our Heavenly Father, and if we so live to be worthy of the companionship of the Holy Spirit, he will guide us into all truth; he will show us things to come; he will bring all things to our remembrance; he will testify of the divinity of the Lord Jesus Christ.

(David O. McKay, *Man May Know for Himself: Teachings of President David O. McKay,* comp. Clare Middlemiss [Salt Lake City: Deseret Book, 1967], 28)

Daily Living

THROUGH FAITH, LOVE, AND OBEDIENCE YOU MAY KNOW THE THINGS YOU SHOULD DO.

- ৩ The Holy Ghost comes by faith in Jesus Christ—1 Nephi 10:17
- ৩ The Holy Ghost comes as a result of our love for God—D&C 76:116
- ৩ The Holy Ghost comes by obedience—D&C 20:77, 79
- ৩ You lose the Holy Ghost through wickedness—Mormon 1:13–14
- ৩ The Holy Ghost will tell you the truth of all things—Moroni 10:5
- ৩ The Holy Ghost will lead you—1 Nephi 4:6

THE POWER OF PRAYER

*If ye would hearken unto the Spirit which teacheth a man to
pray ye would know that ye must pray; for the evil spirit teacheth
not a man to pray. . . . But behold, I say unto you that ye must
pray always . . . ye must not perform any thing unto the Lord
save in the first place ye shall pray unto the Father in the name
of Christ, that he will consecrate thy performance . . . for the
welfare of thy soul.*
2 NEPHI 32:8–9

Christ taught that we should meet in church "oft" and should pray
for all who seek the Church, forbidding or casting out none. As this
discourse concludes, it is clear . . . that the "light" we are to hold up
to the world is the fact that we pray . . . always—as Christ prayed
unto the Father: "Behold I am the light which ye shall hold up—
that which ye have seen me do."

(Jeffrey R. Holland, *Christ and the New Covenant:
The Messianic Message of the Book of Mormon*
[Salt Lake City: Deseret Book, 1997], 273)

Daily Living
PRAY ALWAYS TO DO THE WILL OF GOD.

- ❧ Pray to retain a remission of sins and to be filled with the love
  of God—Mosiah 4:11–12

- ❧ Pray over all things—Alma 34:17–28

- ❧ Pray and fast to teach with the power and authority of God—
  Alma 17:3

- ❧ Pray with all the energy of your heart to be filled with charity—
  Moroni 7:47–48

SPEAK BY THE SPIRIT

*When a man speaketh by the power of the Holy Ghost the power of
the Holy Ghost carrieth it unto the hearts of the children of men.*
2 NEPHI 33:1

You speak by the Spirit, and the Spirit speaks the word of Christ,
which is the mind and the will of God. Do you remember what was
happening about the time of Alma 17:2–3? . . . His friends had
"waxed strong in the knowledge of the truth" and "they were men of
sound understanding." Why? Because "they had searched the scriptures diligently, that they might know the word of God." But this
was not all. They'd also "given themselves to much prayer and fasting," so that when they spoke, they spoke by revelation and by
prophecy, "with power and authority of God."

> (Ed J. Pinegar, *Especially for Missionaries, Volume 3: Teaching
> by the Spirit with the Power of God* [American Fork, UT:
> Covenant Communications, 1997], 4–5)

Daily Living

BE WORTHY OF THE SPIRIT SO AS TO SPEAK BY THE SPIRIT.

- ଚ Only when you have the Spirit can you speak by the Spirit—
  2 Nephi 25:11

- ଚ Fasting and prayer will help you speak by the Spirit—Alma 17:3

- ଚ Hunger and thirst after righteousness and you will be filled
  with the Spirit—3 Nephi 12:6

- ଚ Keep His commandments—3 Nephi 18:7; D&C 20:77, 79

- ଚ The Spirit will bear record of what you say—D&C 100:8

BELIEVE IN CHRIST

*And now, my beloved brethren, . . . hearken unto these words
and believe in Christ; and if ye believe not in these words believe
in Christ. And if ye shall believe in Christ ye will believe in
these words, for they are the words of Christ, . . . and they teach
all men that they should do good.*

2 NEPHI 33:10

The reason his words teach men to do good is that they teach of
Christ. . . . Because of its strong witness for Christ, the Book of
Mormon was designed, as Joseph F. Smith said about Mormonism,
to make "good men better men, and that it takes even bad men and
makes good ones of them."

(Monte S. Nyman and Charles D. Tate Jr., eds.,
Second Nephi: The Doctrinal Structure [Provo, UT:
Religious Studies Center, 1989], 388)

Daily Living

BELIEVE IN CHRIST AND HIS WORDS WHICH WILL TEACH YOU TO DO
GOOD.

- ‍ The word of God will tell you all things to do—2 Nephi 32:3

- ‍ The word of God persuadeth you to do good—2 Nephi 33:4

- ‍ The word of God when entering the heart brings change—
Enos 1:2–12

- ‍ Remember the word of God and it will help you in your hour
of trial—Alma 36:17–19

- ‍ All things spoken by the Spirit are the words of God—D&C
68:3–5

MAGNIFY YOUR CALLINGS

*And we did magnify our office unto the Lord, taking upon us
the responsibility, answering the sins of the people upon our own
heads if we did not teach them the word of God with all diligence;
wherefore, by laboring with our might their blood might not
come upon our garments; otherwise . . . we would not be found
spotless at the last day.*

JACOB 1:19

We magnify our priesthood and enlarge our calling when we serve
with diligence and enthusiasm in those responsibilities to which we
are called by proper authority. I emphasize the words, "diligence and
enthusiasm." This work has not reached its present stature through
indifference on the part of those who have labored in its behalf. The
Lord needs men, both young and old, who will carry the banners of
His kingdom with positive strength and determined purpose.

(Gordon B. Hinckley, "Magnify Your Calling,"
Ensign, May 1989, 47–49)

Daily Living

MAGNIFY YOUR CALLINGS.

- ଊ You waste the days of your probation if you transgress the laws
  of God—2 Nephi 9:27

- ଊ Work with unwearingness in your calling—Helaman 10:4–5

- ଊ Learn your duty—D&C 107:99–100

- ଊ You can be sanctified by magnifying your calling—D&C
  10784:33

THE KINGDOM OF GOD AND RICHES

But before ye seek for riches, seek ye for the kingdom of God. And after ye have obtained a hope in Christ ye shall obtain riches, if ye seek them; and ye will seek them for the intent to do good—to clothe the naked, and to feed the hungry, and to liberate the captive, and administer relief to the sick and the afflicted.
JACOB 2:18–19

Often it is the order of things that is fundamental in the Lord's instructions to us. The Lord is not telling us that we should not be prosperous. This would be inconsistent with the many records we have of his blessing his people with prosperity. But he is telling us that we should seek prosperity only after we have sought and found him. Then, because our hearts are right, because we love him first and foremost, we will choose to invest the riches we obtain in building his kingdom.

(L. Tom Perry, *Living with Enthusiasm*
[Salt Lake City: Deseret Book, 1996], 34–35)

Daily Living

BUILD UP THE KINGDOM OF GOD AND SEEK TO BLESS OTHERS WITH YOUR RICHES.

- Seek first the Kingdom of God—3 Nephi 13:33

- Labor without ceasing to help others come into the Kingdom—Alma 36:24

- Impart of your substance to the poor and needy—Mosiah 18:27–29; Alma 1:27

- Always remember the poor and needy in your prosperity—Mormon 8:39

- Your prayers are in vain if you fail to help the needy—Alma 34:28–29

LOOK UNTO GOD

But behold, I, Jacob, would speak unto you that are pure in heart. Look unto God with firmness of mind, and pray unto him with exceeding faith, and he will console you in your afflictions, and he will plead your cause, and send down justice upon those who seek your destruction.

JACOB 3:1

In days of sunshine it will become us to be humble. In times of storm we shall look to God for strength. This is his work. He will overrule for its blessing in the future as he has in the past. His Spirit will brood over the nations according to his will and wisdom, and hearts will be touched by its power.

(Gordon B. Hinckley, *Be Thou an Example*
[Salt Lake City: Deseret Book, 1981], 116)

Daily Living

LOOK TO GOD IN ALL THINGS AND FOR CONSOLATION OF YOUR AFFLICTIONS.

- ஐ The Lord is always there through His atonement to bless and nurture us—Alma 7:11–12

- ஐ Can you look to God with a pure heart and clean hands?—Alma 5:19

- ஐ Look to God and live—Alma 37:47

- ஐ Pray with sincerity and the Lord will be merciful to you in your afflictions—Alma 33:11

- ஐ Trust in the Lord and you shall be supported in your trials—Alma 36:3

- ஐ Your attitude in your afflictions will determine your response—Alma 62:41

THE LORD COUNSELS IN WISDOM

Wherefore, brethren, seek not to counsel the Lord, but to take counsel from his hand. For behold, ye yourselves know that he counseleth in wisdom, and in justice, and in great mercy, over all his works.

JACOB 4:10

As we counsel with the Lord in all our doings, we will know that in the midst of affliction our table truly is spread. We will sense new power. We will know comfort no matter how severe our tribulations are at the moment.

(Elaine Cannon, *Adversity* [Salt Lake City: Bookcraft, 1987], 120)

Daily Living
COUNSEL WITH THE LORD IN ALL THINGS.

- ଚ Trust in the Lord and not in man—2 Nephi 4:34

- ଚ To be learned is good if you counsel with the Lord—2 Nephi 9:28–29

- ଚ You learn wisdom from the counsel of the Lord—2 Nephi 28:30

- ଚ If you set at naught the counsels of God you will fall—D&C 3:4

- ଚ Don't seek to build yourself up and fail to counsel with the Lord for you shall have no power—D&C 136:19

POWER IN CHRIST'S ATONEMENT

Wherefore, beloved brethren, be reconciled unto him through the atonement of Christ, his Only Begotten Son, and ye may obtain a resurrection, according to the power of the resurrection which is in Christ, and be presented as the first-fruits of Christ.

JACOB 4:11

The peace that accompanies a remission of our sins will come only if we have faith. Faith unto repentance leads us through the steps of repentance because we trust in the power of Christ's atonement, leaving our sins with him, letting go of our guilt, and seeking for a new purity. . . . After "wrestling" before God for a remission of his sins, Enos recorded, "There came a voice unto me, saying: Enos, thy sins are forgiven thee . . . thy faith hath made thee whole" (Enos 1:5–8).

(Victor L. Ludlow, *Principles and Practices of the Restored Gospel* [Salt Lake City: Deseret Book, 1992], 278)

Daily Living

GAIN PEACE AND RECONCILIATION THROUGH THE ATONEMENT.

    Reconciliation comes as you apply the Atonement through the principles and ordinances of the gospel—2 Nephi 33:9

    You are saved through the atoning blood of the Lord Jesus Christ—Helaman 5:9

    Peace comes from your faith on the Lord Jesus Christ—Helaman 5:47

SERVANTS AND LABORERS IN THE VINEYARD

And the Lord of the vineyard said unto them: Go to, and labor in the vineyard, with your might. For behold . . . the end is nigh at hand . . . and if ye labor with your might with me ye shall have joy in the fruit which I shall lay up unto myself against the time which will soon come.

JACOB 5:–71

As we keep the Lord's commandment to introduce the gospel to others . . . the Spirit of the Lord helps overcome the differences between those who teach and those who are taught. The Lord made the process clear when he said, "Wherefore, he that preacheth [by the Spirit] and he that receiveth [by the Spirit], understand one another, and both are edified and rejoice together" (D&C 50:22). One cannot think of the hundreds of millions who have never heard of this work without wondering how our charge to teach all mankind can ever be accomplished. . . . As we put forth our effort and pray humbly for inspiration, we will be blessed in our desires to share the gospel.

(Gordon B. Hinckley, *Faith: The Essence of True Religion*
[Salt Lake City: Deseret Book, 1989], 55–56)

Daily Living

SHARE THE GOSPEL OF JESUS CHRIST.

- ෨ Bringing souls unto Christ is of the greatest worth—D&C 15:6; 16:6

- ෨ It is your duty to warn your neighbor—D&C 88:81

- ෨ Many are kept from the truth because they know not where to find it—D&C 123:12

TEACH YOUR CHILDREN

Behold, it came to pass that I, Enos, knowing my father that he was a just man—for he taught me in his language, and also in the nurture and admonition of the Lord—and blessed be the name of my God for it.

ENOS 1:1

Youth, if you want to be guided by wisdom, stay close to your parents. Listen to the counsel of your father and your mother and lean heavily upon the experience of their lives, because they are entitled to inspiration in the rearing of their family.

(Harold B. Lee, *Stand Ye in Holy Places*
[Salt Lake City: Deseret Book, 1974], 376)

Daily Living

PARENTS, TEACH YOUR CHILDREN. CHILDREN, HEARKEN UNTO YOUR PARENTS.

- ଝ Teach children to walk uprightly before the Lord—D&C 68:25–28

- ଝ Teach your children to love and serve one another—Mosiah 4:14–15

- ଝ Fathers give blessings to your children—2 Nephi 4:5

- ଝ Teach your children concerning our Savior Jesus Christ—2 Nephi 25:16

- ଝ Do all you can do to persuade your children to believe in Christ so as to be reconciled to God—2 Nephi 25:23

- ଝ Pray in your families that your children may be blessed—3 Nephi 18:21

- ଝ Always set a good example less the sins of the children be upon your heads—Jacob 3:10

MARCH

ℰↃ

Therefore, lift up your heads,
and rejoice, and put your
trust in God.

—Mosiah 7:19

POWER OF PRAYER AND FAITH

*I kneeled down before my Maker, and I cried unto him in
mighty prayer . . . and when the night came I did still raise my
voice high that it reached the heavens.
And there came a voice unto me, saying: Enos, thy sins are forgiven
thee. . . .
And I, Enos, knew that God could not lie; wherefore, my guilt
was swept away.*
ENOS 1:4–6

The intent of this last sacrifice would be to "bring about the bowels
of mercy, which overpowereth justice," providing a way for mortals
to have "faith unto repentance" (Alma 34:15–16).
Prayer is the way we begin to exercise faith unto repentance. We
begin by calling upon God to have mercy upon us" (see Alma
34:17).

(Jeffrey R. Holland, *Christ and the New Covenant:
The Messianic Message of the Book of Mormon*
[Salt Lake City: Deseret Book, 1997], 125)

Daily Living

FORGIVENESS OF SINS COMES FROM TRUE REPENTANCE THROUGH MIGHTY
PRAYER AND FAITH.

   ❧ Pray unto the Father that you might be forgiven of your sins—
1 Nephi 7:21

   ❧ Exercise faith unto repentance—Alma 34:15–17

   ❧ Seek mercy through the Atonement of the Lord to be forgiven—
Mosiah 4:2

   ❧ Forgiveness brings peace of conscience through faith in Jesus
Christ—Mosiah 4:3

THE RESULTS OF FORGIVENESS AND TRUE CONVERSION

Now, it came to pass that when I had heard these words I began to feel a desire for the welfare of my brethren . . . I did pour out my whole soul unto God for them.

ENOS 1:9

Referring back to the conversion of Enos, we may now summarize the results of these words in his life as follows: first, receive the words through the Holy Ghost (vv 1–3); second, repent (vv 4–8); third, have charity (vv 9–18); fourth, share the word (vv 19–26); and fifth, endure to the end (vv 25–27). These steps are not unique to Enos but are the true fruits of conversion common to all.

(Monte S. Nyman and Charles D. Tate Jr., eds., *Jacob through Words of Mormon: To Learn with Joy* [Provo, UT: Religious Studies Center, 1990], 243–244)

Daily Living

FORGIVENESS AND TRUE CONVERSION RESULT IN A DEEP CONCERN FOR YOUR FELLOWMEN.

- ❧ You want all to taste and feel the joy of the gospel in their lives—Alma 36:24

- ❧ Good works always follow true repentance—Helaman 12:24

- ❧ You will have the desire to sing the song of redeeming love—Alma 5:26

- ❧ Charity, the attribute of the truly converted, is manifested in a love of your fellowmen—Ether 12:34

- ❧ Pray for the welfare of everyone and act accordingly—Alma 6:6; 34:27–28

THE POWER OF THE WORD CAN PRICK OUR HEARTS

Wherefore, the prophets, and the priests, and the teachers, did labor diligently, exhorting with all long-suffering the people to diligence . . . persuading them to look forward unto the Messiah, and believe in him to come as though he already was. . . .
And it came to pass that by so doing they kept them from being destroyed upon the face of the land; for they did prick their hearts with the word, continually stirring them up unto repentance.
JAROM 1:11–12

Jesus reminded his listeners of the eternal value of such scripture: those who hearken to the Lord's revealed word, repent, and are baptized will be saved (3 Nephi 23:5).

(Kent P. Jackson, ed., *Studies in Scripture, Vol. 8: Alma 30 to Moroni* [Salt Lake City: Deseret Book, 1988], 196)

Daily Living

HEARKEN TO THE WORD OF GOD AND YOU WILL BE INSPIRED TO REPENT.

- ಐ The words of Enos's father sunk deep into his heart—Enos 1:3–4

- ಐ Alma the Younger was able to repent when he recalled the words of his father concerning Christ's Atonement—Alma 36:17–20

- ಐ Pull down pride with the word of God—Alma 4:19

- ಐ The word has the greatest power to cause change—Alma 31:5

- ಐ Hearken to the word and do not procrastinate the day of your repentance—Alma 13:27

- ಐ Searching the scriptures will bring you to repentance—Alma 37:9

THE PRICE OF SALVATION

Come unto him, and offer your whole souls as an offering unto him, and continue in fasting and praying, and endure to the end; and as the Lord liveth ye will be saved.
OMNI 1:26

To offer our "whole soul" to God, we must teach all of the parts of ourselves to serve God; only then can we be said to be giving all our hearts and all our souls, as commanded in the scriptures. . . . The Savior further broke down the commandment to offer all of our hearts and souls, and thereby harmonize ourselves, when he taught, "And thou shalt love the Lord thy God with all thy heart, and with all thy soul, and with all thy mind, and with all thy strength: this is the first commandment" (Mark 12:30).

(Rodney Jay Vessels, *The Zeezrom Syndrome: Let Your Spiritual Awakening Begin* [Salt Lake City: Deseret Book, 2005], 101)

Daily Living

OFFER YOUR "WHOLE SOUL" TO GAIN ETERNAL LIFE.

- ଚଠ Your sacrifice should be a broken heart and contrite spirit—3 Nephi 9:20

- ଚଠ You are saved by grace after all you can do—2 Nephi 25:23

- ଚଠ Work and serve unwearyingly—Helaman 10:4–5

- ଚଠ Seek the will of God rather than your own will—Helaman 10:4

- ଚଠ Press forward with steadfastness—2 Nephi 31:20

- ଚଠ Enter the king of heaven by doing the will of the Father—3 Nephi 14:21

THE LORD KNOWS ALL THINGS

And I do this [make this record] for a wise purpose; for thus it whispereth me, according to the workings of the Spirit of the Lord which is in me. And now, I do not know all things; but the Lord knoweth all things which are to come; wherefore, he worketh in me to do according to his will.

WORDS OF MORMON 1:7

Moreover, God, since "all things are present" with him, is not simply predicting based solely on the past. In ways that are not clear to us, he sees rather than foresees the future, because all things are at once present before him . . . We need to develop both the understanding and the trust that Mormon had when he was dealing with something that he sensed had a relationship to events yet future.

(Neal A. Maxwell, *Things As They Really Are* [Salt Lake City: Deseret Book, 1978], 28)

Daily Living

TRUST IN THE LORD IN FAITH FOR HE KNOWETH ALL THINGS.

- ✺ The Lord knoweth all things from the beginning and prepares a way to accomplish His work—1 Nephi 9:6

- ✺ All things are done according to the wisdom of God—2 Nephi 2:24

- ✺ Trust in the Lord for He shall lift thee up in the last day—Mosiah 23:22

- ✺ Trust in the Lord and ye shall be supported in your trials—Alma 36:3

- ✺ You will be blessed and prospered as you put your trust in God—Helaman 12:1

BLESSINGS CONTAINED IN THE RECORDS OF GOD

*I would that ye should remember that were it not for these
plates, which contain these records and these commandments,
we must have suffered in ignorance, even at this present time,
not knowing the mysteries of God.*
MOSIAH 1:3

That morning in scripture reading the Lord sent the blessing we
sought—a blessing that came by the power of love, of testimony, of
the scriptures, and of his words. There are few times when parents
have a better opportunity to teach and to testify than during family
scripture time. In fact, that is one of the major blessings of family
scripture study—it gives parents a golden opportunity, day after day,
to instill in their children the truths that are most important to
them.

(Gene R. Cook, *Searching the Scriptures: Bringing Power
to Your Personal and Family Study* [Salt Lake City:
Deseret Book, 1997], 150)

Daily Living

SEARCH THE SCRIPTURES AND RECEIVE DIRECTION IN YOUR LIFE.

- ဆ The iron rod will lead you to the tree of life—1 Nephi 8:19

- ဆ The word of God is like a Liahona to our lives—Alma
  37:44–47

- ဆ The word will tell you all things to do—2 Nephi 32:3

- ဆ Ponder the scriptures—2 Nephi 4:15

- ဆ The word will give you the power of God unto salvation—
  D&C 68:4

THE PROPHET SPEAKS FOR GOD

*I have not commanded you to come up hither to trifle with the
words which I shall speak, but that you should hearken unto
me, and open your ears that ye may hear, and your hearts that
ye may understand, and your minds that the mysteries of God
may be unfolded to your view.*

MOSIAH 2:9

Gratefully, we follow prophets who have been given a divine commission: "Whatsoever they shall speak when moved upon by the
Holy Ghost shall be scripture, shall be the will of the Lord, shall be
the mind of the Lord, shall be the word of the Lord, shall be the
voice of the Lord, and the power of God unto salvation" [D&C
68:4]. While we follow prophetic teachings, we can develop our
spiritual capacities by emulating one such as President Gordon B.
Hinckley. I thank God for this prophet. He is the Lord's anointed.
Willingly I follow him. I love him and sustain him.

(Russell M. Nelson, "Spiritual Capacity,"
Ensign, November 1997, 16)

Daily Living

FOLLOW THE PROPHETS IN RIGHTEOUSNESS OR REJECT THEM AND PERISH.

- ❧ You perish if you cast out the prophets—2 Nephi 26:3

- ❧ If you reject the words of the prophets the Lord will not receive
  you—3 Nephi 28:34

- ❧ The righteous hearken to the words of the prophets—2 Nephi 26:8

- ❧ Search the words of the prophet and obtain hope and faith—
  Jacob 4:6

- ❧ The prophets always speak of Christ—Jacob 7:11; Mosiah 15:11

- ❧ The prophets words shall all be fulfilled—3 Nephi 29:2

SERVICE

*When ye are in the service of your fellow beings ye are only in
the service of your God.*
Mosiah 2:17

Service to a friend, neighbor, stranger, or others is service to God
and has eternal implications. Those who balk at service opportunities should sensitize themselves by reading these words of the Savior,
as related to the judgment day: "Inasmuch as ye have done it unto
one of the least of these my brethren, ye have done it unto me. . . .
And these [who turned away the stranger in need] shall go away into
everlasting punishment: but the righteous [those who fed, clothed,
and administered to the needs of the stranger] into life eternal"
(Matthew 25:40, 46; see verses 31–46).

(Carlos E. Asay, *Family Pecan Trees: Planting a Legacy of
Faith at Home* [Salt Lake City: Deseret Book, 1992], 181)

Daily Living

You serve God as you serve others.

ᵍ Teach your children to serve one another—Mosiah 4:15

ᵍ Succor those who stand in need—Mosiah 4:16

ᵍ We must bear one another's burdens, mourn with those that
mourn, and comfort those who stand in need of comfort—
Mosiah 18:8–9

YOU ARE BLESSED MORE THAN YOU DESERVE

*I say unto you that if ye should serve him who has created you
from the beginning, and is preserving you from day to day, by
lending you breath, that ye may live and move and do according
to your own will, and even supporting you from one moment to
another—I say, if ye should serve him with all your whole souls
yet ye would be unprofitable servants.*

MOSIAH 2:21; SEE ALSO VERSES 19–20, 22–24

My life has been rich with challenges and associations. I have wrestled with problems large and small. I have known something of discouragement and on a few occasions have felt the exhilaration of achievement. I feel a deep sense of gratitude for the marvelous and generous blessings of the Lord. Among these is the opportunity to be associated with His great cause and kingdom.

(Sheri L. Dew, *Go Forward with Faith: The Biography
of Gordon B. Hinckley* [Salt Lake City:
Deseret Book, 1996], 448)

Daily Living

RECOGNIZE YOUR BLESSINGS WITH GRATITUDE, FOR YOU ARE ALWAYS IN
DEBT TO THE LORD.

ᏸ Render thanks with your whole soul—Mosiah 2:20

ᏸ Live in thanksgiving daily for the mercies and goodness of
God—Alma 34:38

ᏸ Acknowledge your unworthiness of all your blessings before
God—Alma 38:14

ᏸ The goodness and mercy of God are over all the people of the
earth—1 Nephi 1:14

LOSS OF THE SPIRIT

After ye have known and have been taught all these things, if ye should transgress and go contrary to that which has been spoken, that ye do withdraw yourselves from the Spirit of the Lord, that it may have no place in you to guide you in wisdom's paths that ye may be blessed, prospered, and preserved— . . . the same cometh out in open rebellion against God.
MOSIAH 2:36–37

As a man grows and increases in the things of this world, if he is not careful, he will lose the Spirit of the Lord, and he will set his heart upon the things of this world. . . . The great trouble is that there are many people who, as they grow and increase in the things of this world, set their hearts upon them and lose the Spirit of the Lord.

(Heber J. Grant, *Gospel Standards: Selections from the Sermons and Writings of Heber J. Grant,* comp. G. Homer Durham [Salt Lake City: Deseret Book, 1981], 181)

Daily Living

YOU LOSE THE SPIRIT WHEN YOU BREAK THE COMMANDMENTS.

   ⁞ If you reject the prophets you lose the Spirit—1 Nephi 7:14

   ⁞ The Spirit leaves when you are prideful or choose works of darkness—2 Nephi 26:10–11

   ⁞ If your heart is hardened you lose the Spirit—2 Nephi 33:2

   ⁞ If you go contrary to what you know is right, you withdraw yourselves from the Spirit—Mosiah 2:36

BECOMING AN ENEMY TO GOD

Therefore if that man repenteth not, and remaineth and dieth an enemy to God, the demands of divine justice do awaken his immortal soul to a lively sense of his own guilt, which doth cause him to shrink from the presence of the Lord, and doth fill his breast with guilt, and pain, and anguish, which is like an unquenchable fire, whose flame ascendeth up forever and ever.
MOSIAH 2:38

Therefore, if we desire to repent and thus stop being an enemy to God, we must repent of even the tiniest of our sins, thoughts and actions both, and become "clean every whit" (John 13:10) before the Lord.

(Blaine and Brenton Yorgason, *Spiritual Survival in the Last Days* [Salt Lake City: Deseret Book, 1990], 92)

Daily Living

STRIVE TO KEEP YOUR THOUGHTS AND ACTIONS PURE.

- ଠ The natural man (the unrepentant man) is an enemy to God— Mosiah 3:19

- ଠ When you love Satan more than God you are carnal, sensual and devilish—Moses 5:13

- ଠ You become the covenant people of the Lord when you repent— 2 Nephi 30:2

- ଠ If you don't repent and be baptized, you are damned—3 Nephi 11:34

HAPPINESS IN RIGHTEOUSNESS

And moreover, I would desire that ye should consider on the blessed and happy state of those that keep the commandments of God. For behold, they are blessed in all things, both temporal and spiritual; and if they hold out faithful to the end they are received into heaven, that thereby they may dwell with God in a state of never-ending happiness.

MOSIAH 2:41

Keep the faith. Your happiness lies in following the gospel of Jesus Christ. That's the case with all of us. "Wickedness never was happiness" (Alma 41:10), said Alma to his son Corianton. That's as true as the sunrise in the morning. . . . There is no happiness in sin. There is misery and pain and regret and heartache and suffering. Happiness lies in walking in righteousness. Happiness lies in faithfulness and in righteousness. (Juneau Alaska Fireside, June 18, 1995.)

(Gordon B. Hinckley, *Teachings of Gordon B. Hinckley*
[Salt Lake City: Deseret Book, 1997], 256)

Daily Living

KEEPING THE COMMANDMENTS BRINGS THE BLESSINGS OF HAPPINESS.

- ❧ If you keep the commandments you will prosper in the land—Jarom 1:9

- ❧ Partaking of the love of God brings happiness—1 Nephi 8:10

- ❧ Good works bring forth eternal life and happiness—Mosiah 16:11

- ❧ The righteous are received into a state of happiness—Alma 40:12

- ❧ You cannot find happiness in sin—Mormon 2:13

CHRIST OFFERS SALVATION TO ALL

And lo, he cometh unto his own, that salvation might come
unto the children of men even through faith on his name; and
even after all this they shall consider him a man, and say that
he hath a devil, and shall scourge him, and shall crucify him.
And he shall rise the third day from the dead; and behold, he
standeth to judge the world; and behold, all these things are done
that a righteous judgment might come upon the children of men.
MOSIAH 3:9–10

Faith in Jesus Christ, the Redeemer of mankind, is the key to salvation and a knowledge of all things. Those who walk the strait and narrow way with "an eye of faith" shall be perfected in all the knowledge of God. . . . Thus, from the tiny seed of mortal faith in the Son of Man will come an immortal knowledge of God and his unimaginable mysteries. It only remains for us to plant that seed and nourish it with diligence.

(Kent P. Jackson, ed., *Studies in Scripture, Vol. 8: Alma 30 to Moroni* [Salt Lake City: Deseret Book, 1988], 26)

Daily Living

SALVATION IS OFFERED TO ALL MANKIND.

- ಏ You will be saved if you hearken to the voice of the Lord—2 Nephi

- ಏ Christ inviteth all to come unto Him and partake of His goodness—2 Nephi 26:33

- ಏ Salvation can come to all that believe in Christ—Alma 34:15

- ಏ We can't be saved without each other—D&C 128:15

PROPHETS PREACH REPENTANCE AND FAITH

*Salvation cometh to none such except it be through repentance
and faith on the Lord Jesus Christ.
And the Lord God hath sent his holy prophets among all the
children of men, to declare these things to every kindred, nation,
and tongue, that thereby whosoever should believe that Christ
should come, the same might receive remission of their sins, and
rejoice with exceedingly great joy, even as though he had already
come among them.*

MOSIAH 3:12–13

The prophets teach faith—through the power of the Holy
Ghost.
They teach repentance by the same power. . . .
They help us to obtain "the knowledge of the Son of God,
unto a perfect man, unto the measure of the stature of the ful-
ness of Christ."

(Mark E. Petersen, *Faith* [Salt Lake City:
Deseret Book, 1983], 33)

Daily Living

YOU MUST REPENT AND EXERCISE FAITH IN OUR SAVIOR JESUS CHRIST.

- Alma preached faith and repentance on the Lord Jesus Christ—
  Mosiah 18:7; 25:15, 22

- Faith unto repentance is the key to salvation—Alma 34:15–17

- Alma counsels Helaman to preach repentance and faith in
  Christ—Alma 37:33

- Nothing can save you save it be repentance and faith on the
  Lord Jesus Christ—Helaman 13:6

THE NATURAL MAN

*For the natural man is an enemy to God . . . unless he yields to
the enticings of the Holy Spirit, and putteth off the natural man
and becometh a saint through the atonement of Christ the Lord,
and becometh as a child, submissive, meek, humble, patient,
full of love, willing to submit to all things which the Lord seeth
fit to inflict upon him, even as a child doth submit to his father.*
MOSIAH 3:19

As the descendants of Adam and Eve then become accountable for
their own sins at the age of eight, they all taste sin to one degree or
another as the result of their curiosity and their experiences with
temptation in a free environment. Those . . . who accept Christ's
grace by their faith, repentance, baptism, and continued striving will
yield to the "enticings of the Holy Spirit," put off "the natural man,"
and become "saint[s] through the atonement of Christ the Lord"
(Mosiah 3:19).

(Bruce C. Hafen and Marie K. Hafen, *The Belonging Heart:
The Atonement and Relationships with God and Family*
[Salt Lake City: Deseret Book, 1994], 111–112)

Daily Living

TAKE HIS YOKE UPON YOU, YIELD UNTO CHRIST, FOR HIS YOKE IS EASY,
HIS BURDEN LIGHT.

- The Holy Ghost will show you all things to do—2 Nephi 32:5

- Be easily entreated—Alma 7:23

- If you put off the Spirit the devil has power over you—Alma
  30:42

DEPENDENCE ON THE ATONEMENT

*Salvation might come to him that should put his trust in the
Lord, and should be diligent in keeping his commandments,
and continue in the faith even unto the end of his life.*
MOSIAH 4:6

This total dependence on the atonement of Jesus Christ was no doubt
known in the premortal world by the spirits who would be coming
to earth to gain mortal bodies and was a trial to those who had not
strong faith in and a testimony of Jesus Christ. It was no doubt a
factor in causing some to align themselves with the "guaranteed,"
"no-risk," "no-effort," "no-individual-responsibility" seduction of
Lucifer.

Our relationship to Jesus Christ is just that vital and critical. He is
our Redeemer, and without him we could do nothing (cf. John
15:1–6). Even with the atonement we must give our best efforts, but
without him, no one could have ever attained to even a particle of
salvation.

(Robert L. Millet and Kent P. Jackson, eds., *Studies in
Scripture, Vol. 2: The Pearl of Great Price* [Salt Lake City:
Randall Book, 1985], 117–118)

Daily Living

RECOGNIZE THE GOODNESS OF GOD AND YOUR DEPENDENCE UPON THE
ATONEMENT OF JESUS CHRIST AND THEN ACT UPON IT.

- ∞ Without the Atonement you would be like unto the devil—
  2 Nephi 9:9

- ∞ The goodness of God prepareth a way to escape death and
  hell—2 Nephi 9:10

- ∞ Remember by grace are you saved after all you can do—2 Nephi
  25:23

REPENTANCE

And again, believe that ye must repent of your sins and forsake them, and humble yourselves before God; and ask in sincerity of heart that he would forgive you.

MOSIAH 4:10

If sin has deprived us of peace within, we can repent and seek forgiveness. The Lord said that he "cannot look upon sin with the least degree of allowance; nevertheless, he that repents and does the commandments of the Lord shall be forgiven" (D&C 1:31–32). President Spencer W. Kimball wrote: "The essence of the miracle of forgiveness is that it brings peace to the previously anxious, restless, frustrated, perhaps tormented soul. In a world of turmoil and contention this is indeed a priceless gift" (Spencer W. Kimball, *The Miracle of Forgiveness* [Salt Lake City: Deseret Book, 1969], 363).

(Joseph B. Wirthlin, *Finding Peace in Our Lives*
[Salt Lake City: Deseret Book, 1995], 9)

Daily Living

HIS HAND IS EVER STRETCHED OUT.

- ☙ Everyone must repent—2 Nephi 9:23

- ☙ You must pay the price to repent—Enos 1:2–8

- ☙ If you truly repent the Lord will forgive and remember the sin no more—D&C 58:42–43

- ☙ You must repent and be born again—Alma 7:14

- ☙ Confess your sins and repent and the Lord will forgive you—Mosiah 26:29

GOODNESS OF GOD

If ye have known of his goodness and have tasted of his love, and have received a remission of your sins, which causeth such exceedingly great joy in your souls, even so I would that ye should remember, and always retain in remembrance, the great-ness of God, and your own nothingness, and his goodness and long-suffering towards you, unworthy creatures, and humble yourselves even in the depths of humility, calling on the name of the Lord daily, and standing steadfastly in the faith of that which is to come, which was spoken by the mouth of the angel.
MOSIAH 4:11

How can you and I remember, always, the goodness of God, that we can retain a remission of our sins? . . . The Holy Ghost brings back memories of what God has taught us. And one of the ways God teaches us is with his blessings; and so, if we choose to exercise faith, the Holy Ghost will bring God's kindnesses to our remembrance.
(Henry B. Eyring, *To Draw Closer to God: A Collection of Discourses* [Salt Lake City: Deseret Book, 1997], 77–78)

Daily Living

ALWAYS REMEMBER THE GREATNESS OF GOD AND HIS WORDS.

- ℰ Remember the Savior, His paths and His words—2 Nephi 9:40, 41,44

- ℰ Remember to search the word of God diligently—Mosiah 1:7

- ℰ Remember what the Lord has done for you—Alma 29:10; 62:50

- ℰ Remember His mercy, the gifts He has blessed you with, and that He is always there—Moroni 10:3, 18–19

REJOICE IN THE LORD

And behold, I say unto you that if ye do this ye shall always rejoice, and be filled with the love of God, and always retain a remission of your sins; and ye shall grow in the knowledge of the glory of him that created you, or in the knowledge of that which is just and true.

MOSIAH 4:12

Forsaking sin involves not only a turning from evil practices but also a turning to God in greater righteousness and service. . . . The resulting "works meet for repentance" are naturally two-directional—we cannot demonstrate greater love and worship of God without also gaining an intensified desire to serve and bless the lives of others. Alma taught that the covenants associated with baptism for the remission of sins require devotion on our part to both God and our fellowmen (see Mosiah 18:8–10).

(Brent L. Top, in *Doctrines of the Book of Mormon:
1991 Sperry Symposium on the Book of Mormon*
[Salt Lake City: Deseret Book, 1992], 204)

Daily Living

REJOICE IN THE LORD THROUGH REPENTANCE AND SERVICE TO YOUR
FELLOWMEN.

- ∞ Repentance is personified through good works—Helaman 12:24

- ∞ Rejoice in the Lord because of His goodness—2 Nephi 4:28–30; 2 Nephi 9:13

- ∞ Rejoice in the Lord for He is the source for your remission of sins—2 Nephi 25:26

- ∞ Rejoice in the service of the Lord and your fellowmen—Alma 25:17; 26:11,13,16

FRUITS OF POSSESSING THE LOVE OF GOD

And ye will not have a mind to injure one another, but to live peaceably, and to render to every man according to that which is his due.

And ye will not suffer your children that they go hungry, or naked; neither will ye suffer that they transgress the laws of God, and fight and quarrel one with another. . . .

And also, ye yourselves will succor those that stand in need of your succor; ye will administer of your substance unto him that standeth in need.

MOSIAH 4:13–14, 16

Yes, charity is the bringing together of knowledge and service, learning and love. If the greatest of the commandments has to do with love of God, its full meaning implies far more than sincerity and good will. . . . It is not enough that we love; we must also come to a knowledge of the truth and pray with all the energy of our hearts that we may be filled with that love which is called charity, the pure love of Christ, so that when He comes again, we shall be like Him.

(Barbara B. Smith, et al., *A Woman's Choices: The Relief Society Legacy Lectures* [Salt Lake City: Deseret Book, 1984], 23)

Daily Living

PRAY TO BE FILLED WITH CHARITY, THE GREATEST GIFT.

ဆ Without charity you are nothing—2 Nephi 26:30

ဆ With the love of God you can be happy in all things—4 Nephi 1:15–18

ဆ The love of God is the most desirable above all things—1 Nephi 11:22

DEPENDENCE UPON GOD

Ye have been calling on his name, and begging for a remission
of your sins. And has he suffered that ye have begged in vain?
Nay; he has poured out his Spirit upon you, and has caused that
your hearts should be filled with joy. . . .
And now, if God, who has created you, on whom you are
dependent for your lives and for all that ye have and are, doth
grant unto you whatsoever ye ask that is right, in faith, believing
that ye shall receive, O then, how ye ought to impart of the
substance that ye have one to another.

MOSIAH 4:20–21

I heard a man of prominence say the other day, "I have amended the
language of my prayers. Instead of saying, "Bless the poor and the sick
and the needy," I now say, "Father, show me how to help the poor and
the sick and the needy, and give me resolution to do so."

(Gordon B. Hinckley, *Teachings of Gordon B. Hinckley*
[Salt Lake City: Deseret Book, 1997], 458)

Daily Living

MAKE A PLAN TO GIVE FREELY TO THOSE IN NEED.

- ಐ Be merciful to all and do good continually—Alma 41:14

- ಐ Beware of materialism to the extent of forgetting the needy—
  Mormon 8:39

- ಐ Give with a pure heart and not grudgingly—Moroni 7:6–10

- ಐ Give according to your ability of your own free will—Mosiah
  18:27–28

JUDGING OTHERS

*And if ye judge the man who putteth up his petition to you for
your substance that he perish not, and condemn him, how much
more just will be your condemnation for withholding your substance, which doth not belong to you but to God, to whom also
your life belongeth; and yet ye put up no petition, nor repent of
the thing which thou hast done.*

MOSIAH 4:22

A Christian's . . . loyalty goes beyond his own family and church
community. Like Jesus, he is concerned with Jew and Gentile, with
people in the larger community and in the third world. He is willing to share his time and means with people anywhere who need his
interest and help. He is interested in the retarded, the mentally ill,
the elderly, the poor, the lonely, the "sinner." He does not judge others. He will serve some of these people as his strength permits.

(Lowell L. Bennion, *The Best of Lowell L. Bennion:
Selected Writings 1928–1988,* ed. Eugene England
[Salt Lake City: Deseret Book, 1988], 271–272)

Daily Living

NEVER SUPPRESS A GENEROUS THOUGHT.

ಏ Judge not, for as you judge so shall you be judged—3 Nephi
14:1–2

ಏ Give freely of your substance—Jacob 2:17

ಏ Be liberal to all—Alma 1:30

ಏ If you don't remember to be charitable, your prayers are in
vain—Alma 34:29

WISDOM AND ORDER

And see that all these things are done in wisdom and order; for it is not requisite that a man should run faster than he has strength. And again, it is expedient that he should be diligent, that thereby he might win the prize; therefore, all things must be done in order.

MOSIAH 4:27

We can learn to become like him [Christ] as we use his ways to teach our children: establishing regular communications with them; listening, guiding, prompting; watching over them always; protecting but not manipulating; allowing them to learn by experience; correcting them in such a way that they learn to obey—not because it is our will, but because they have learned to do what is right to do to grow in wisdom.

We can plan our lives and, to the degree that it is possible, determine the end from the beginning by building upon God-given principles to provide the security of truth.

(Barbara B. Smith, *LDS Women's Treasury: Insights and Inspiration for Today's Woman* [Salt Lake City: Deseret Book, 1997], 277)

Daily Living

PLAN WELL, BE DILIGENT, AND ORGANIZE EVERY NEEDFUL THING.

- ❧ Organize and prepare every needful thing—D&C 88:119

- ❧ Diligently seek and ye shall find—1 Nephi 10:19

- ❧ Diligently seek happiness—Alma 27:18

- ❧ Seek first the Kingdom of God—3 Nephi 13:33

WATCH YOURSELVES IN ALL THINGS

But this much I can tell you, that if ye do not watch yourselves, and your thoughts, and your words, and your deeds, and observe the commandments of God, and continue in the faith of what ye have heard concerning the coming of our Lord, even unto the end of your lives, ye must perish. And now, O man, remember, and perish not.
MOSIAH 4:30

Watch yourselves day by day, hour by hour and minute by minute. Keep a guard over yourselves so that you will never do or say anything that you will regret hereafter, and your lives will be filled with usefulness, and you will increase your own peace and promote it among your neighbors, and this will insure a great degree of salvation here, and prepare for a higher degree hereafter.

(Brigham Young, in *Journal of Discourses* [London: Latter-day Saints' Book Depot, 1854–1886], 13:253)

Daily Living
EVALUATE YOUR LIFE.

ᘓ Have you experienced a change of heart?—Alma 5 (the great evaluation chapter)

ᘓ What manner of men ought ye to be?—3 Nephi 27:27

ᘓ Consider the happy state of those who keep the commandments—Mosiah 2:41

ᘓ Do you feel a desire for the welfare of others?—Enos 1:9

ᘓ What are your real intentions?—Moroni 7:6

THE MIGHTY CHANGE

And they all cried with one voice, saying: Yea, we believe all the words which thou hast spoken unto us; and also, we know of their surety and truth, because of the Spirit of the Lord Omnipotent, which has wrought a mighty change in us, or in our hearts, that we have no more disposition to do evil, but to do good continually.

MOSIAH 5:2

As we become affirmatively purified and perfected—beyond having achieved remission of our sins—our hearts and minds begin to change, for our very nature is changing.

It was this taste of the divinely bestowed power of godliness that then caused Benjamin's people to . . . experience . . . the rebirth of the Spirit, and King Benjamin counseled them then to seek a course of growth leading from spiritual rebirth to full spiritual maturity.

(Bruce C. Hafen, *The Broken Heart: Applying the Atonement to Life's Experiences* [Salt Lake City: Deseret Book, 1989], 173)

Daily Living

EXPERIENCE THE MIGHTY CHANGE AND HAVE NO DESIRE TO DO EVIL.

- ࠔ Have ye been spiritually been born of God?—Alma 5:14

- ࠔ All must be born again from their fallen state—Mosiah 27:25

- ࠔ You must repent in order to be born again—Alma 7:14; 22:15

- ࠔ You know the things of God when you are born again—Alma 36:5

EXERCISE FAITH

*And it is the faith which we have had on the things which our king
has spoken unto us that has brought us to this great knowledge,
whereby we do rejoice with such exceedingly great joy.*
MOSIAH 5:4

We frequently hear it said that faith is imperfect knowledge; that the
first disappears as the second takes its place; that now we walk by
faith but some day we shall walk by the sure light of knowledge. In
a sense this is true; yet it must be remembered that knowledge may
be as dead and unproductive in good works as is faithless belief.

(James E. Talmage, *Articles of Faith* [Salt Lake City:
Deseret Book, 1981], 98)

Daily Living

YOU CAN GAIN SURE KNOWLEDGE AS YOU EXERCISE YOUR FAITH.

- ෨ You can gain knowledge through prayer—2 Nephi 4:23

- ෨ You cannot gain knowledge if you fail to search for it—2 Nephi 32:7; Ether 4:13

- ෨ Stand steadfastly in faith and ye shall grow in the knowledge of that which is just and true—Mosiah 4:12

- ෨ Faith and prayer can help others be brought to the knowledge of truth—Mosiah 27:14; Alma 17:9

- ෨ The Spirit giveth knowledge and power according to your faith—Alma 18:35

- ෨ Perfect knowledge of something makes your faith in it dormant but you must never lay aside your faith, diligence or patience in nourishing the word of God—Alma 32:34–43

BORN OF CHRIST

And now, because of the covenant which ye have made ye shall be called the children of Christ, his sons, and his daughters; for behold, this day he hath spiritually begotten you; for ye say that your hearts are changed through faith on his name; therefore, ye are born of him and have become his sons and his daughters.

MOSIAH 5:7

Through "the covenant" of baptism, those who are actually born again, become "the children of Christ, his sons, and his daughters"; they are "spiritually begotten" by him; their "hearts are changed through faith on his name"; thus they "are born of him and have become his sons and his daughters" (Mosiah 5:7).

(Bruce R. McConkie, *Doctrinal New Testament Commentary*
[Salt Lake City: Bookcraft, 1965–1973], 1:74)

Daily Living
SEEK TO BECOME HIS CHILDREN.

- ෨ If you receive and believe in Christ you become His children—3 Nephi 9:17

- ෨ Lay hold to every good thing and become a child of Christ—Moroni 7:19

- ෨ By faith you become His child—Moroni 7:26

- ෨ Pray with all the energy of heart to possess charity and when He appears you will be like Him—Moroni 7:48

FREEDOM FROM SIN

*There is no other name given whereby salvation cometh; therefore,
I would that ye should take upon you the name of Christ, all
you that have entered into the covenant with God that ye should
be obedient unto the end of your lives.*
MOSIAH 5:8

The doctrine delivered to them was the gospel of repentance and of obedience. "Being then made free from sin, ye became the servants of righteousness." When the saints repent, their sins flee away; they then become righteous, pure, holy, fit candidates to go where God and Christ are and to inherit eternal life. "Now being made free from sin, and become servants to God, ye have your fruit unto holiness, and the end [for all such is an inheritance of] everlasting life. For the wages of sin is death; but the gift of God is eternal life through Jesus Christ our Lord" (Romans 6:16–23).

(Bruce R. McConkie, *A New Witness for the Articles
of Faith* [Salt Lake City: Deseret Book, 1985], 216)

Daily Living

TAKE UPON YOURSELF THE NAME OF JESUS CHRIST AND OBEDIENTLY
ENDURE TO THE END.

ɞ There is no other way whereby mankind can be saved—2 Nephi 31:21

ɞ You must repent, be baptized and exercise faith in order to be saved—2 Nephi 9:23

ɞ Remember you are saved by grace after all you can do—2 Nephi 25:23

ɞ Blessed are those who repent and hearken to the voice of the Lord—Helaman 12:23

ABOUND IN GOOD WORKS

Therefore, I would that ye should be steadfast and immovable,
always abounding in good works, that Christ, the Lord God
Omnipotent, may seal you his, that you may be brought to
heaven, that ye may have everlasting salvation and eternal life,
through the wisdom, and power, and justice, and mercy of him
who created all things, in heaven and in earth, who is God
above all. Amen.

MOSIAH 5:15

Significantly, those who look forward to a next and better world are usually "anxiously engaged" in improving this one, for they "always abound in good works" (D&C 58:27; Alma 7:24). . . . We should not let the gray mists of the moment obscure the bright promises and prospects of eternity.

(Cory H. Maxwell, ed., *The Neal A. Maxwell Quote Book*
[Salt Lake City: Bookcraft, 1997], 265)

Daily Living

BE STEADFAST AND ABOUND IN GOOD WORKS.

- ಋ Remember you will be judged by your works—1 Nephi 15:32

- ಋ Through faith, hope and charity you will always abound in good works—Alma 7:24

- ಋ You can know the mysteries of God through faith and good works—Alma 26:22

- ಋ Now is the time to perform your labors—Alma 34:22

- ಋ If you fail to do your duty you shall be under condemnation—Moroni 9:6

BLESSINGS OF A DEDICATED LIFE

But if ye will turn to the Lord with full purpose of heart, and put your trust in him, and serve him with all diligence of mind, if ye do this, he will, according to his own will and pleasure, deliver you out of bondage.
MOSIAH 7:33

Nephi taught that we must walk the path of faith "with full purpose of heart, acting no hypocrisy and no deception before God." We know that "a double minded man is unstable in all his ways" and that we cannot "serve two masters." President Marion G. Romney wisely observed that there are too many of us "who try to serve the Lord without offending the devil."

"The Lord requireth the heart and a willing mind.". . . Only when we give our all and overcome our pride and walk the path of faith without deviation can we honestly sing, "Lord, accept our true devotion."
(Joseph B. Wirthlin, "True to the Truth,"
Ensign, May 1997, 16)

Daily Living
STRIVE TO SERVE GOD WITH FULL PURPOSE OF HEART.

- Follow the Savior with full purpose of heart with no hypocrisy—2 Nephi 31:13

- Come unto the Savior with full purpose of heart and be healed—3 Nephi 18:32

- Worship God and Christ with all your might, mind and strength—2 Nephi 25:29

- Serve others with all your might, mind and strength—Mosiah 2:11

- Love God, and by His grace you may become perfect in Christ—Moroni 10:32

CARNAL NATURE

But remember that he that persists in his own carnal nature,
and goes on in the ways of sin and rebellion against God,
remaineth in his fallen state and the devil hath all power over
him. Therefore, he is as though there was no redemption made,
being an enemy to God; and also is the devil an enemy to God.
MOSIAH 16:5

We believe that men will be punished for their own sins (Article of Faith 2). Through the prophet Isaiah, the Lord said he would "punish the inhabitants of the earth for their iniquity" (Isaiah 26:21). God's law could not exist "save there was a punishment" (Alma 42:17). . . . Amulek explained that "he that exercises no faith unto repentance is exposed to the whole law of the demands of justice" (Alma 34:16). Justice requires that the unrepentant sinner suffer for his own sins. "If they would not repent," the Savior said, "they must suffer even as I" (D&C 19:17).

(Dallin H. Oaks, *The Lord's Way* [Salt Lake City: Deseret Book, 1991], 222)

Daily Living

REPENT AND BELIEVE IN THE PROMISE OF THE ATONEMENT.

- ∞ The unrepentant are enemies to God—Mosiah 2:38

- ∞ You become devilish when you don't believe in the Redemption—Moses 5:13

- ∞ The natural man is an enemy to God—Mosiah 3:19

- ∞ If you don't repent you must perish—1 Nephi 14:5

APRIL

&

And they gave thanks to God, yea, all their men and all their women and all their children that could speak lifted their voices in the praises of their God.

—MOSIAH 24:22

DUTIES OF CHURCH MEMBERS

And now, as ye are desirous to come into the fold of God, and to be called his people, and are willing to bear one another's burdens, that they may be light;
Yea, and are willing to mourn with those that mourn; yea, and comfort those that stand in need of comfort, and to stand as witnesses of God at all times and in all things, and in all places that ye may be in, even until death, that ye may be redeemed of God, and be numbered with those of the first resurrection, that ye may have eternal life—

MOSIAH 18:8–9

It occurs to me that we are never invited to participate in acts of kindness without the promise that we'll receive ideas to help in our response. It's as if with the invitation, the feeling of compassion, comes an increase in our ability to respond in a helpful, kind, Christlike way. We become more whole and complete ourselves as we reach out to lift and bless others, to comfort them and mourn with them, to do what we can to make their burdens bearable.

(Mary Ellen Edmunds, *Love Is a Verb*
[Salt Lake City: Deseret Book, 1995], 43–44)

Daily Living

REMEMBER YOUR BAPTISMAL DUTIES AND OBLIGATIONS.

ဆ Ponder the qualifications to be baptized—Moroni 6:1–4; D&C 20:37

ဆ You must press forward steadfastly after baptism—2 Nephi 31:19–20

ဆ You must renew your covenant of baptism—Moroni 4:3; 5:2

ဆ Your baptism is a witness that you will serve God—Mosiah 21:35

RESPONSIBILITIES OF A TEACHER

And he commanded them that they should teach nothing save it were the things which he had taught, and which had been spoken by the mouth of the holy prophets.
Yea, even he commanded them that they should preach nothing save it were repentance and faith on the Lord, who had redeemed his people.
MOSIAH 18:19–20

To others he commanded: "Take upon you mine ordination, even that of an elder, to preach faith and repentance and remission of sins, according to my word, and the reception of the Holy Spirit by the laying on of hands" (D&C 53:3; see also 55:2). It is evident from these scriptures that when a man receives the Melchizedek Priesthood, he accepts the responsibility to preach the restored gospel to the children of God.

(H. Dean Garrett, *The Heavens Are Open: The 1992 Sperry Symposium on the Doctrine and Covenants and Church History* [Salt Lake City: Deseret Book, 1993], 131)

Daily Living

TEACH THE WORD OF GOD BY THE SPIRIT FROM THE SCRIPTURES AND PROPHETS OF GOD.

- ❧ Teach your children and others to walk in the ways of truth—Mosiah 4:15

- ❧ As a teacher, walk in the ways of the Lord and keep the commandments—Mosiah 23:14

- ❧ Teach with the power and authority of God by the Spirit—Alma 17:3

- ❧ Speak as moved upon by the Holy Ghost—D&C 68:3–7

TEACHERS, BE WORTHY OF TRUST

And also trust no one to be your teacher nor your minister,
except he be a man of God, walking in his ways and keeping his
commandments.
MOSIAH 23:14

Of course, the principle of common consent has always played an important role in encouraging individual Church members to express themselves about sustaining those called to Church positions. Moreover, Church leaders at any level seek to be worthy of the members' trust. Yet the accountability of these leaders is not only to the members of their congregations but to the Lord and his authorized representatives.

(Bruce C. Hafen and Marie K. Hafen, *The Belonging Heart:*
The Atonement and Relationships with God and Family
[Salt Lake City: Deseret Book, 1994], 128)

Daily Living

BE A GOOD EXAMPLE THAT YOU MIGHT BETTER SERVE YOUR FELLOWMEN.

  ❧ Children can lose confidence in their parents because of their example—Jacob 2:35

  ❧ A bad example can hinder a person's willingness to hear the gospel—Alma 39:11

  ❧ Let your light shine that you might bless others and glorify your Heavenly Father—3 Nephi 12:15–16

FORGIVENESS OF OTHERS

Yea, and as often as my people repent will I forgive them their trespasses against me.
And ye shall also forgive one another your trespasses; for verily I say unto you, he that forgiveth not his neighbor's trespasses when he says that he repents, the same hath brought himself under condemnation.
MOSIAH 26:30–31

These words came to me with such clarity that I wrote them down. I keep them in my scriptures: "Forgiveness is one of our tasks as we partake of the sacrament. If we would be forgiven, we must, ourselves, forgive. To truly forgive, I must identify the hurt, the pain—honestly, not denying it—and then offer that pain as a willing sacrifice to God. Then it can disappear. Once I've given it away, my attitude toward the person who inflicted it is also changed; no grievance or wound remains, and he or she can be seen in a new Light. The other person need do nothing for this to happen. It is in my heart that the 'mighty change' can take place."

(Dawn Anderson, Dlora Dalton, and Susette Green, eds.,
Every Good Thing: Talks from the 1997 BYU Women's Conference [Salt Lake City: Deseret Book, 1998], 306)

Daily Living
STRIVE TO FORGIVE OTHERS.

ᔆ Reconcile yourself with others that you may have offended—3 Nephi 12:23–24

ᔆ If you forgive, your Heavenly Father will forgive you—3 Nephi 13:14

ᔆ Remember it is required of us to forgive all men—D&C 64:10

BLESSINGS THROUGH FAITHFUL PRAYERS

*And again, the angel said: Behold, the Lord hath heard . . . the
prayers of his servant, Alma, who is thy father; for he has prayed
with much faith concerning thee that thou mightest be brought to
the knowledge of the truth; therefore, for this purpose have I come
to convince thee of the power and authority of God, that the
prayers of his servants might be answered according to their faith.*

MOSIAH 27:14

Suppose . . . you are a mother or father with a son who is straying from
the path of righteousness. . . . You can do much to pray him home . . .
to fast him home. You can repent enough of your own sins that,
through your sacrifice, the Lord may intervene more in his life and save
the boy. It's not that you're paying for your own sins—Jesus did that.
But through your agency, through your sacrifice, you are able to receive
blessings that you otherwise would not be able to obtain. (Of course,
these things still depend on the agency of others—our prayers can't
supersede the agency of those we're praying for. But sacrifice and fervent
prayer can do much to help. With such prayer we can accomplish
much—even if it doesn't bring our loved ones all the way home.)

(Gene R. Cook, *Receiving Answers to Our Prayers*
[Salt Lake City: Deseret Book, 1996], 25)

Daily Living

PRAY FOR OTHERS BUT REMEMBER THAT AGENCY IS SUPREME; GOD WILL
FORCE NO ONE.

- ❧ Pray for all those who know not God—Alma 6:6

- ❧ Through the prayers of the righteous many blessings are received—
  Alma 10:23

- ❧ Fast and pray for the Spirit to help bring souls unto Christ—
  Alma 17:9

BORN AGAIN

And the Lord said unto me: Marvel not that all mankind, yea, men and women, all nations, kindreds, tongues and people, must be born again; yea, born of God, changed from their carnal and fallen state, to a state of righteousness, being redeemed of God, becoming his sons and daughters.

MOSIAH 27:25

We need to be born again, and have new hearts put in us. There is too much of the old leaven about us. We are not born again as we should be. Do you not believe that we ought to be born again? Do you not believe that we should become new creatures in Christ Jesus, under the influence of the Gospel? All will say yes, who understand the Gospel. You must be born again. You must have new desires, new hearts, so to speak, in you.

(George Q. Cannon, quoted in Rulon T. Burton, *We Believe* [Salt Lake City: Tabernacle Books, 1994], 128)

Daily Living

STRIVE TO KEEP THE COVENANTS YOU MADE AT BAPTISM.

- ∞ Preach repentance to all that they might repent and be born again—Alma 5:49

- ∞ You must be born again else you cannot inherit the kingdom of Heaven—Alma 7:14

- ∞ Being born again is being born of the Spirit—Mosiah 27:24

- ∞ You become the sons and daughters of Christ through baptism—Mosiah 5:7

WORTH OF SOULS

*Now they were desirous that salvation should be declared to
every creature, for they could not bear that any human soul
should perish; yea, even the very thoughts that any soul should
endure endless torment did cause them to quake and tremble.*
MOSIAH 28:3

Much of the Church's resources are expended on teaching the Saints
concerning the "welfare of their souls." This instruction is not given
just to increase gospel scholarship but is designed to lead men and
women a partake of Christ's atonement in their own lives—which
in turn leads to greater compassion and concern for the welfare of
the souls of others.

(Joseph Fielding McConkie and Robert L. Millet, *Doctrinal
Commentary on the Book of Mormon* [Salt Lake City:
Bookcraft, 1987–1992], 4:330)

Daily Living

THE SIGN OF TRUE CONVERSION IS CONCERN FOR THE WELFARE OF OTHERS.

- ◊ Concern for others is expressed following conversion—Enos 1:9, 11

- ◊ You want people to taste the joy that you taste in the gospel—Alma 36:24

- ◊ Labor for the welfare of others—Alma 48:12

- ◊ Succor those that stand in need of succor—Mosiah 4:16

- ◊ Bear one another's burdens—Mosiah 18:8

IN LEARNING, ALL ARE IMPORTANT

And when the priests left their labor to impart the word of God unto the people, the people also left their labors to hear the word of God. And when the priest had imparted unto them the word of God they all returned again diligently unto their labors; and the priest, not esteeming himself above his hearers, for the preacher was no better than the hearer, neither was the teacher any better than the learner; and thus they were all equal, and they did all labor, every man according to his strength.

Alma 1:26

Whether the classroom is a seat on the plane, a hotel room, a home, a chapel, the Mission Training Center, the Salt Lake Tabernacle, or a satellite audience, reverence and a receptive heart must be present if this teacher is to teach and the learner learn.

(Lucile C. Tate, *Boyd K. Packer: A Watchman on the Tower*
[Salt Lake City: Bookcraft, 1995], 278)

Daily Living

WE NEED THE SPIRIT AS BOTH TEACHERS AND LEARNERS.

- Both are edified by the Spirit—D&C 50:17–23

- The word enlightens and enlarges your soul—Alma 32:28

- The Spirit gives you knowledge—Alma 18:35

- You can know the truth of all things by the power of the Holy Ghost—Moroni 10:5

- The Spirit will show you all things to do—2 Nephi 32:5

DISCIPLINE BRINGS BLESSINGS

*And it came to pass that by thus exercising the law upon them,
every man suffering according to that which he had done, they
became more still, and durst not commit any wickedness if it
were known; therefore, there was much peace among the people
of Nephi until the fifth year of the reign of the judges.*
ALMA 1:33

With every law, there is a blessing. It is through obedience to a specific law that we receive a specific blessing. When we understand the
law and the blessings, we can better discipline ourselves to abide the
law. As we strive to live in complete harmony with the laws of God,
we are on our way to self-mastery and to becoming more like our
Savior. Obedience to the laws of God brings harmony within, happiness and peace; while disobedience to the laws of God brings misery, unhappiness, and disunity within.
(Ardeth Greene Kapp, *My Neighbor, My Sister, My Friend*
[Salt Lake City: Deseret Book, 1990], 161)

Daily Living

EVERY LAW OBEYED BRINGS BLESSINGS INTO YOUR LIFE.

- All blessings are predicated by obedience to law—D&C
130:20–21

- If you keep the commandments you will prosper—Jarom 1:9;
Mosiah 2:22

- If you keep the commandments you will be saved at the last
day—1 Nephi 22:31

- Discipline and bridle your passions that you may be filled with
love—Alma 38:12

THE MIGHTY CHANGE

*And behold, he preached the word unto your fathers, and a
mighty change was also wrought in their hearts, and they
humbled themselves and put their trust in the true and living
God. And behold, they were faithful until the end; therefore
they were saved.*

ALMA 5:13

When Joseph Smith said "the Book of Mormon was the most correct of any book on earth," it seems evident that he was not talking about grammar, punctuation, or spelling. He was referring to the clarity and depth of doctrine, to the mission and message of the book, to the spirit of inspiration that it fosters, to the divine desire that it sparks in the soul to make the "mighty change," and to the abiding love of the Lord that it brings into our hearts.

(George A. Horton Jr., in *The Book of Mormon: The Keystone
Scripture,* ed. Paul R. Cheesman [Provo, UT: Religious
Studies Center, 1988], 251)

Daily Living

STRIVE TO BE HUMBLE, TO TRUST IN GOD, AND TO FAITHFULLY KEEP THE
COMMANDMENTS.

- ಇಲ್ When you make the mighty change you have no desire to do evil—
  Mosiah 5:2

- ಇಲ್ The word is the greatest power to cause change—Alma 31:5

- ಇಲ್ Pray for humility—Helaman 3:35

- ಇಲ್ Trust in God and be supported in your trials—Alma 36:3

- ಇಲ್ Hold out faithful to the end and you are received into heaven—
  Mosiah 2:41

QUESTIONS FOR YOUR SOUL

And now behold, I ask of you, my brethren of the church, have ye spiritually been born of God? Have ye received his image in your countenances? Have ye experienced this mighty change in your hearts?

ALMA 5:14

Each day I pray that you'll take a moment to look in the mirror (maybe the mirror could even have a picture of Christ taped to it) and evaluate your life. Then go and do as Jesus would do. Every day, let us be as the Savior Jesus Christ would have us be.

And what manner of men and women ought we to be? The Savior answered: "Therefore I would that ye should be perfect even as I, or your Father who is in heaven is perfect" (3 Nephi 12:48).

(Ed J. Pinegar, *Especially for Missionaries, Volume 4: Your Capacity and Potential as a Missionary* [American Fork, UT: Covenant Communications, 1997], 7)

Daily Living

EVALUATE YOUR LIFE EACH DAY.

- ଚ୍ଚ Do you plan and organize every needful thing?—D&C 88:119

- ଚ୍ଚ Do you live by every word that proceedeth forth from the mouth of God?—D&C 84:43–46

- ଚ୍ଚ Do you learn and do your duty?—D&C 107:99–100

- ଚ୍ଚ Do you seek and pray for the Holy Spirit?—3 Nephi 19:9

THERE WILL BE A JUDGMENT DAY

*I say unto you, can you imagine to yourselves that ye hear the voice
of the Lord, saying unto you, in that day: Come unto me ye blessed,
for behold, your works have been the works of righteousness
upon the face of the earth? Or do ye imagine to yourselves that
ye can lie unto the Lord in that day, and say—Lord, our works
have been righteous works upon the face of the earth—and that
he will save you?*

ALMA 5:16–17

But after the resurrection, then we have to be judged according to
the deeds of the flesh, good or bad. On the judgment day we will
receive our rewards or punishments; we must pay for our own sins
[Sec. 76:110–11].

(J. Reuben Clark Jr., in *Latter-day Prophets and the Doctrine
and Covenants,* comp. Roy W. Doxey [Salt Lake City:
Deseret Book, 1978], 1:224–225)

Daily Living

PREPARE FOR THE JUDGMENT DAY.

- ᴇᴏ You will stand before God to be judged of your works—1 Nephi 15:33

- ᴇᴏ You will face the Lord Jesus Christ for He is the gatekeeper—2 Nephi 9:41

- ᴇᴏ Prepare for the day of judgment. It will be glorious if you are righteous—2 Nephi 9:46

- ᴇᴏ Out of the books that are written shall all mankind be judged—3 Nephi 27:25–26

- ᴇᴏ Now is the time to prepare to meet God—Alma 34:32

PREPARE TO MEET GOD

*Have ye walked, keeping yourselves blameless before God? Could
ye say, if ye were called to die at this time, within yourselves,
that ye have been sufficiently humble? That your garments have
been cleansed and made white through the blood of Christ, who
will come to redeem his people from their sins?
Behold, are ye stripped of pride? I say unto you, if ye are not ye
are not prepared to meet God. Behold ye must prepare quickly;
for the kingdom of heaven is soon at hand, and such an one
hath not eternal life.*

ALMA 5:27–28

To be in control of your life, to be a success regardless of your situation,
whether happily married, unhappily married, a single parent, a widow,
or a wife of an inactive husband, I recommend that you come to know
your Father in heaven. . . . Include Him in your decision making.
Include Him when you take inventory of your personal worth.

(Marvin J. Ashton, *Be of Good Cheer* [Salt Lake City:
Deseret Book, 1987], 29)

Daily Living

LIVE EACH DAY AS IF IT WERE YOUR LAST. DON'T PROCRASTINATE.

- ℬ Now is the time for you to perform your labors—Alma 34:32

- ℬ Don't procrastinate the day of repentance—Alma 34:33–35

- ℬ Remember the Lord will prepare a way for you to keep the
  commandments—1 Nephi 3:7

- ℬ Organize yourself and prepare every needful thing—D&C
  88:119

CHRIST CALLS AFTER US

Behold, I say unto you, that the good shepherd doth call you;
yea, and in his own name he doth call you, which is the name
of Christ; and if ye will not hearken unto the voice of the good
shepherd, to the name by which ye are called, behold, ye are not
the sheep of the good shepherd.
ALMA 5:38

The Savior invites all his earthly brothers and sisters to return to that heavenly family of which they were once a part, to take again the family name, and become heirs of the blessings associated with it. Thus salvation centers in our accepting Christ as our Savior, being born again into the family of the Father through the waters of baptism, and living worthy of all the ordinances of the house of the Lord wherein we are endowed with the powers of heaven.

(Joseph Fielding McConkie and Robert L. Millet, *Doctrinal Commentary on the Book of Mormon* [Salt Lake City: Bookcraft, 1987–1992], 3:37)

Daily Living

FIND WAYS TO HEARKEN UNTO GOD, THROUGH PRAYERS, SCRIPTURE STUDY, AND SERVICE.

ɞ There will be one fold and one Shepherd—1 Nephi 22:25

ɞ If you harden your heart you will not hearken to the voice of the Good Shepherd—Helaman 7:18

ɞ The Lord will manifest himself unto you as you hearken to Him—1 Nephi 14:1

ɞ Be faithful and choose eternal life—2 Nephi 2:28

KNOW THE TRUTH

Behold, I say unto you they [these eternal truths] are made known unto me by the Holy Spirit of God. Behold, I have fasted and prayed many days that I might know these things of myself. And now I do know of myself that they are true; for the Lord God hath made them manifest unto me by his Holy Spirit; and this is the spirit of revelation which is in me.

ALMA 5:46

Moroni has taught us, "And when ye shall receive these things, I would exhort you that ye would ask God, the Eternal Father, in the name of Christ, if these things are not true; and if ye shall ask with a sincere heart, with real intent, having faith in Christ, he will manifest the truth of it unto you, by the power of the Holy Ghost. And by the power of the Holy Ghost ye may know the truth of all things."

(Moroni 10:4–5)

Daily Living

SEEK TO KNOW THE TRUTH OF ALL THINGS.

ꙮ The Holy Ghost will manifest the truth of all things—Moroni 10:5

ꙮ The Lord is full of grace and truth—2 Nephi 2:6

ꙮ Search the scriptures to wax strong in the knowledge of truth—Alma 17:2

ꙮ People are brought to the knowledge of the truth by preaching the word—Alma 23:6

CONCERN FOR OTHERS

Nevertheless the children of God were commanded that they should gather themselves together oft, and join in fasting and mighty prayer in behalf of the welfare of the souls of those who knew not God.

ALMA 6:6

"I give unto you a commandment," the Savior stated in 1832, "that ye shall continue in prayer and fasting from this time forth" (D&C 88:76). . . . The Saints of the Most High are counseled to employ the law of the fast to break the heavy burdens of sin and sickness and personal struggles (see Isaiah 58); . . . the people of the Lord are encouraged to fast and pray for deeper spirituality; . . . the household of faith fast and pray often for those who know not God or who have strayed from the path of peace (Alma 6:6; Moroni 6:5).

(Joseph Fielding McConkie and Robert L. Millet, *Doctrinal Commentary on the Book of Mormon* [Salt Lake City: Bookcraft, 1987–1992], 4:201)

Daily Living

YOU SHOULD FAST AND PRAY FOR THE WELFARE OF OTHERS.

- ✌ Fast and pray for struggling souls—Mosiah 27:14

- ✌ Pray to be an instrument in the hand of the Lord to bless others—Alma 29:9–10

- ✌ Fast and pray to help others come to the knowledge of the truth—Alma 17:9

CHRIST SUFFERED ALL THINGS IN THE FLESH

And he shall go forth, suffering pains and afflictions and
temptations of every kind; . . . he will take upon him the pains
and the sicknesses of his people.
And he will take upon him death, that he may loose the bands
of death which bind his people; and he will take upon him
their infirmities, that his bowels may be filled with mercy,
according to the flesh, that he may know according to the flesh
how to succor his people according to their infirmities.
ALMA 7:11–12

Jesus, being sinless, could not have known suffering caused by sin—
but the agonies of the atonement made it possible for Christ to succor
us in our weaknesses and infirmities!

You and I on a much lesser scale may also need to undergo certain
experiences "according to the flesh" in order to increase our capacity to
help other people, bringing experiences we may not want, but which
the Lord in His wisdom may insist upon.

(Neal A. Maxwell, *Notwithstanding My Weakness*
[Salt Lake City: Deseret Book, 1981], 120)

Daily Living

RECOGNIZE AND APPRECIATE THE SUFFERING AND SACRIFICE OF YOUR
SAVIOR.

- ∞ Give thanks unto God for all things—Mosiah 26:39

- ∞ Show gratitude by offering a broken heart and contrite spirit—
  3 Nephi 9:20

- ∞ Give thanks and serve Him with your whole soul—Mosiah
  2:20–21; Alma 26:8

- ∞ Live in thanksgiving daily—Alma 34:38

FOLLOW THE PROPHETS AND STAND BLAMELESS

*And now my beloved brethren, I have said these things unto you
that I might awaken you to a sense of your duty to God, that ye
may walk blameless before him, that ye may walk after the holy
order of God, after which ye have been received.*

ALMA 7:22

Gratefully, we follow prophets who have been given a divine commission: "Whatsoever they shall speak when moved upon by the Holy Ghost shall be scripture, shall be the will of the Lord, shall be the mind of the Lord, shall be the word of the Lord, shall be the voice of the Lord, and the power of God unto salvation [D&C 68:4]." While we follow prophetic teachings, we can develop our spiritual capacities by emulating one such as President Gordon B. Hinckley. I thank God for this prophet. . . . Willingly I follow him. I love him and sustain him.

(Russell M. Nelson, "Spiritual Capacity,"
Ensign, November 1997, 16)

Daily Living

STRIVE TO FOLLOW THE PROPHETS' COUNSEL IN ALL THINGS.

ɞ If you don't accept the words of the prophets you don't accept Christ—3 Nephi 28:34

ɞ Hearken unto the words of the prophets and ye shall not perish—2 Nephi 26:8

ɞ Search the words of the prophets thus obtaining hope and faith in the Lord—Jacob 4:6

ɞ Prophets can prick your conscience and your heart unto repentance—Jarom 1:11–12

ɞ The words of the prophets are God's word—3 Nephi 1:20; D&C 1:38

QUALITIES OF RIGHTEOUSNESS

And now I would that ye should be humble, and be submissive and gentle; easy to be entreated; full of patience and long-suffering; being temperate in all things; being diligent in keeping the commandments of God at all times; asking for whatsoever things ye stand in need, both spiritual and temporal; always returning thanks unto God for whatsoever things ye do receive.
ALMA 7:23

These virtues, brothers and sisters, are cardinal; they are portable; and they are eternal. They reflect in each of us the seriousness of our discipleship. After all, true disciples will continue to grow spiritually because they have "faith unto repentance" (Alma 34:16, 17; see also Alma 13:10).

(Monte S. Nyman and Charles D. Tate Jr., eds.,
Mosiah: Salvation Only through Christ [Provo, UT:
Religious Studies Center, 1991], 11–12)

Daily Living
QUALITIES THAT LEAD TO RIGHTEOUSNESS

- ೞ Humility . . . pray and fast for humility—Helaman 3:35

- ೞ Submissive to the Lord in all things—Mosiah 3:19

- ೞ Patient . . . bear all things in patience with the Lord—Alma 38:4

- ೞ Diligence and temperance . . . at all times and in all things—Alma 38:10

- ೞ Prayer . . . pray always lest ye be tempted—3 Nephi 18:18

- ೞ Thanksgiving . . . give thanks in all things—Mosiah 26:39

PEACE OF GOD

And now, may the peace of God rest upon you, and upon your houses and lands, and upon your flocks and herds, and all that you possess, your women and your children, according to your faith and good works, from this time forth and forever. And thus I have spoken. Amen.

ALMA 7:27

It has ever had but one purpose, and now, under able and inspired leadership, it is pursuing that purpose more vigorously than at any time in its history. That objective is to bring men and women to a knowledge of the eternal truth that Jesus Christ is the Savior and Redeemer of the world, and to a realization that only through the cultivation of faith which actively manifests itself in good works can men and nations enjoy peace.

(Gordon B. Hinckley, *What of the Mormons?*
[Salt Lake City: Deseret Book, 1947], 222)

Daily Living

LIVE IN PEACE THROUGH FAITH AND GOOD WORKS.

ဢ Through faith, hope and charity you will always abound in good works—Alma 7:24

ဢ Be steadfast and immovable, always abounding in good works—Mosiah 5:15

ဢ You are prepared to serve and be called through your faith and good works—Alma 13:3

ဢ Peace comes from faith in the Lord Jesus Christ—Helaman 5:47

ဢ Through faith in Jesus Christ can all good things be done—Ether 12:7–23

THE TENDER MERCIES OF GOD

*Do ye not remember that our father, Lehi, was brought out of
Jerusalem by the hand of God? Do ye not remember that they
were all led by him through the wilderness?
And have ye forgotten so soon how many times he delivered our
fathers out of the hands of their enemies?*
ALMA 9:9–10

The simpleness, the sweetness, and the constancy of the tender mercies of the Lord will do much to fortify and protect us in the troubled times in which we do now and will yet live. When words cannot provide the solace we need or express the joy we feel, when it is simply futile to attempt to explain that which is unexplainable, when logic and reason cannot yield adequate understanding about the injustices and inequities of life . . . and when it seems that perhaps we are so totally alone, truly we are blessed by the tender mercies of the Lord and made mighty even unto the power of deliverance (see 1 Nephi 1:20).

(David A. Bednar, "The Tender Mercies of the Lord,"
Ensign, May 2005, 100)

Daily Living

NEVER FORGET THE GOODNESS OF GOD AND HIS TENDER MERCY OVER
HIS CHILDREN.

- ∾ The mercy and goodness of God is over all the inhabitants of the earth—1 Nephi 1:14

- ∾ Through the mercy of our Savior you are able to return the presence of God—2 Nephi 2:8

- ∾ If you repent you lay claim to the mercy of our Savior Jesus Christ—Alma 12:3

PRAYER OF THE RIGHTEOUS

*I say unto you that if it were not for the prayers of the righteous,
who are now in the land, that ye would even now be visited
with utter destruction.*

ALMA 10:22

Alma the Younger was a rebel. He was struck down by an angel who told him, "Behold, the Lord hath heard the prayers of his people, and also the prayers of his servant, Alma, who is thy father; for he has prayed with much faith concerning thee that thou mightest be brought to the knowledge of the truth; therefore, for this purpose have I come to convince thee of the power and authority of God, that the prayers of his servants might be answered according to their faith" (Mosiah 27:14).

(Boyd K. Packer, "The Golden Years," *Ensign,* May 2003, 83)

Daily Living

STRIVE TO LIVE SO THAT YOUR PRAYERS MAY BE ANSWERED ACCORDING TO YOUR FAITH.

- ও Pray in faith and you can be consoled in your afflictions—Jacob 3:1

- ও Pray in faith for those who are struggling—Mosiah 27:14

- ও Through repentance, faith, good works and prayer you can know the mysteries of God—Alma 26:22

- ও Afflictions and trials can be swallowed up through faith in Christ—Alma 31:38

- ও Remember prayers are answered according to your faith—Mormon 9:37

POWER OF AGENCY

*But Amulek stretched forth his hand, and cried the mightier
unto them, saying: O ye wicked and perverse generation, why
hath Satan got such great hold upon your hearts? Why will ye
yield yourselves unto him that he may have power over you, to
blind your eyes, that ye will not understand the words which are
spoken, according to their truth?*

ALMA 10:25

Just as light is of God (1 John 1:5), darkness is of the devil, for he "is
an enemy unto God, and fighteth against him continually" (Moro.
7:12). Darkness represents the evil influence of the devil's domain. It
symbolizes that which does not edify (D&C 50:23). John declared
that the devil's kingdom is full of darkness (Rev. 16:10). Those whose
deeds are evil love darkness and reject light (D&C 10:21; 29:45;
John 3:19). An ancient prophet proclaimed the fate of those who
yield to the enticings of the devil and "choose works of darkness
rather than light": they "must go down to hell" (2 Ne. 26:10).

(Hoyt W. Brewster Jr., *Doctrine and Covenants
Encyclopedia* [Salt Lake City: Bookcraft, 1988], 120)

Daily Living

SEEK FOR UNDERSTANDING THAT YE MAY NOT BE LED ASTRAY.

- ༄ To yield to the devil is to be carnally-minded—2 Nephi 9:39

- ༄ Destruction comes because you choose darkness—2 Nephi 26:10

- ༄ Be firm in not yielding to temptations but always serve the
Lord—Mormon 9:28

- ༄ Remember the devil enticeth you to sin and do evil continually—
Moroni 7:12

STAND BEFORE GOD

The spirit and the body shall be reunited again in its perfect form; both limb and joint shall be restored to its proper frame, even as we now are at this time; and we shall be brought to stand before God, knowing even as we know now, and have a bright recollection of all our guilt.

ALMA 11:43

Let us live with the certain knowledge that someday "we shall be brought to stand before God, knowing even as we know now, and have a bright recollection of all our guilt" (Alma 11:43). Let us live today knowing that we shall live forever. Let us live with the conviction that whatever principle of intelligence and beauty and truth and goodness we make a part of our life here, it will rise with us in the resurrection.

(Gordon B. Hinckley, "What Shall I Do Then with Jesus Which Is Called Christ?" *Ensign,* December 1983, 4)

Daily Living

BEST REPENT RATHER THAN SUFFER WITH GUILT.

- ☙ Guilt can be swept away through faith in the Lord Jesus Christ if you repent—Enos 1:5–8

- ☙ You will have a perfect knowledge of your deeds—2 Nephi 9:14

- ☙ Remember that mercy can overpower justice; if you repent the Lord will remember your sins no more—D&C 58:42–43

- ☙ The view of your guilt, if you fail to repent, will cause you to shrink from the presence of the Lord—Mosiah 3:25

HEED THE WORD

He that will not harden his heart, to him is given the greater portion of the word, until it is given unto him to know the mysteries of God until he know them in full.
And they that will harden their hearts, to them is given the lesser portion of the word until they know nothing concerning his mysteries; and then they are taken captive by the devil, and led by his will down to destruction. Now this is what is meant by the chains of hell.

ALMA 12:10–11

It has pleased God to make covenants with his people, from time to time, according to the heed and diligence that they give unto him. Those who devote themselves to righteousness receive more of his word and inherit greater rewards; those who harden their hearts and stiffen their necks are denied what otherwise would be theirs.

(Bruce R. McConkie, *The Promised Messiah: The First Coming of Christ* [Salt Lake City: Deseret Book, 1978], 438)

Daily Living

STRIVE TO BE HUMBLE AND TEACHABLE.

- ଚ Prophets exhort you to heed the word of God—1 Nephi 15:25

- ଚ As you diligently heed the word the blessings are forthcoming—Alma 7:26–27

- ଚ As you heed the word you will be zealous in keeping the commandments—Alma 21:23

- ଚ As you heed the word it will point you in a straight course to eternal bliss—Alma 37:44

- ଚ Peace is a great reward for heeding with diligence the word of God—Alma 49:30

CONDEMNED OR BLESSED

For our words will condemn us, yea, all our works will condemn us; we shall not be found spotless; and our thoughts will also condemn us; and in this awful state we shall not dare to look up to our God; and we would fain be glad if we could command the rocks and the mountains to fall upon us to hide us from his presence.

Alma 12:14

The final judgment is the final point of eternal accountability for all voluntary actions, words, thoughts, desires, and works of the individual. The full significance of such an accounting cannot be adequately assessed unless it is realized that all judgments granted from the seat of God's justice are of infinite scope and eternal consequence (3 Ne. 26:4; D&C 76:112).

(Daniel H. Ludlow, ed., *Encyclopedia of Mormonism*
[New York: Macmillan, 1992], 3:774)

Daily Living

Watch yourselves; your words, works, and the thoughts of your heart.

- ✇ Imagine the joy of God calling you forth for your works of righteousness—Alma 5:16

- ✇ A covetous heart will condemn you—Mosiah 4:25

- ✇ If your heart is hardened against the word then is your state awful—Alma 12:13

- ✇ Remember you bring your own condemnation upon yourself—Helaman 14:29

- ✇ Be careful lest lusting shall lead you to sin—3 Nephi 12:28

MORTALITY, A PROBATIONARY STATE

Nevertheless there was a space granted unto man in which he might repent; therefore this life became a probationary state; a time to prepare to meet God; a time to prepare for that endless state which has been spoken of by us, which is after the resurrection of the dead.

Alma 12:24

Knowingly we wanted the risks of mortality, which would allow the exercise of agency and accountability. "This life [was to become] a probationary state; a time to prepare to meet God." But we regarded the returning home as the best part of that long-awaited trip, just as we do now. Before embarking on any journey, we like to have some assurance of a round-trip ticket. Returning from earth to life in our heavenly home requires passage through—and not around—the doors of death. We were born to die, and we die to live. As seedlings of God, we barely blossom on earth; we fully flower in heaven.

(Russell M. Nelson, *Perfection Pending, and Other Favorite Discourses* [Salt Lake City: Deseret Book, 1998], 137)

Daily Living

Now is the time to prepare to meet God in hopes of a glorious Resurrection.

- ✀ Your time here upon the earth is lengthened to give you time to repent—2 Nephi 2:30

- ✀ When you know the law and commandments, don't waste your time—2 Nephi 9:27

- ✀ Prepare to meet God today—Alma 34:32–35

FOREKNOWLEDGE OF GOD

*They were . . . prepared from the foundation of the world
according to the foreknowledge of God, on account of their
exceeding faith and good works. . . .
And thus they have been called, . . . while others would reject
the Spirit of God on account of the hardness of their hearts and
blindness of their minds, while, if it had not been for this they
might have had as great privilege as their brethren.*

ALMA 13:3–4

The extent of such lost blessings is attested by Jude, who spoke to
the "angels which kept not their first estate," having been cast out of
that habitation for their wickedness (Jude 1:6).

(Joseph F. McConkie, "Premortal Existence,
Foreordinations, and Heavenly Councils," in *Apocryphal
Writings and the Latter-day Saints,* ed. C. Wilfred Griggs
[Provo, UT: Religious Studies Center, 1986], 178–179)

Daily Living

LIVE SO THAT YOUR SECOND ESTATE HONORS THE CHOICES OF YOUR FIRST.

ຂ Remember the Lord knoweth all things from the beginning—
1 Nephi 9:6

ຂ Callings were prepared from the foundation of the world—
Alma 13:5–7

ຂ You receive a reward according to your works—Alma 9:28

ຂ Prayers are answered according to your faith—Mosiah 27:14

SANCTIFICATION

Now they, after being sanctified by the Holy Ghost, having their garments made white, being pure and spotless before God, could not look upon sin save it were with abhorrence; and there were many, exceedingly great many, who were made pure and entered into the rest of the Lord their God.

Alma 13:12

Men and women who come unto Christ through the appropriate ordinances are in time "sanctified by the reception of the Holy Ghost" (3 Nephi 27:20), meaning they are made pure and holy. Filth and dross—the elements of the natural world—are burned out of their souls as though by fire, thus giving rise to the expression "the baptism of fire." . . . In time, through being sanctified, members of the Church come to abhor sin and cleave unto righteousness (see Alma 13:12).

(Monte S. Nyman and Charles D. Tate Jr., eds.,
Third Nephi 9–30: This Is My Gospel [Provo, UT:
Religious Studies Center, 1993], 17)

Daily Living

SEEK TO BECOME SANCTIFIED, CLEAN, AND PURE BY THE POWER OF THE HOLY GHOST.

- ❧ Become sanctified by the Holy Ghost—Alma 5:54

- ❧ Sanctification comes by yielding your heart to God—Helaman 3:35

- ❧ Through the reception of the Holy Ghost you may become sanctified—3 Nephi 27:20

- ❧ Ye are sanctified in Christ by the grace of God—Moroni 10:33

PLEADINGS OF A PROPHET

*But that ye would humble yourselves before the Lord, and call
on his holy name, and watch and pray continually, that ye may
not be tempted above that which ye can bear, and thus be led by
the Holy Spirit, becoming humble, meek, submissive, patient,
full of love and all long-suffering.*
ALMA 13:28

Alma instructed his brethren to humble themselves before the Lord,
to pray continually about temptation, and be led by the Holy Spirit.
And if they did these three things, they would become "humble,
meek, submissive, patient, full of love and all long-suffering" (Alma
13:28; emphasis added). In sum, basically, Alma instructs us to
humble ourselves, to pray, and then to listen as we are led by the
Holy Spirit. Following these three steps will assist us in acquiring the
ability to become full of love.

(Paul R. Cheesman, ed., *The Book of Mormon: The Keystone
Scripture* [Provo, UT: Religious Studies Center, 1988], 153)

Daily Living
SEEK TO BE LED BY THE SPIRIT IN ALL THINGS.

- ༀ Power of the Holy Ghost comes through faith in the Lord Jesus
  Christ—1 Nephi 10:17

- ༀ Yield to the enticings of the Holy Spirit and become a saint
  through the Atonement of the Lord Jesus Christ—Mosiah 3:19

- ༀ Remember the Spirit will show you all things to do—2 Nephi
  32:5

- ༀ If worthy, you can be led by the Spirit at all times—1 Nephi 4:6

MAY

&

*My brothers and my brethren,
behold I say unto you, how great reason have we to rejoice; for could we
have supposed when we started from
the land of Zarahemla that God
would have granted unto us such
great blessings?*

—ALMA 26:1

STRENGTH IN THE LORD

*And Alma cried, saying: How long shall we suffer these great
afflictions, O Lord? O Lord, give us strength according to our
faith which is in Christ, even unto deliverance. And they broke
the cords with which they were bound; and when the people saw
this, they began to flee, for the fear of destruction had come
upon them.*
Alma 14:26

Living members give heed to the Spirit, which quickens the inner
life. They constantly seek its direction. They pray for strength and
overcome difficulties. Their hearts are not set upon the things of this
world but upon the infinite. Spiritual renewal is not sacrificed for
physical gratification.

(Howard W. Hunter, *The Teachings of Howard W. Hunter,*
ed. Clyde J. Williams [Salt Lake City: Bookcraft, 1997],
264)

Daily Living

PRAY FOR STRENGTH ACCORDING TO YOUR FAITH.

- Pray to overcome temptation—3 Nephi 18:18

- Pray for strength that you might be delivered from your enemies—
  1 Nephi 7:17

- Pray that you might not be tempted above that which you can
  bear—Alma 13:28

- Pray to be strong in humility and firm in your faith—Helaman
  3:35

- Pray with all the energy of your heart that you may filled with
  charity—Moroni 7:48

FORSAKE ALL

And it came to pass that . . . Amulek [forsook] all his gold, and silver, and his precious things, which were in the land of Ammonihah, for the word of God, he being rejected by those who were once his friends and also by his father and his kindred.
ALMA 15:16

As we hear the Lord's answers, they are not always easy to bear. For example, Jesus' discourse on the dangers of wealth produced anxiety and inquiry among His followers: "When his disciples heard it, they were exceedingly amazed, saying, Who then can be saved?" (Matthew 19:25). Note the Savior's response as rendered by the Joseph Smith Translation: "But Jesus beheld their thoughts, and said unto them, With men this is impossible; but if they will forsake all things for my sake, with God whatsoever things I speak are possible" (JST, Matthew 19:26). We can succeed, if we will forsake the world.

(Neal A. Maxwell, *Men and Women of Christ* [Salt Lake City: Bookcraft, 1991], 123–124)

Daily Living

YOU MUST SACRIFICE ALL THINGS FOR THE BUILDING UP OF THE KINGDOM OF GOD.

- ᛞ Offer you whole soul as an offering to the Lord—Omni 1:26
- ᛞ You must work with unwearyingness and seek the will of the Lord—Helaman 10:4
- ᛞ Your sacrifice should be a broken heart and contrite spirit—3 Nephi 9:20
- ᛞ Seek to build up the kingdom of God—3 Nephi 13:33

BLESSINGS OF UNITY

And there was no inequality among them; the Lord did pour out his Spirit on all the face of the land to prepare the minds of the children of men, or to prepare their hearts to receive the word which should be taught among them at the time of his coming—
ALMA 16:16

God bless you men of the priesthood, you teachers of youth, you parents, and all good people everywhere. May the ecclesiastical groups of the Church be blessed with the spirit of unity and harmony. May there be banished from their hearts the spirit of enmity, backbiting, and evil speaking, and may they keep in their hearts the truth expressed by Jesus when he said, ". . . if ye are not one ye are not mine" (D&C 38:27).

(David O. Mckay, Conference Report,
April 1967, 87–88)

Daily Living

SEEK THE SPIRIT OF THE LORD BY BEING UNIFIED AND CHARITABLE.

- ଌ You will lose the Spirit through contention and obey the evil spirit—3 Nephi 11:29; Mosiah 2:32

- ଌ Through purity and the love of God you can be blessed with the Spirit—D&C 76:116

- ଌ As you hunger and thirst after righteousness you will be filled—3 Nephi 12:6

- ଌ Through iniquity and wickedness you can lose the Spirit—Mormon 1:14

PREPARATION TO TEACH

But this is not all; they had given themselves to much prayer,
and fasting; therefore they had the spirit of prophecy, and the
spirit of revelation, and when they taught, they taught with
power and authority of God.

ALMA 17:3

I promise you that as you more diligently study modern revelation on gospel subjects, your power to teach and preach will be magnified and you will so move the cause of Zion that added numbers will enter into the house of the Lord as well as the mission field.

(Ezra Taft Benson, *The Teachings of Ezra Taft Benson*
[Salt Lake City: Bookcraft, 1988], 115)

Daily Living

PREPARE TO TEACH WITH THE SPIRIT BY GAINING KNOWLEDGE, BY SEARCHING
THE SCRIPTURES, AND THROUGH FASTING AND PRAYER.

- ೮ Seek first to obtain the word of God—D&C 11:21

- ೮ Treasure up the word and it will be given to you the moment you need it—D&C 84:85

- ೮ Pray to know the things of God—Alma 5:46

- ೮ Pray for the Spirit for you and those you teach—Alma 17:9

FAST AND PRAY FOR THE SPIRIT

And it came to pass that they journeyed many days in the wilderness, and they fasted much and prayed much that the Lord would grant unto them a portion of his Spirit to go with them, and abide with them, that they might be an instrument in the hands of God to bring, if it were possible, their brethren, the Lamanites, to the knowledge of the truth, to the knowledge of the baseness of the traditions of their fathers, which were not correct.
ALMA 17:9

There are special gifts and endowments reserved for those who study and ponder the scriptures; for those who treasure up the Lord's word; for those who fast and pray and seek knowledge by the power of the Spirit. They receive guidance and enlightenment that can be gained in no other way. They become men of sound understanding. They gain the spirit of revelation and of prophecy and teach and speak with power from on high.

(Marion G. Romney, *Learning for the Eternities*
[Salt Lake City: Deseret Book, 1977], viii)

Daily Living

SEEK TO BE AN INSTRUMENT IN GOD'S HANDS BY OBTAINING THE SPIRIT.

- ৪০ The Spirit will always encourage you to pray—2 Nephi 32:8

- ৪০ The Spirit will show you all things to do—2 Nephi 32:5

- ৪০ The Spirit will give you utterance—2 Nephi 1:27

- ৪০ The Spirit manifests truth according to your faith—Jarom 1:4; Moroni 10:5

- ৪০ The Spirit can bring about the mighty change in you—Mosiah 5:2

BE A READY INSTRUMENT FOR GOOD

And the Lord said unto them also: Go forth among the *Take action* *Lamanites, thy brethren, and establish my word; yet ye shall be patient in long-suffering and afflictions, that ye may show forth good examples unto them in me, and I will make an instrument of thee in my hands unto the salvation of many souls.*
ALMA 17:11

Wise shepherds exemplify the courage they wish others to emulate. They try hard not to show fear or disquietude, though they may well feel them. They do not flag or fail; they struggle on to the end. They set a good example, knowing with Edmund Burke that "example is the school of mankind" (Bartlett's Familiar Quotations, p. 374) and a powerful teacher.

(Alexander B. Morrison, *Feed My Sheep: Leadership Ideas for Latter-day Shepherds* [Salt Lake City: Deseret Book, 1992], 124)

Daily Living

SET A GOOD EXAMPLE . . . THE LORD CAN THEN USE YOU TO BUILD UP THE KINGDOM.

- ఴ Jesus Christ has set the perfect example for you—2 Nephi 31:9–10; 3 Nephi 18:16

- ఴ Follow the example of your Savior and be saved—2 Nephi 31:16; 3 Nephi 27:21

- ఴ Bad examples of members cause people to not believe the word of God—Alma 39:11

- ఴ Let your light shine that they may see your good works—3 Nephi 12:16

POWER OF GOD

Now they wept because of the fear of being slain. Now when Ammon saw this his heart was swollen within him with joy; for, said he, I will show forth my power unto these my fellow-servants, or the power which is in me, in restoring these flocks unto the king, that I may win the hearts of these my fellow-servants, that I may lead them to believe in my words.

ALMA 17:29

We have received living testimonies in our hearts, and we know that all the gifts, powers and blessings pertaining to the Gospel of Christ are with us today, for the power of God is made manifest in our families. Our children are growing up to realize that God is with us as a people, that He sanctifies the ministrations of the Elders and that the power of God is amongst this people.

(Benjamin F. Goddard., Conference Report,
October 1905, 64)

Daily Living

STRIVE TO LIVE SO THAT THE POWER OF GOD IS MADE MANIFEST IN YOU.

- ಐ The power of God can be made manifest in you—1 Nephi 17:48
- ಐ You can have the power to teach with the power and authority of God—Alma 17:2–3
- ಐ Armed with righteous you have the power of God—1 Nephi 14:14
- ಐ The righteous will inherit the Kingdom of God—2 Nephi 9:18
- ಐ The righteous are received into a state of happiness—Alma 40:12
- ಐ You can be delivered out of danger by the power of God— Mosiah 23:13

POWER OF FAITH

Ammon said unto him: I am a man; and man in the beginning
was created after the image of God, and I am called by his Holy
Spirit to teach these things unto this people, that they may be
brought to a knowledge of that which is just and true;
And a portion of that Spirit dwelleth in me, which giveth me
knowledge, and also power according to my faith and desires
which are in God.
ALMA 18:34–35

Each of us enters the scene of mortality for a brief season. We are born. We grow. We encounter tests and trials. We win a few, lose a few, and then we pass on. We came to earth for two reasons: to get a body and to develop faith, which is sometimes best measured as the power of the spirit over the appetites of the body.

(Russell M. Nelson, *The Power within Us* [Salt Lake City: Deseret Book, 1988], 123)

Daily Living

MAKE THE MOST OF EACH DAY BY UTILIZING THE GIFT OF THE HOLY GHOST.

- You can speak by the power of the Holy Ghost—1 Nephi 10:17

- The Holy Spirit will manifest things to you according to your faith—Jarom 1:4

- The Spirit can give you knowledge and power according to your faith—Alma 18:35

- Increase in your faith that the Holy Ghost shall be in your heart that you might have power to do what is expedient in the Lord—Moroni 7:32–33

BLESSINGS FROM THE LORD

And thus the work of the Lord did commence among the Lamanites; thus the Lord did begin to pour out his Spirit upon them; and we see that his arm is extended to all people who will repent and believe on his name.

ALMA 19:36

There are some areas of truth that the natural man cannot know because he does not have the medium for acquiring them. Spiritual truth is made known only by the Spirit and only to those who believe, repent, and prepare themselves to obtain it.

(Robert J. Matthews, *A Bible! A Bible!* [Salt Lake City: Bookcraft, 1990], 163)

Daily Living

PREPARE YOURSELF TO BE GUIDED BY THE SPIRIT.

- ɤ You must repent to be born again to receive the Spirit—Alma 7:14

- ɤ You must repent or the word and the Spirit will be taken away—Helaman 13:8

- ɤ You are blessed with the Holy Ghost if you believe and are baptized—3 Nephi 12:1

- ɤ Heavenly Father gives the Holy Ghost to those who believe in His Son Jesus Christ—3 Nephi 19:22

POWER OF LOVE

*And when he saw that Ammon had no desire to destroy him,
and when he also saw the great love he had for his son Lamoni,
he was astonished exceedingly, and said: Because this is all that
thou hast desired, that I would release thy brethren, and suffer
that my son Lamoni should retain his kingdom, behold, I will
grant unto you that my son may retain his kingdom from this
time and forever; and I will govern him no more—*

ALMA 20:26

Love is one of the chief characteristics of Deity, and ought to be
manifested by those who aspire to be the sons of God. A man filled
with the love of God, is not content with blessing his family alone,
but ranges through the whole world, anxious to bless the whole
human race.

(Joseph Smith, *History of The Church of Jesus Christ of Latter-day
Saints,* comp. B. H. Roberts [Salt Lake City: The Church of Jesus
Christ of Latter-day Saints, 1932–1951], 4:227)

Daily Living

WHEN YOUR LOVE IS EXPRESSED AND FELT, IT IS THE TRUE MOTIVATOR FOR
RIGHTEOUSNESS.

- ∞ You will feel gratitude for the Father and the Son as They
  express Their love for you—John 3:16; 2 Nephi 26:24

- ∞ Charity brings forth many qualities of righteousness—Moroni
  7:45

- ∞ The Holy Ghost can fill you with perfect love—Moroni 8:26

- ∞ Your love for the Lord will make you an instrument in His
  hands—Alma 17:11

LED BY THE SPIRIT

*And they went forth whithersoever they were led by the Spirit of
the Lord, preaching the word of God in every synagogue. . . .
And it came to pass that the Lord began to bless them, insomuch
that they brought many to the knowledge of the truth.*
ALMA 21:16–17

The greatest challenge we have today is to teach the members of this
church to keep the commandments of God. Never before has there
been such a challenge to the doctrine of righteousness and purity
and chastity. The moral standards are being eroded by powers of
evil. There is nothing more important for us to do than to teach as
powerfully, led by the Spirit of the Lord, as we can in order to persuade our people in the world to live close to the Lord in this hour
of great temptation (72–17, p. 4).

(Harold B. Lee, *The Teachings of Harold B. Lee,* ed. Clyde J.
Williams [Salt Lake City: Bookcraft, 1996], 85)

Daily Living

BE A POWERFUL FORCE FOR RIGHTEOUSNESS BY LIVING WORTHY OF THE
HOLY GHOST.

- The Holy Spirit gives you knowledge to impart to others—
Alma 18:34–35

- The Holy Spirit can soften hearts so people will listen—Alma
24:8–9

- Remember you cannot teach without the Spirit—D&C 42:14

- The Holy Ghost will manifest the truth of all things—Moroni
10:5

BLESSINGS AND POWER OF HOPE

But Aaron said unto him: If thou desirest this thing, if thou wilt bow down before God, yea, if thou wilt repent of all thy sins, and will bow down before God, and call on his name in faith, believing that ye shall receive, then shalt thou receive the hope which thou desirest.

ALMA 22:16

For in the absence of God's mercy, why should anyone have faith? Life would still be a dead-end street leading to death, hell, and the devil. (See 2 Ne. 9:7–9; Jacob 7:12.) Thus God's mercy justifies human faith. And faith, in turn, begets the hope of eternal life. This hope is justified by the works of divine love that complete the triangle of salvation: faith, hope, and charity. (See Alma 34:27–29; Moro. 7:38–48.)

(Kent P. Jackson, ed., *Studies in Scripture, Vol. 8: Alma 30 to Moroni* [Salt Lake City: Deseret Book, 1988], 33–34)

Daily Living

FIND HOPE AS YOU COME TO UNDERSTAND THE ATONEMENT.

- ✤ You can press forward with a perfect brightness of hope—2 Nephi 31:20

- ✤ Remember that hope is integrally connected with faith and charity—Alma 7:24

- ✤ Hope cometh of faith—Ether 12:4

- ✤ Without hope you cannot receive an inheritance from Heavenly Father—Ether 12:32

- ✤ Hope is through Atonement of the Lord Jesus Christ—Moroni 7:40–43

GRATITUDE TO GOD

And I also thank my God, yea, my great God, that he hath granted unto us that we might repent of these things, and also that he hath forgiven us of those our many sins and murders which we have committed, and taken away the guilt from our hearts, through the merits of his Son.

ALMA 24:10

King Benjamin's teaching had a miraculous effect. Gratitude for what they had led to faith unto repentance. That led to forgiveness. That produced new gratitude. And then King Benjamin taught that, if we can remember and so remain grateful, we will retain a remission of our sins through all the losses and the gains of life.

(Henry B. Eyring, "Remembrance and Gratitude,"
Ensign, November 1989, 12)

Daily Living

GIVE THANKS, ACKNOWLEDGING HIS HAND IN ALL THINGS.

- ဢ Give thanks in your prayers and let your hearts rejoice—2 Nephi 9:52

- ဢ Be grateful for the words of God and learn from them—Jacob 4:3

- ဢ Serve Heavenly Father with thanksgiving—Mosiah 2:19–21

- ဢ Praise Heavenly Father for the mercy He extends to us—Mosiah 24:21–22

- ဢ Rejoice in the Lord and you can do all things in His strength—Alma 26:11–12

- ဢ Gratitude to the Lord gives you the desire to serve and help others—Alma 29:9–10; 36:24

STRENGTH IN THE LORD

*But Ammon said unto him: I do not boast in my own strength,
nor in my own wisdom; but behold, my joy is full, yea, my
heart is brim with joy, and I will rejoice in my God.
Yea, I know that I am nothing; as to my strength I am weak;
therefore I will not boast of myself, but I will boast of my God,
for in his strength I can do all things; yea, behold, many mighty
miracles we have wrought in this land, for which we will praise
his name forever.*
Alma 26:11–12

I will go where the Lord and the leaders of His Church want me to go, I will do what they want me to do, I will teach what they want me to teach, and I will strive to become what I should and must become. In the strength of the Lord and through His grace, I know that you and I can be blessed to accomplish all things.

(David A. Bednar, "In the Strength of the Lord," *Ensign,*
November 2004, 78)

Daily Living

REALIZE THAT IN THE STRENGTH OF THE LORD YOU CAN DO ALL THINGS.

- ࠔ The Lord is your strength and salvation—2 Nephi 22:2

- ࠔ You can receive strength of the Lord in your trials according to your faith—Alma 14:22

- ࠔ In the strength of the Lord you can do all things—Alma 20:4

- ࠔ Pray for strength to bear your infirmities—Alma 31:30–33, 38

- ࠔ Fast and pray for humility and faith—Helaman 3:35

GLORY IN THE LORD

Therefore, let us glory, yea, we will glory in the Lord; yea, we will rejoice, for our joy is full; yea, we will praise our God forever. Behold, who can glory too much in the Lord? Yea, who can say too much of his great power, and of his mercy, and of his long-suffering towards the children of men? Behold, I say unto you, I cannot say the smallest part which I feel.

Alma 26:16

I stand before you today grateful for our Redeemer, Jesus Christ, grateful for this gospel, grateful for the priesthood that blesses our lives, and for the goodness of all of you. This gathering of Saints at general conference reminds me of Isaiah's joyous proclamation, "Holy, holy, holy, is the Lord of hosts: the whole earth is full of his glory (Isa. 6:3). Righteous Saints are the glory of God, and there are mighty legions gathered here and in many lands.

(Elaine L. Jack, "Walk with Me," *Ensign,* May 1994,15)

Daily Living

GLORY IN HIS GOODNESS.

- ෨ Rejoice in the revelations of the Lord—1 Nephi1:15

- ෨ Remember the greatness of God and His goodness toward you—Mosiah 4:11

- ෨ Remember what the Lord has done for you—Alma 29:10–11

- ෨ Remember to trust in the Lord and He will deliver you out of your trials—Alma 38:5

- ෨ Remember how merciful the Lord has been and ponder it in your heart—Moroni 10:3

KNOW THE MYSTERIES OF GOD

Yea, he that repenteth and exerciseth faith, and bringeth forth good works, and prayeth continually without ceasing—unto such it is given to know the mysteries of God; yea, unto such it shall be given to reveal things which never have been revealed; yea, and it shall be given unto such to bring thousands of souls to repentance.

ALMA 26:22

In the scriptures, the Lord has specified how we learn by faith. We must be humble, cultivate faith, repent of our sins, serve our fellow-men, and keep the commandments of God. (See Ether 12:27; D&C 1:28; 12:8; 50:28; 63:23; 136:32–33.) As the Book of Mormon says, "Yea, he that repenteth and exerciseth faith, and bringeth forth good works, and prayeth continually without ceasing—unto such it is given to know the mysteries of God" (Alma 26:22).

(Dallin H. Oaks, "Alternate Voices," *Ensign,* May 1989, 29–30)

Daily Living

PRAY WITHOUT CEASING TO KNOW THE MYSTERIES OF GOD.

- Diligently seek to know the mysteries of God—1 Nephi 10:19

- Without the scriptures you can never know the mysteries of God—Mosiah 1:3

- Open your ears and hearts that you may understand the mysteries of God—Mosiah 2:9

- Understand mysteries of God according to your heed and diligence—Alma 12:9–10

- Seek for wisdom that God's mysteries be unfolded—D&C 6:7

NEVER GIVE UP

Now when our hearts were depressed, and we were about to turn back, behold, the Lord comforted us, and said: Go amongst thy brethren, the Lamanites, and bear with patience thine afflictions, and I will give unto you success.

ALMA 26:27

To those scattered around the world, may I say a word of encouragement? Be of good cheer, be diligent, trust in the Lord, and he will help you. You were probably placed where you are to do a special work in gathering records or to fulfill a special missionary assignment. If you will let him, the Lord will give you success in your work and much happiness in so doing.

(Eldred G. Smith, "Family Research," *Ensign,* November 1975, 108)

Daily Living

LEARN TO TRUST IN THE LORD'S TIMING.

- ℰ Remember that you may tried and tested in your patience and faith but if you trust in the Lord you shall be blessed—Mosiah 23:21–22

- ℰ The Lord will bless you as you exercise patience with faith—Mosiah 24:15–16

- ℰ As you are patient and long-suffering in the work of the Lord you can become an instrument in His hands to bless others—Alma 17:11; 26:28–31

- ℰ Labor with unwearyingness to do the will of the Lord—Helaman 4–5

TEACH THE GOSPEL EVERYWHERE

*And we have entered into their houses and taught them, and we
have taught them in their streets; yea, and we have taught them
upon their hills; and we have also entered into their temples and
their synagogues and taught them; and we have been cast out,
and mocked, and spit upon, and smote upon our cheeks; and we
have been stoned, and taken and bound with strong cords, and
cast into prison; and through the power and wisdom of God we
have been delivered again.*

ALMA 26:29

The answer has been given by a Prophet of God. Every member of The
Church of Jesus Christ of Latter-day Saints should be a missionary.
Each member should bring one or more of his neighbors and friends
into the Church each year. Each member must increase his faith and
turn up his divine luster and candle power and let his light so shine
before men that they may see his good works, and glorify their Father
which is in heaven (Matt. 5:16).

(Bernard P. Brockbank, Conference Report,
October 1966, 89)

Daily Living

OPEN YOUR MOUTH AND IT WILL BE FILLED.

   ᴃ Open your mouth and it will be filled—D&C 33:8–11

   ᴃ It is your duty to warn your neighbor—D&C 88:81

   ᴃ Stand as a witness at all times and places—Mosiah 18:9

   ᴃ Pray for all those who know not God—Alma 6:6

   ᴃ Your joy and glory is to be an instrument in the hands of the
Lord—Alma 29:9–20

WORTH OF SOULS

And we have suffered all manner of afflictions, and all this, that perhaps we might be the means of saving some soul; and we supposed that our joy would be full if perhaps we could be the means of saving some.

ALMA 26:30

This is God's work. He wants us to participate with Him and His Beloved Son in bringing the gospel into the lives of all of His children. The Lord has promised us that our joy will be great if we bring just one soul unto Him (see D&C 18:15–16). Let us exercise greater faith and work together, members and missionaries, to bring many more souls unto Him. Let every family in the Church include as part of their daily family prayers a plea with the Lord to go before your family members and help them to find someone prepared to receive the message of the restored gospel of Jesus Christ.

(M. Russell Ballard, "Now Is the Time,"
Ensign, November 2000, 76–77)

Daily Living

SEEK TO BRING ALL SOULS TO CHRIST.

- ☙ Seek the welfare of every soul because you truly care—Mosiah 28:3

- ☙ Remember the worth of souls—D&C 18:10

- ☙ Your can help souls come unto Christ—D&C 18:15–16

- ☙ Seek first to build up the kingdom of God—3 Nephi 13:33

RESULTS OF TRUE CONVERSION

*Now behold, we can look forth and see the fruits of our labors;
and are they few? I say unto you, Nay, they are many; yea, and
we can witness of their sincerity, because of their love towards
their brethren and also towards us.*

ALMA 26:31

The scriptures confirm that the truly converted do more than just
forsake the enticements of the world. They love God and their fellowmen. Their minds and hearts are centered on the Savior's atoning sacrifice. From the moment of their respective conversions,
Enos, Alma the Younger, Paul, and others turned wholeheartedly to
the task of bringing themselves and their fellowmen to God.
Worldly power and possessions lost their former significance. . . .
These faithful sons were driven by the hope that they might be able
to help save even one soul—thus winning for themselves and their
brethren a place in God's eternal kingdom.

(Robert D. Hales, "The Covenant of Baptism: To Be in the
Kingdom and of the Kingdom," Ensign, November 2000, 8)

Daily Living

WHEN YOU ARE TRULY CONVERTED YOU DESIRE THE WELFARE OF YOUR
FELLOWMEN.

- ɞ True disciples of Jesus Christ have love one to another—John 13:34–35

- ɞ Think of others like unto yourselves and be free with your sub-stance—Jacob 2:17

- ɞ Be filled with love towards God and all men—Mosiah 2:4

- ɞ As you are filled with charity you will love all men—Ether 12:34

REASON TO REJOICE

Now have we not reason to rejoice? Yea, I say unto you, there never were men that had so great reason to rejoice as we, since the world began; yea, and my joy is carried away, even unto boasting in my God; for he has all power . . . and he is a merciful Being, even unto salvation, to those who will repent and believe on his name.

ALMA 26:35

Since our last General Epistle, we have received intelligence of the general success and spread of the Gospel of Christ, with few exceptions, wherever it has been preached; which is cheering to our souls, and causes our hearts to rejoice in the goodness of God towards our fellow men, by inclining the honest in heart among the nations of the earth, unto the truth as it is in Christ Jesus.

(Brigham Young, Heber C. Kimball, Jedediah M. Grant, James R. Clark, comp., *Messages of the First Presidency of The Church of Jesus Christ of Latter-day Saints 1833–1964* [Salt Lake City: Bookcraft, 1965], 2:127)

Daily Living

STRIVE TO PLAY AN ACTIVE ROLE IN BUILDING UP THE KINGDOM OF GOD.

- ৵ Use your life to bless and serve your fellowmen—Alma 2:30

- ৵ Live so that the Lord can use you as an instrument in His hands—Alma 17:9

- ৵ Converts as well as you will rejoice as they come unto Christ—Alma 26:3–4

- ৵ Receive and feel joy as you serve the Lord as an instrument in His hands—Alma 29:9–10

GOD LOVES ALL OF HIS CHILDREN

*Now my brethren, we see that God is mindful of every people,
whatsoever land they may be in; yea, he numbereth his people,
and his bowels of mercy are over all the earth. Now this is my
joy, and my great thanksgiving; yea, and I will give thanks unto
my God forever. Amen.*

ALMA 26:37

Some have questioned why our missionaries would be sent to all
parts of the world, even among our fellow Christians. In the third
chapter of John, verse 16, we read the familiar scripture, "For God
so loved the world, that he gave his only begotten Son, that whosoever believeth in him should not perish, but have everlasting life."
Our missionaries go to all nations and all people because they have
a firm, unshakable testimony that God still loves the world and that
He has spoken again as an indication of that love.

(Richard C. Edgley, "We Care Enough to Send Our Very
Best," *Ensign,* November 1996, 63)

Daily Living

YOU SHOULD SEEK TO EMULATE THE LOVE OF GOD FOR ALL MANKIND.

- ଚ Rejoice and be filled with love towards God and all men—
  Mosiah 2:4

- ଚ Love your neighbor as yourself—Mosiah 27:4

- ଚ Love your enemies—3 Nephi 12:44

- ଚ With the love of God in your hearts you will be lifted up at the
  last day—Alma 13:29

JOY IN THE LORD

I know that which the Lord hath commanded me, and I glory in it. I do not glory of myself, but I glory in that which the Lord hath commanded me; yea, and this is my glory, that perhaps I may be an instrument in the hands of God to bring some soul to repentance; and this is my joy.

And behold, when I see many of my brethren truly penitent, and coming to the Lord their God, then is my soul filled with joy; then do I remember what the Lord has done for me, yea, even that he hath heard my prayer; yea, then do I remember his merciful arm which he extended towards me.

ALMA 29:9–10

Brethren and sisters, in serving the Lord we reap everlasting joy. We are not striving for the praise of men, but for the praise and honor that comes from God only.

(Charles A. Callis, Conference Report, October 1910, 74)

Daily Living

SEEK TO BE AN INSTRUMENT IN THE HANDS OF GOD TO HELP PEOPLE REPENT.

- ଓ Fast and pray for the Spirit to help you to be an instrument— Alma 17:9

- ଓ Be patient and long-suffering so the Lord can use you—Alma 17:11

- ଓ Seek to persuade others to come unto Christ—Jacob 1:7

- ଓ Remember that the thing of greatest worth unto you is to declare repentance—D&C 15:6

JOY IN THE SUCCESS OF OTHERS

Yea, and that same God did establish his church among them;
yea, and that same God hath called me by a holy calling, to
preach the word unto this people, and hath given me much success,
in the which my joy is full.
ALMA 29:13

Find joy in the success of others. Said Alma: "I do not joy in my own success alone, but my joy is more full because of the success of my brethren. . . . Behold, they have labored exceedingly, and have brought forth much fruit; and how great shall be their reward! . . . When I think of the success of these my brethren . . . great is my joy" (Alma 29:14–16).

Look for the good in others and learn. Give sincere credit where credit is due. Spend less time fault-finding and more time identifying strengths. Yes, try to catch others doing good!

(Carlos E. Asay, *In the Lord's Service: A Guide to Spiritual Development* [Salt Lake City: Deseret Book, 1990], 95)

Daily Living

JOY IN THE SUCCESS AND HAPPINESS OF OTHERS.

  You want others to taste of the joy of the gospel in their lives—Alma 36:24

  There is joy in knowing your children walk in truth—3 John 1:4

  Remember that man is that he might have joy—2 Nephi 2:25

  Rejoice that others have success in bringing souls to Christ—Alma 29:16

THERE IS A GOD IN HEAVEN

*But Alma said unto him: Thou hast had signs enough; will ye
tempt your God? Will ye say, Show unto me a sign, when ye
have the testimony of all these thy brethren, and also all the holy
prophets? The scriptures are laid before thee, yea, and all things
denote there is a God; yea, even the earth, and all things that
are upon the face of it, yea, and its motion, yea, and also all the
planets which move in their regular form do witness that there
is a Supreme Creator.*

ALMA 30:44

The Lord has blessed us with sufficient perception to recognize in
the creations a witness that he lives, so that anyone could have faith
and believe on his name. All over the world men and women believe
in some kind of superior being who created the heavens and the
earth. They do not know what he is or who he is, but they at least
believe in him. That is a great witness to me that the Lord set things
up so that with nothing but his creations, we could have faith that
he exists.

(Gene R. Cook, *Living by the Power of Faith* [Salt Lake City:
Deseret Book, 1985], 33)

Daily Living

LOOK AROUND YOU AND MARVEL AT GOD'S HAND.

- ❧ Recognize that God has all power, all wisdom, all understanding—
  Alma 26:35

- ❧ The Lord is able to do all things according to His will—1 Nephi
  7:12

- ❧ You can be preserved according to His miraculous power—
  Alma 57:26

WORD OF GOD

The preaching of the word had a great tendency to lead the people to do that which was just—yea, it had had more powerful effect upon the minds of the people than the sword, or anything else, which had happened unto them—therefore Alma thought it was expedient that they should try the virtue of the word of God.

ALMA 31:5

[The Book of Mormon] reminds us of the power of God's word, the power to change our lives. . . . We . . . are reminded of the promise of President Ezra Taft Benson: . . . "I bless you with increased discernment to judge between Christ and anti-Christ. I bless you with increased power to do good and resist evil. I bless you with increased understanding of the Book of Mormon. I promise you . . . if we will daily sup from its pages and abide by its precepts, God will pour out upon each child of Zion and the Church a blessing hitherto unknown."

(Gerald N. Lund, *Selected Writings of Gerald N. Lund: Gospel Scholars Series* [Salt Lake City: Deseret Book, 1999], 132)

Daily Living

SEEK TO OBTAIN HIS WORD AND THEN STRIVE TO LIVE IT.

ๆ Live by God's every word—D&C 84:43–46

ๆ The word of God, the iron rod, will lead you in a straight course—1 Nephi 11:25

ๆ Remember that you must nurture the word of God—Alma 32:40–43

ๆ The word of God is like a compass that can lead you to eternal bliss—Alma 37:44

SOULS ARE PRECIOUS

Behold, O Lord, their souls are precious, and many of them are our brethren; therefore, give unto us, O Lord, power and wisdom that we may bring these, our brethren, again unto thee.

ALMA 31:35

First, cultivate an awareness; bring others to a knowledge. President Gordon B. Hinckley teaches us: "Let there be cultivated an awareness in every member's heart of his [or her] own potential for bringing others to a knowledge of the truth. . . . Let him pray with great earnestness about it. Let each member pray."

(Yoshihiko Kikuchi, "Find the Lambs, Feed the Sheep," *Ensign,* May 1999, 106)

Daily Living

HELP OTHERS COME TO THE SAVIOR BY REALIZING THEIR DIVINE WORTH.

- ∞ Pray for all those who know not God—Alma 6:6

- ∞ Lift up the hands that hang down—D&C 81:5

- ∞ Strengthen others in conversation, in prayer, in all your doings—D&C 108:7

- ∞ Labor to assist others to taste of the joy of the gospel—Alma 36:24

- ∞ Seek the welfare of the souls of your fellowmen—2 Nephi 6:3

- ∞ Pray for others and their well being—Enos 1:9, 11, 16

BLESSINGS IN AFFLICTIONS

And now when Alma heard this, he turned him about, his face immediately towards him, and he beheld with great joy; for he beheld that their afflictions had truly humbled them, and that they were in a preparation to hear the word.
ALMA 32:6

Alma preaches to the poor and afflicted who were cast out of their own synagogues because of their extreme poverty. When Alma sees that the people are penitent and that their afflictions have truly humbled them, he explains: ". . . Yea, he that truly humbleth himself, and repenteth of his sins, and endureth to the end, the same shall be blessed" (Alma 32:15).

(Richard L. Bednar and Scott R. Peterson,
Spirituality and Self-Esteem: Developing the Inner Self
[Salt Lake City: Deseret Book, 1990], 28)

Daily Living
ALLOW YOUR AFFLICTIONS TO TURN YOU TOWARD GOD.

⽤ The Lord can consecrate your afflictions for your gain—2 Nephi 2:2

⽤ The Lord will console you in your afflictions—Jacob 3:1; Alma 7:11–12

⽤ Your attitude determines how you respond to afflictions—Alma 62:41

⽤ Remember that sometimes the Lord will chasten you with afflictions—Helaman 12:3

⽤ Remember that all these things will give you experience and be for your good—D&C 121:7

WORSHIP GOD

*Behold I say unto you, do ye suppose that ye cannot worship
God save it be in your synagogues only?
And moreover, I would ask, do ye suppose that ye must not
worship God only once in a week?*
ALMA 32:10–11

And every dispensation entered on its pathway to apostasy when the
people compromised the worship of God with the conventions of
men. To love and serve God—to worship him alone—at all times
meant keeping his commandments, not in isolation from the world,
but in puritanical contrast to universal and prevailing custom.

(Avraham Gileadi, "Twelve Diatribes of Modern Israel," in *By
Study and Also by Faith,* eds. John M. Lundquist and Stephen
D. Ricks [Salt Lake City: Deseret Book, 1990], 2:355)

Daily Living

MAKE SURE NOTHING TAKES PRECEDENCE OVER GOD.

ත Worship Heavenly Father in the name of Jesus Christ—Jacob
4:5

ත Worship Heavenly Father through prayer—Alma 33:3

ත Worship Heavenly Father wherever you may be; live in thanksgiving daily—Alma 34:38

ත Beware of worshiping idols and things of the world—2 Nephi
12:8

BLESSINGS OF HUMILITY

And now, because ye are compelled to be humble blessed are ye;
for a man sometimes, if he is compelled to be humble, seeketh
repentance; and now surely, whosoever repenteth shall find
mercy; and he that findeth mercy and endureth to the end the
same shall be saved.

ALMA 32:13

The blessings of the Lord are given to all who will come unto him.
Seek his guidance in prayer and faith and humility, that the blessings of the Lord shall be unto you as you draw near to him with your
hearts.

(Eldred G. Smith, Conference Report, April 1958, 34)

Daily Living

BE HUMBLE AND THE LORD WILL LEAD YOU INTO SALVATION.

- ࢤ Humble yourselves by always remembering the goodness of
  God through a remission of your sins—Mosiah 4:11

- ࢤ Ask your self continually if you have been sufficiently humble—
  Alma 5:27

- ࢤ You are blessed when you humble yourself—Alma 32:16;
  48:20

- ࢤ Fast and pray to be stronger in your humility—Helaman 3:35

- ࢤ You can be made strong through your humility and faith—
  Ether 12:27

MORE BLESSED

Therefore, blessed are they who humble themselves without being compelled to be humble; or rather, in other words, blessed is he that believeth in the word of God, and is baptized without stubbornness of heart, yea, without being brought to know the word, or even compelled to know, before they will believe.

ALMA 32:16

Most of us seem to have the "Nephite cycle" as part of our character. There is a point when we are teachable; our humility enables us to grow and to ride the crest of spirituality. Then there are other times when we begin to feel self-sufficient and puffed up with pride. These times cause us to fall of our own weight and ill-doing into pits of spiritual darkness. How much better it would be if we kept in remembrance our God and our religion and broke the cycle by consistent worship and righteous living.

(Carlos E. Asay, *Family Pecan Trees: Planting a Legacy of Faith at Home* [Salt Lake City: Deseret Book, 1992], 193–194)

Daily Living

YOU ARE BLESSED MORE BY BEING HUMBLED BY THE WORD RATHER THAN BY CIRCUMSTANCE.

- ✺ You can be humbled by the preaching of the word—Alma 5:13

- ✺ When you are humbled you are in preparation to hear the word of God—Alma 32:6

- ✺ Act with faith as you receive the word of God—Mosiah 26:15–16

- ✺ You are blessed when you heed the words of the Lord's servants— 3 Nephi 12:1

JUNE

ℰഌ

*. . . they brought them to the
knowledge of the Lord their God,
and to rejoice in Jesus Christ
their Redeemer.*

—Alma 37:9

FAITH

And now as I said concerning faith—faith is not to have a perfect knowledge of things; therefore if ye have faith ye hope for things which are not seen, which are true.

ALMA 32:21

The same power of an early choice to exercise faith and to be persistent in obedience applies to gaining the faith to resist temptation and to gain forgiveness. The best time to resist temptation is early. The best time to repent is now. The enemy of our souls will place thoughts in our minds to tempt us. We can decide early to exercise faith, to cast out evil thoughts before we act on them. And we can choose quickly to repent when we do sin, before Satan can weaken our faith and bind us. Seeking forgiveness is always better now than later.

(Henry B. Eyring, "Spiritual Preparedness: Start Early and
Be Steady," Ensign, November 2005, 40)

Daily Living

SEEK TO GAIN AND EXERCISE FAITH IN THE LORD JESUS CHRIST.

- ℘ You exercise your faith unto repentance and forgiveness—Enos 1:8; Alma 34:15–17

- ℘ Salvation comes through faith in the Lord Jesus Christ—Mosiah 3:9

- ℘ Prayers are answered according to your faith—Mosiah 27:14

- ℘ Strength is given according to our faith—Alma 14:26

- ℘ Fast and pray to increase and make firm your faith—Helaman 3:35

- ℘ Through faith in the Lord Jesus Christ you can do all things— Moroni 7:33

EXPERIMENT UPON THE WORD

But behold, if ye will awake and arouse your faculties, even to an experiment upon my words, and exercise a particle of faith, yea, even if ye can no more than desire to believe, let this desire work in you, even until ye believe in a manner that ye can give place for a portion of my words."

ALMA 32:27

We know that both members and nonmembers are more likely to be thoroughly converted to the gospel of Jesus Christ when there is a willingness to experiment upon the word (see Alma 32:27). This is an attitude of both mind and heart that includes a desire to know the truth and a willingness to act on that desire. For those investigating the Church, the experiment can be as simple as agreeing to read the Book of Mormon, to pray about it, and to earnestly seek to know if Joseph Smith was the Lord's prophet.

True conversion comes through the power of the Spirit. . . . These experiences with the Spirit follow naturally when a person is willing to experiment upon the word.

(M. Russell Ballard, "Now Is the Time," *Ensign,* November 2000, 75)

Daily Living

EXERCISE A LITTLE FAITH SO THAT THE BLESSINGS OF HIS WORDS CAN BE PART OF YOUR LIFE.

- ✢ Seek diligently and the mysteries of God will be unfolded to you— 1 Nephi 10:19

- ✢ The Lord granteth unto men according to their desires—Alma 29:4

- ✢ If you exercise faith you can cleave to every good thing—Moroni 7:28

THE WORD COMPARED TO A SEED

*Now, we will compare the word unto a seed. Now, if ye give place,
that a seed may be planted in your heart, behold, if it be a true
seed, or a good seed, if ye do not cast it out by your unbelief . . .
behold, it will begin to swell within your breasts; and when you
feel these swelling motions, ye will begin to say within yourselves—
It must needs be that this is a good seed . . . for it beginneth to
enlarge my soul . . . to enlighten my understanding, yea, it
beginneth to be delicious to me.*

ALMA 32:28

Alma invites his hearers to plant the word as a seed in their hearts and
not to "cast it out by [their] unbelief" (Alma 32:28). The sprouting
and growing of the seed then gives the experimenter knowledge that it
is good (verses 33–35). . . . If one will "nourish the word" with "great
diligence" he will be able to harvest the fruit, "which is most precious"
(verses 33–42).

(Stephen D. Ricks and John W. Welch, eds.,
*The Allegory of the Olive Tree: The Olive, the Bible,
and Jacob 5* [Salt Lake City and Provo, UT: Deseret Book
and FARMS, 1994], 45–46)

Daily Living

NOURISH AND OBEY THE WORD OF GOD.

- ಬಿ Nourish the word with faith, diligence, and patience—Alma
  32:40–43

- ಬಿ Nourish the word with faith that you may enjoy everlasting
  life—Alma 33:23

- ಬಿ All members need to be nourished by the good word of God—
  Moroni 6:4

- ó You must live by every word that proceedeth forth from the
  mouth of God—D&C 84:44

STRENGTHENING YOUR FAITH

*But behold, as the seed swelleth, and sprouteth, and beginneth
to grow, then you must needs say that the seed is good; for
behold it swelleth, and sprouteth, and beginneth to grow. And
now, behold, will not this strengthen your faith? Yea, it will
strengthen your faith: for ye will say I know that this is a good
seed; for behold it sprouteth and beginneth to grow.*

ALMA 32:30

It does not require a calling more than being a member to nourish
by reaching out in kindness. And even those who have no calling to
teach or to preach can nourish with the good word of God if we prepare for it. We can do it every time we speak with a new member
and every time we participate in a class discussion. Every word we
speak can strengthen or weaken faith. We need help from the Spirit
to speak the words which will nourish and which will strengthen.

(Henry B. Eyring, "Feed My Lambs," *Ensign,*
November 1997, 83)

Daily Living

NURTURE THE WORD BY YOUR FAITH.

- ෩ Faith comes by hearing the word—Romans 10:17

- ෩ Stay on the strait and narrow path with unshaken faith—2 Nephi
31:19

- ෩ Help the seed take root in your heart with faith, diligence, and
patience—Alma 32:40–43

- ෩ You obtain the word as you exercise your faith—Ether 12:20

KNOWLEDGE COMES OF FAITH

*And now, behold, is your knowledge perfect? Yea, your knowledge
is perfect in that thing, and your faith is dormant; and this
because you know, for ye know that the word hath swelled your
souls, and ye also know that it hath sprouted up, that your
understanding doth begin to be enlightened, and your mind
doth begin to expand.*

ALMA 32:34

Learning by faith is not easy. To one schooled in the doctrines of salvation and the history of the Restoration and with a testimony of the divine origin of this church, we would remind you that the acquiring of knowledge by faith. . . . demands strenuous effort and a continual striving. . . .

In short, learning by faith is no task for a lazy man. . . . Such a process requires the bending of the whole soul, the calling up from the depths of the human mind and linking it with God—the right connection must be formed. Then only comes "knowledge by faith" (71–29, p. 119).

(Harold B. Lee, *The Teachings of Harold B. Lee,* ed. Clyde J.
Williams [Salt Lake City: Bookcraft, 1996], 331)

Daily Living

SEEK TO INCREASE IN YOUR FAITH, AND AS IT IS EXERCISED YOU WILL GAIN
KNOWLEDGE.

- ✵ Plead for faith; fast and pray—Luke 17:5; Helaman 3:35

- ✵ Remember knowledge is hid up through unbelief, the lack of faith—Ether 4:13

- ✵ Remember the just live by faith—Romans 1:17

- ✵ If you have faith you can do all things that are expedient in the Lord—Moroni 7:33

NOURISH THE WORD

Now, this is not because the seed was not good, neither is it because the fruit thereof would not be desirable; but it is because your ground is barren, and <u>ye will not nourish the tree,</u> therefore ye cannot have the fruit thereof.

Alma 32:39

Through scripture study we hold to the iron rod, which will guide us through the mists of darkness and the temptations of Satan. Scripture study will be a fortress around us as we study and apply the scriptures to our lives and nurture the word of God through faith, diligence, and patience. A caring mother feels peace when she walks by her child's room and sees her child studying the scriptures. She knows that the power of the word will fortify her daughter.

(Ed and Patricia Pinegar, "Avoiding Temptation," in
*Why Say No When the World Says Yes? Resisting Temptation
in an Immoral World,* comp. Randal A. Wright
[Salt Lake City: Deseret Book, 1993], 7)

Daily Living

BE DILIGENT IN YOUR EFFORTS TO NURTURE THE WORD OF GOD.

- ಬಿ Ponder the word and the things of the Lord—2 Nephi 4:15–16

- ಬಿ Follow the Lord with full purpose of heart—2 Nephi 31:13

- ಬಿ You nurture the word with faith, diligence, and patience—Alma 32:40–43

- ಬಿ You are blessed with the fruit of the tree by nurturing the word—Alma 32:42–43

PARTAKE OF THE FRUIT

*And because of your diligence and your faith and your patience
with the word in nourishing it, that it may take root in you,
behold, by and by ye shall pluck the fruit thereof, which is most
precious . . . and ye shall feast upon this fruit even until ye are
filled, that ye hunger not, neither shall ye thirst.*

Alma 32:42

We can partake of the "love of God," "the tree of life," and drink from
"the fountain of living waters" daily by communing with our Holy
Father, immersing ourselves in the scriptures, and meditation. Then
the Lord will bless us to be more sensitive to speak to those souls
which He has prepared for us.

(Yoshihiko Kikuchi, "Heavenly Father Has a Special Plan,"
Ensign, May 2000, 79)

Daily Living

MAKE SCRIPTURE STUDY A DAILY FEAST.

- The fruit is desirable above all other things to make one happy—1 Nephi 8:10

- You will have a desire that others might partake also—1 Nephi 8:11–12; Alma 36:24

- When your heart is full of love, you will be blessed beyond measure—4 Nephi 1:15–16

- The love of God will encourage you to search the scriptures—Jacob 7:23

- Follow Mosiah's counsel and you will be filled with the love of God—Mosiah 4:11–12

PRAYER

Thou hast heard my prayer, even when I was in the wilderness;
yea, thou wast merciful when I prayed concerning those who
were mine enemies. . . . I did cry unto thee in my field, . . .
[and] when I did turn to my house thou didst hear me in my
prayer. . . . When I did turn unto my closet . . . thou didst
hear me. . . . Thou hast . . . heard my cries in the midst of thy
congregations . . . thou hast also heard me when I have been
cast out and have been despised by mine enemies, . . . therefore I
will cry unto thee in all mine afflictions, for in thee is my joy;
for thou hast turned thy judgments away from me, because of
thy Son.
ALMA 33:4–11

My patriarchal blessing tells me to pray at all times, in all places, and
regarding all things. Those words suddenly had new meaning, and I
prayed constantly for the strength and serenity to get through each
night, each morning, each afternoon, and often each hour. . . . And
as my need increased, so did His sustenance.

(Donna Lee Bowen Barnes, *As Women of Faith:*
Talks Selected from the BYU Women's Conferences
[Salt Lake City; Deseret Book, 1989], 77)

Daily Living

LET YOUR HEART BE CONTINUOUSLY DRAWN OUT TO GOD IN PRAYER.

- ෨ Remember that the Spirit teaches you to pray—2 Nephi 32:8

- ෨ Watch and pray continually that you not be tempted—Alma 13:28

- ෨ Counsel with the Lord in all your doings—Alma 37:37

THE INFINITE ATONEMENT

For it is expedient that an atonement should be made; for according to the great plan of the Eternal God there must be an atonement made, or else all mankind must unavoidably perish; . . . yea, all are fallen and are lost . . . except it be through the atonement which it is expedient should be made.

ALMA 34:9

I was reading in the book of 2 Nephi when I realized that if Jacob had been in that earlier class meeting he would have said something like this: "Now, wait a minute. This is what the atonement of Jesus does for us: It not only brings the body forth from the grave but also redeems the spirit from what otherwise would have been an endless, miserable condition with the devil." Or, in other words, if Jesus Christ had not performed the infinite atonement, every man, woman, and child—everybody who belongs to the family of Adam—would have become a son of perdition.

(Robert J. Matthews, *A Bible! A Bible!*
[Salt Lake City: Bookcraft, 1990], 286)

Daily Living

LIVE SO AS NEVER TO TAKE THE ATONEMENT FOR GRANTED.

- ✑ You are redeemed from hell because of the Lord's atoning sacrifice—2 Nephi 1:15

- ✑ Remember the Atonement brings to pass the Resurrection—Alma 42:23

- ✑ You can be saved through the Atonement of the Lord—Helaman 5:9

- ✑ Through the Atonement of the Lord we are drawn unto Him—3 Nephi 27:14

OUR RESPONSIBILITIES IN GOD'S PLAN

And thus mercy can satisfy the demands of justice, and encircles them in the arms of safety, while he that exercises no faith unto repentance is exposed to the whole law of the demands of justice; therefore only unto him that has faith unto repentance is brought about the great and eternal plan of redemption.
ALMA 34:16

It is in the home that one learns that faith is intimately related to the Atonement. . . . Without the effects of the Atonement in our lives, it would be impossible to develop the type of faith necessary for repentance, and so we would remain outside the marvelous plan of mercy since "only unto him that has faith unto repentance is brought about the great and eternal plan of redemption" (Alma 34:16).

(Francisco J. Viñas, "Applying the Simple and Plain Gospel Principles in the Family," *Ensign,* May 2004, 39)

Daily Living

MAKE THE ATONEMENT EFFICACIOUS IN YOUR LIFE BY EXERCISING FAITH UNTO REPENTANCE.

- ফ If you don't repent you must perish—1 Nephi 14:5
- ফ The process of repentance and forgiveness always hinges upon faith—Enos 1:8
- ফ Remember that you can become an enemy to God for not repenting—Mosiah 2:38
- ফ Heavenly Father has commanded everyone to repent—3 Nephi 11:32–34

PRAYER

Ye must pour out your souls in your closets, and your secret places, and in your wilderness.
Yea, and when you do not cry unto the Lord, let your hearts be full, drawn out in prayer unto him continually for your welfare, and also for the welfare of those who are around you.
ALMA 34:26–27

We would say . . . seek to know God in your closets, call upon him in the fields. Follow the directions of the Book of Mormon, and pray over, and for your families, your cattle, your flocks, your herds, your corn, and all things that you possess; ask the blessing of God upon all your labors, and everything that you engage in.

(Joseph Smith, *Teachings of the Prophet Joseph Smith,* selected and arranged by Joseph Fielding Smith [Salt Lake City: Deseret Book, 1976], 247)

Daily Living

YOU SHOULD PRAY FOR AND OVER ALL THINGS.

- ✍ Pray for forgiveness—Enos 1:4–8
- ✍ Pray for strength—Alma 14:26
- ✍ Pray in your families—3 Nephi 18:21
- ✍ Watch and pray so as to not be tempted—3 Nephi 18:18
- ✍ Pray for charity—Moroni 7:48
- ✍ Pray to know the truth of all things—Moroni 10:4–5

PRAYER IS NOT ENOUGH

And now behold, my beloved brethren, I say unto you, do not suppose that this is all; for after ye have done all these things, if ye turn away the needy, and the naked, and visit not the sick and afflicted, and impart of your substance, if ye have, to those who stand in need—I say unto you, if ye do not any of these things, behold, your prayer is vain, and availeth you nothing, and ye are as hypocrites who do deny the faith.
ALMA 34:28

You will recall that Amulek, in his great sermon to the multitude, told us the things about which we might pray. This great message is worth reading and rereading, and I would like to call your particular attention to the admonition which he gave to the multitude when he recounted how vain would be their prayers if they turned away the needy and the naked and visited not the sick and afflicted and imparted not of their substance (Alma 34:17 ff).

(J. Reuben Clark Jr., *Behold the Lamb of God* [Salt Lake City: Deseret Book, 1991], 324)

Daily Living

CONSCIENTIOUSLY BE AWARE OF THOSE AROUND YOU AND GIVE FREELY OF YOUR SUBSTANCE.

- ∞ Be free with your substance—Jacob 2:17

- ∞ Give freely according to your ability—Mosiah 4:26; 18:27

- ∞ Remember, all are beggars, so judge not—Mosiah 4:19

- ∞ Don't give to be seen of men—3 Nephi 13:1

- ∞ Be careful lest you love things more than the poor and needy—Mormon 8:37

SCRIPTURES TESTIFY OF CHRIST

*And now, my brethren, I would that, after ye have received so
many witnesses, seeing that the holy scriptures testify of these
things, ye come forth and bring fruit unto repentance.
Yea, I would that ye would come forth and harden not your
hearts any longer; for behold, now is the time and the day of
your salvation; and therefore, if ye will repent and harden not
your hearts, immediately shall the great plan of redemption be
brought about unto you.*

ALMA 34:30–31

To emphasize the spiritual dimension is not to reject the study of
scriptures and the doctrines. The scriptures testify of Christ. Study
is an important element, of course, but there must be much prayer
and reaching associated with study, and then revelation comes.

(Spencer W. Kimball, *President Kimball Speaks Out* [Salt
Lake City: Deseret Book, 1981], 25)

Daily Living

SEARCH THE SCRIPTURES, HARDEN NOT YOUR HEARTS AND REPENT, AND BE
GRATEFUL FOR THE PLAN OF REDEMPTION.

- ಐ Give heed to the word of God—1 Nephi 15:25

- ಐ Remember to liken the scriptures to your life—1 Nephi 19:23

- ಐ The Book of Mormon can bring you unto salvation—2 Nephi 3:15

- ಐ Delight in the scriptures and ponder them—2 Nephi. 4:15

- ಐ Search the scriptures diligently—Mosiah 1:7

- ಐ Search the scriptures that you might know the word of God—Alma 17:2

MORTALITY

For behold, this life is the time for men to prepare to meet God; yea, behold the day of this life is the day for men to perform their labors.

ALMA 34:32

Now is the time to prepare to meet God. Tomorrow may be too late. Prophets through the ages have so declared: "This life is the time for men to prepare to meet God. . . . Do not procrastinate the day of your repentance"(Alma 34:32–33; see also Alma 13:27).

(Russell M. Nelson, "Now Is the Time to Prepare,"
Ensign, May 2005, 16)

Daily Living

NOW IS THE TIME TO PREPARE TO MEET GOD . . . MAKE A PLAN FOR A RIGHTEOUS LIFE.

ဆ Prepare your souls for the judgment—2 Nephi 9:46

ဆ You must prepare quickly for the hour is close at hand—Alma 5:28–29

ဆ Life is a probationary state to prepare to meet God—Alma 12:24

ဆ Remember to prepare every needful thing—D&C 88:119

PROCRASTINATION

*And now, as I said unto you before, as ye have had so many wit-
nesses, therefore, I beseech of you that ye do not procrastinate the
day of your repentance until the end; for after this day of life,
which is given us to prepare for eternity, behold, if we do not
improve our time while in this life, then cometh the night of
darkness wherein there can be no labor performed.*

Alma 34:33

Procrastination is the father of a countless family of things that
come too late. Procrastination means making an appointment with
opportunity to "call again tomorrow." It kills self-control, saps men-
tal energy, makes man a creature of circumstances instead of their
creator. There is one brand of procrastination that is a virtue. It is
never doing today a wrong that can be put off till tomorrow, never
performing an act today that may make tomorrow ashamed.

(William George Jordan, "The Power of Truth,"
Improvement Era, May 1934, 273)

Daily Living

Learn to overcome procrastination. Do it now.

- Don't procrastinate the day of your repentance—Alma 13:27

- Now is the time to repent, for the same spirit will possess your
  body in the hereafter—Alma 34:34

- Remember you can not have happiness in wickedness. Don't
  procrastinate—Helaman 13:38

OVERCOME TEMPTATION

Yea, and I also exhort you, my brethren, that ye be <u>watchful</u> <u>unto prayer continually</u>, that ye may not be <u>led away</u> by the <u>temptations of the devil</u>, that he may not <u>overpower you</u>, that ye may not become his <u>subjects</u> at the last day; for behold, <u>he</u> <u>rewardeth you no good thing</u>.

ALMA 34:39

With the help of the Holy Ghost, we can watch over ourselves. We can <u>pray to recognize and reject the first thoughts of sin.</u> We can pray to recognize a warning not to speak words which would hurt or tempt someone else. And we can, when we must, pray for the humility and the faith to repent. There will surely be some who hear my voice who will have this thought come into their minds: "But the temptations are too great for me. I have resisted as long as I can. For me, the commandments are too hard. The standard is too high." That is not so. The Savior is our Advocate with the Father. He knows our weaknesses. He knows how to succor those who are tempted.

(Henry B. Eyring, "As a Child," *Ensign,* May 2006, 17)

Daily Living

PRAY TO OVERCOME TEMPTATION.

- ℵ Hearken to the word of God and the temptations of the devil will not overpower you—1 Nephi 15:24

- ℵ <u>The righteous shall not yield to temptation</u>—Alma 11:23

- ℵ <u>Pray so as not to yield to or be overcome with temptation</u>— Alma 13:28; 31:10; 34:39; 3 Nephi 13:12; 18:18

- ℵ Remember that <u>temptation is part of the test</u>—D&C 29:39

PATIENCE AND HOPE

But that ye have patience, and bear with those afflictions, with a firm hope that ye shall one day rest from all your afflictions.
ALMA 34:41

They were to be watchful in prayer, and were not to be led away by the temptations of the devil. Amulek ended his important doctrinal discourse by exhorting his audience to have patience, to bear with all manner of afflictions, and not to revile those who had cast them out because of their poverty, lest they also become sinners. They were to bear their afflictions in patience, with a firm hope that one day they would rest from all of them (34:36–41).

(Sidney B. Sperry, *Book of Mormon Compendium*
[Salt Lake City: Bookcraft, 1968], 353)

Daily Living
DEVELOP PATIENCE AND LIVE WITH HOPE.

- ৪৩ Be patient and long-suffering that you might be a good example—Alma 17:11

- ৪৩ Patience a virtue that leads to charity—D&C 4:6; 2 Peter 1:3–12

- ৪৩ A perfect brightness of hope helps you press forward with steadfastness—2 Nephi 31:20

- ৪৩ Have hope through the Atonement of the Lord Jesus Christ—Moroni 7:41

- ৪৩ Remember, the Holy Ghost fills you with hope and perfect love—Moroni 8:26

FATHER'S BLESSINGS

Therefore, he caused that his sons should be gathered together, that he might give unto them every one his charge, separately, concerning the things pertaining unto righteousness. And we have an account of his commandments, which he gave unto them according to his own record.

ALMA 35:16

Another blessing that can come is a father's blessing, which can help us face some of life's greatest challenges. One of the sweetest experiences of my life came to me when my oldest daughter, then a university student and faced with some of life's greatest decisions, came to my office and asked if I would give her a father's blessing (56–07, p. 117).

(Harold B. Lee, *The Teachings of Harold B. Lee,* ed. Clyde J. Williams [Salt Lake City: Bookcraft, 1996], 502)

Daily Living

FATHERS AND MOTHERS, SEEK TO TEACH AND BLESS YOUR CHILDREN. CHILDREN, SEEK TO BE TAUGHT AND RECEIVE BLESSINGS FROM YOUR FATHER AND MOTHER.

- ◊ Labor diligently to persuade your children to believe in Christ— 2 Nephi 25:23

- ◊ Honor your father and mother—Mosiah 13:20

- ◊ Teach your children—1 Nephi 1:1; Alma 56:47; D&C 68:25–31

- ◊ See examples of blessings of fathers to children—2 Nephi 1–4; Alma 36–42

KEEP THE COMMANDMENTS

My son, give ear to my words; for I swear unto you, that inasmuch as ye shall keep the commandments of God ye shall prosper in the land.

ALMA 36:1

[From a letter by a young man who served a mission in Bolivia:] "This is our opportunity, and we cannot fail. The Lord trusts us. I have read many times in the Book of Mormon the words the Lord told the prophets, that as we keep the commandments, we would prosper in the land. This is being fulfilled. I am so grateful to God for this great opportunity to receive what my brothers and sisters did not have, to help my family, to accomplish my goals. And I am excited to repay the loan to see others be so blessed. I know the Lord will bless me as I do it."

(Gordon B. Hinckley, "Reaching Down to Lift Another," *Ensign,* November 2001, 53)

Daily Living

AS YOU KEEP THE COMMANDMENTS THE LORD WILL BLESS YOU.

- ෨ The Lord will help you keep the commandments—1 Nephi 3:7

- ෨ The Lord will bless and prosper you as you keep the commandments—Mosiah 2:22

- ෨ You can enter into a state of never ending happiness if you keep the commandments—Mosiah 2:41

- ෨ You can always have His Spirit to be with you—Moroni 4:3; 5:2

REMEMBER

*I would that ye should do as I have done, in remembering the
captivity of our fathers; for they were in bondage, and none
could deliver them except it was the God of Abraham, and the
God of Isaac, and the God of Jacob; and he surely did deliver
them in their afflictions.*
ALMA 36:2

What might help us to remember the standards the Lord has given
us? Moroni used the Title of Liberty to remind his people. What can
we do to make sure we keep the commandments? How can we avoid
temptation? Perhaps we can make ourselves little reminders, like a
note on the mirror with the simple word *Remember.*

(Randal A. Wright, comp., *Why Say No When the World Says
Yes? Resisting Temptation in an Immoral World* [Salt Lake
City: Deseret Book, 1993], 13–14)

Daily Living

LEARN TO CONTINUALLY REMEMBER THE GOODNESS OF GOD.

- හ Give heed to the word and you'll remember to keep the commandments—1 Nephi 15:25

- හ You are free to choose eternal life and be reconciled to God—
  2 Nephi 10:22–24

- හ Remember the greatness of God and your own nothingness—
  Mosiah 4:11–16

- හ When you recognize good being done then you remember what
  good things the Lord has done for you—Alma 29:10–12

CHILDREN WANT DIRECTION

And now, O my son Helaman, behold, thou art in thy youth, and therefore, I beseech of thee that thou wilt hear my words and learn of me; for I do know that whosoever shall put their trust in God shall be supported in their trials, and their troubles, and their afflictions, and shall be lifted up at the last day.

ALMA 36:3

Love your children, let them know that you love them; but remember that it is no favor to a child to let him do things he should not do. I have seen the results of many surveys and know from personal experience that children want some direction and control in their lives and want to live up to the expectations of those who are responsible for directing their lives.

(N. Eldon Tanner, "Obeying the Right Voice," *Ensign,*
November 1977, 43)

Daily Living

LEARN FROM YOUR PARENTS, TRUST IN THE LORD; YOU SHALL BE SUPPORTED IN YOUR TRIALS.

- ֍ Learn from your parents—1 Nephi 1:1; Enos 1:1
- ֍ Fathers, bless your children—2 Nephi 1–4; Alma 36–42
- ֍ Parents teach Jesus Christ, that your children may know from what source their blessings come—2 Nephi 25:26
- ֍ Parents are expected to care for and teach their children—Mosiah 4:14–15
- ֍ You are to honor your parents—1 Nephi 17:55; Mosiah 13:20

THE PROCESS OF REPENTANCE

As I was thus racked with torment, while I was harrowed up by
the memory of my many sins, behold, I remembered also to have
heard my father prophesy unto the people concerning the coming of
one Jesus Christ, a Son of God, to atone for the sins of the world.
Now, as my mind caught hold upon this thought, I cried within
my heart: O Jesus, thou Son of God, have mercy on me, who
am . . . encircled about by the everlasting chains of death.
And now, behold, when I thought this, I could remember my
pains no more; yea, I was harrowed up by the memory of
my sins no more.
ALMA 36:17–19

True repentance is a process requiring sincere faith, recognition of
sin, "godly sorrow" (2 Cor. 7:10), confession, restitution for sin, and
a forsaking or turning away from evil.

("Repentance," in *The Book of Mormon Reference*
Companion, ed. Dennis L. Largey [Salt Lake City: Deseret
Book, 2003], 677)

Daily Living

UNDERSTAND THE PROCESS OF REPENTANCE AND FORGIVENESS.

- Repentance and remission of sins is through our Savior Jesus Christ—3 Nephi 7:16

- Nephi felt sorrow and grief for his sins—2 Nephi 4:17

- Confess your sins that you might be forgiven—Mosiah 26:29, 35

- Forsake your sins, humble yourselves before God, ask for forgiveness—Mosiah 4:10

- A restoration to grace is brought about by good works—Helaman 12:24

JOY IN FREEDOM FROM SIN

*Yea, I say unto you, my son, that there could be nothing so
exquisite and so bitter as were my pains. Yea, and again I say
unto you, my son, that on the other hand, there can be nothing
so exquisite and sweet as was my joy.*

ALMA 36:21

In mortality men experience joy only in righteousness—that is, in obedience to the laws and ordinances of the gospel—the gospel being the "glad tidings of great joy." Joy is characteristic of the presence of the Holy Ghost, from whom it comes. It is experienced only when the Spirit is present, and that most acutely in the manifestation that our sins have been remitted, in the knowledge that our path is pleasing to and approved by God, and in our helping others find the way to light and salvation (see Mosiah 4:3; D&C 18:13).

(Joseph Fielding McConkie and Robert L. Millet, *Doctrinal
Commentary on the Book of Mormon* [Salt Lake City:
Bookcraft, 1991], 3:188–189)

Daily Living

MAKE REPENTANCE A DAILY PART OF YOUR LIFE SO YOU CAN FEEL JOY.

   ଐ   You are enemy to God if you don't repent—Mosiah 2:38

   ଐ   If you don't repent you will feel guilt, pain, and anguish—Mosiah 2:38

   ଐ   The righteous have sorrow for the sins of others—3 Nephi 28:9

   ଐ   Your soul will be filled with joy over repentance and forgiveness—Alma 36:20

   ଐ   The Savior experiences great joy over the repentant soul—D&C 18:1

RESULTS OF TRUE REPENTANCE

Yea, and from that time even until now, I have labored without ceasing, that I might bring souls unto repentance; that I might bring them to taste of the exceeding joy of which I did taste; that they might also be born of God, and be filled with the Holy Ghost.

ALMA 36:24

How do we know if we are truly converted? Self-examination tests are available in the scriptures. One measures the degree of conversion prerequisite to baptism. Another measures our willingness to serve others. To His disciple Peter, the Lord said, "I have prayed for thee, that thy faith fail not: and when thou art converted, strengthen thy brethren." Willingness to serve and strengthen others stands as a symbol of one's readiness to be healed.

(Russell M. Nelson, "Jesus Christ—the Master Healer," *Ensign,* November 2005, 87)

Daily Living

TRUE CONVERSION TO CHRIST CAUSES YOU TO SEEK TO BLESS OTHERS THAT THEY MIGHT PARTAKE OF THE JOY THAT YOU FEEL.

- ✺ You have deep concern for the welfare of others—Enos 1:9, 11; Mosiah 28:3

- ✺ You will seek to comfort and bless others—Mosiah 18:8–9

- ✺ You will feel joy over others as they are righteous—Alma 7:4–5

- ✺ You will look upon sin with abhorrence—Alma 13:12

- ✺ You seek to be an instrument in the hands of the Lord—Alma 29:9–10

- ✺ Souls are precious and you will seek to bless others—Alma 31:34–35

JOY IN SERVICE

*Yea, and now behold, O my son, the Lord doth give me
exceedingly great joy in the fruit of my labors.*
ALMA 36:25

Serving others in any way is an indication of our desire to respond
to His invitation to come unto Him. How about a checkup on our
service to others? Let's ask ourselves, Will I make that visit to my
homebound friend? Will I open my mouth to defend and testify
of the truth? Will I give of my worldly goods? Do I share some of
my fresh, productive time with my children? Do I serve with joy
in my Church calling?

(Betty Jo N. Jepsen, "'By Way of Invitation'
[Alma 5:62]," *Ensign,* November 1992, 77)

Daily Living

STRIVE TO LOVE AND SERVE IN THE HOME, BY HELPING ANYONE AT ANY
TIME, BY DOING MISSIONARY SERVICE, ETC.

- ∞ When you serve your fellowmen you are serving God—Mosiah
  2:17

- ∞ Parents joy is in serving their children and seeing them prosper
  in the gospel—3 John 1:4

- ∞ Have joy in the fruits of your labor—Jacob 5:60, 71, 75

- ∞ You an feel joy in blessing others as you serve the Lord—Alma
  26:11, 16, 30

- ∞ Serving is often difficult but your afflictions will be swallowed
  up in joy—Alma 31:38

- ∞ The Lord experiences joy over you as you increase your faith—
  3 Nephi 17:20

THE POWER OF THE WORD

*For because of the word which he has imparted unto me,
behold, many have been born of God, and have tasted as I have
tasted, and have seen eye to eye as I have seen; therefore they do
know of these things of which I have spoken, as I do know; and
the knowledge which I have is of God.*

ALMA 36:26

Since feasting on the word of God has a "more powerful effect upon the
minds of the people than . . . anything else" (Alma 31:5), the more of
the word of God we have and act upon, the more we will press forward.
Much spiritual energy is necessary for the marathon of discipleship.
As a great blessing, the word of God has been richly given to us in the
Restoration. It provides a full and firm basis for real faith, especially in
a world in which many are struggling to believe.

(Neal A. Maxwell, *A Wonderful Flood of Light* [Salt Lake
City: Bookcraft, 1990], 11)

Daily Living

BE PREPARED TO RECEIVE THE WORD OF GOD THAT YOU MIGHT IMPART IT
TO OTHERS.

- Wo unto you if you reject the word of God—2 Nephi 27:14

- You receive line upon line and precept upon precept—2 Nephi
28:30

- The prophets speak in plainness concerning the word of God—
Jacob 2:11

- If you are unbelieving you cannot understand the word of
God—Mosiah 26:3

- Diligently teach and admonish others with the word of God—
Mosiah 26:38–39

- Nurture others with the word of God—Moroni 6:4

SUPPORTED IN YOUR TRIALS

And I have been supported under trials and troubles of every kind, yea, and in all manner of afflictions; yea, God has delivered me from prison, and from bonds, and from death; yea, and I do put my trust in him, and he will still deliver me.

ALMA 36:27

I know, as did Alma of old, that "whosoever shall put their trust in God shall be supported in their trials, and their troubles, and their afflictions, and shall be lifted up at the last day" (Alma 36:3).

Our Heavenly Father is a powerful, moving, directing being. While we may, at times, bear burdens of sorrow, pain, and grief; while we may struggle to understand trials of faith we are called to pass through; while life may seem dark and dreary—through faith, we have absolute confidence that a loving Heavenly Father is at our side.

(Joseph B. Wirthlin, "Shall He Find Faith on the Earth?"
Ensign, November 2002, 85)

Daily Living

TRUST IN THE LORD.

ε᛫ Trust in the Lord and you will be supported in your trials— Alma 36:5

᛫᛫ You will be delivered out of your trials as you trust in the Lord—Alma 38:5

᛫᛫ Trust in the Lord with full purpose of heart and serve Him and you can be delivered out of bondage—Mosiah 7:33

THE BOOK OF MORMON

*Behold, it has been prophesied by our fathers, that they should
be kept and handed down from one generation to another, and
be kept and preserved by the hand of the Lord until they should
go forth unto every nation, kindred, tongue, and people, that
they shall know of the mysteries contained thereon.*
ALMA 37:4

As another important phase of "a marvelous work and a wonder," the
Prophet was commanded that he and the Church members should take
the gospel and the Book of Mormon to every nation, kindred, tongue,
and people, searching out the honest in heart, in order that all of the
covenants that had been made with Abraham, Isaac, and Jacob and
others of the house of Israel might be fulfilled. Thus through this missionary work, Christ would fulfill his covenants which he had made
with the children of men by sending his messengers throughout the
earth.

(Milton R. Hunter, Conference Report, October 1958, 29)

Daily Living

TAKE THIS GLORIOUS BOOK OF MORMON TO EVERY NATION, KINDRED,
TONGUE AND PEOPLE.

- ᐄ Go ye into all the world, and preach my gospel to every creature—
Mormon 9:22

- ᐄ The Book of Mormon will shine forth—Mormon 8:16

- ᐄ The Book of Mormon will stand as a testimony against the world—
Ether 5:4

- ᐄ Teach people to pray to know that the Book of Mormon is true—
Moroni 10:4

- ᐄ Do not treat lightly the Book of Mormon—D&C 84:57

PREACH THE GOSPEL

Preach unto them repentance, and faith on the Lord Jesus
Christ; teach them to humble themselves and to be meek and
lowly in heart; teach them to withstand every temptation of the
devil, with their faith on the Lord Jesus Christ.

ALMA 37:33

As I study the utterances of the prophets through the centuries, their pattern is very clear. We seek, in the words of Alma, to teach people "an everlasting hatred against sin and iniquity." We "preach repentance, and faith on the Lord Jesus Christ" (Alma 37:32, 33). We praise humility. We seek to teach people "to withstand every temptation of the devil, with their faith on the Lord Jesus Christ" (Alma 37:33). We teach our people "to never be weary of good works" (Alma 37:34).

(Spencer W. Kimball, "The Stone Cut without Hands,"
Ensign, May 1976, 6)

Daily Living

PREACH THE GOSPEL; TEACH FAITH AND REPENTANCE TO EVERYONE.

- ଚ Teach that redemption cometh through faith and repentance in Christ—Mosiah 18:7

- ଚ Teach the word of God—Alma 23:4

- ଚ The gospel is preached so all might know Jesus Christ—2 Nephi 30:5; 3 Nephi 28:23

- ଚ Build upon the gospel, repent, and come unto Christ—3 Nephi 27:8–22

- ଚ The gospel shall go forth to the scattered remnant—Mormon 5:15

REST AND PEACE IN OUR SOULS

*Teach them to never be weary of good works, but to be meek
and lowly in heart; for such shall find rest to their souls.*
ALMA 37:34

Christ begins, through his Spirit, to live in them, to prompt and
guide and motivate them to good works, to his works. Those who
live in Christ seldom become weary of good works, at least of those
good works which flow from a regenerate heart. Truly the meek and
lowly of heart, those who have surrendered their will and acknowl-
edged Christ as Lord of their lives—these find peace and rest here
and qualify for that ultimate rest hereafter.

(Joseph Fielding McConkie and Robert L. Millet, *Doctrinal
Commentary on the Book of Mormon* [Salt Lake City:
Bookcraft, 1987–1992], 3:280)

Daily Living

LOOK TO SERVE AND TO BE GUIDED BY THE LORD.

- ❧ Peace comes as you give heed and diligence to the word of God—
  Alma 49:30

- ❧ Peace comes from faith in the Lord Jesus Christ—Helaman 5:47

- ❧ As you possess the love of God you will find joy and happiness—
  4 Nephi 1:15–16

- ❧ Learn from the Lord and His word in meekness and you shall
  have peace in Him—D&C 19:23

JULY

୧୨

And it came to pass that there were many who died, firmly believing that their souls were redeemed by the Lord Jesus Christ; thus they went out of the world rejoicing.

—ALMA 46:39

LEARN WISDOM

*O, remember, my son, and learn wisdom in thy youth; yea,
learn in thy youth to keep the commandments of God.*
ALMA 37:35

There are many things for which I am grateful today, and I acknowledge the love, respect, and devotion that I have for a mother and father who taught me as Alma instructed his son Helaman: "Never be weary of good works, but . . . be meek and lowly in heart, . . . learn wisdom in [my] youth, to keep the commandments of God" (Alma 37:34–35). I will be eternally grateful for their love and its profound influence in my life.

(Jack H. Goaslind Jr., "Never Be Weary of Good Works,"
Ensign, November 1978, 23)

Daily Living

LEARN ALL YOU CAN AND ENCOURAGE YOUR CHILDREN TO DO THE SAME.

- ℰℴ In all your learning always remember to counsel with the Lord—2 Nephi 8:28–29

- ℰℴ As you hearken to the precepts of God you will learn wisdom—2 Nephi 28:30

- ℰℴ As you learn wisdom you realize that as you serve your fellowmen you are serving God—Mosiah 2:17

- ℰℴ Seek wisdom, and the mysteries of God will be revealed to you—D&C 6:7

COUNSEL WITH THE LORD

Counsel with the Lord in all thy doings, and he will direct thee for good; yea, when thou liest down at night lie down unto the Lord, that he may watch over you in your sleep; and when thou risest in the morning let thy heart be full of thanks unto God; and if ye do these things, ye shall be lifted up at the last day.
ALMA 37:37

Let us counsel with the Lord in all our undertakings. Let us be better neighbors. Let us be better employers and employees. Let us be men and women of integrity and honesty in business, in education, in government, in the professions, whatever is our place in life.
(Gordon B. Hinckley, "Latter-day Saints in Very Deed,"
Ensign, November 1997, 85)

Daily Living

COUNSEL WITH THE LORD AND CONTINUALLY EXPRESS GRATITUDE IN ALL THINGS.

- ᚙ Remember the learning of man is foolishness unless we counsel with God—2 Nephi 9:28–19

- ᚙ Give ear to the counsel of the Lord and you shall learn wisdom—2 Nephi 28:30

- ᚙ Seek not to counsel the Lord but to take counsel from Him—Jacob 4:10

- ᚙ Remember the Lord counsels you in wisdom according to what is just and true—Alma 29:8

WHY MIRACLES CEASE

They were slothful, and forgot to exercise their faith and diligence and then those marvelous works ceased, and they did not progress in their journey.
ALMA 37:41

Faith and righteousness are the powers by which miracles are wrought (2 Ne. 26:13; Mosiah 8:18), and miracles are not manifest until after the foundation of faith has been securely built (Ether 12:15–16, 18). Miracles cease when wickedness prevails among a people (Morm. 1:13); their absence is thus conclusive proof of the apostate status of any church or people. "There was not any man who could do a miracle in the name of Jesus," the Nephite record states, "save he were cleansed every whit from his iniquity" (3 Ne. 8:1).
(Bruce R. McConkie, *Mormon Doctrine,* 2nd ed. [Salt Lake City: Bookcraft, 1966], 507)

Daily Living

REMEMBER TO EXERCISE FAITH AND BE DILIGENT IN ALL THINGS.

- ࢷ The Lord can do all things according to His will if you exercise faith—1 Nephi 7:12

- ࢷ If you forget God you will be led away by the devil—Alma 46:8

- ࢷ Beware so that the ease of the way doesn't make you forget the Lord—Helaman 12:2

- ࢷ Do you exercise faith in the redemption of Him who hath created you?—Alma 5:15

- ࢷ Remember to exercise faith unto repentance—Alma 34:15–17

- ࢷ As you exercise your faith you can be sanctified in the Lord—Ether 4:7

DIRECTION IN LIFE

For behold, it is as easy to give heed to the word of Christ,
which will point to you a straight course to eternal bliss, as it
was for our fathers to give heed to this compass, which would
point unto them a straight course to the promised land.
And now I say . . . just as surely as this director did bring our
fathers, by following its course, to the promised land, shall the
words of Christ, if we follow their course, carry us beyond this
vale of sorrow into a far better land of promise.
ALMA 37:44–45

The application of the symbolism of the Liahona to our personal
lives was recorded about five hundred years later. The chapter head-
ing of Alma 37 reads: "As the Liahona guided the Nephites, so the
word of Christ leads men to eternal life."

(Robert E. Wells, "The Liahona Triad," in *Doctrines of the*
Book of Mormon: 1991 Sperry Symposium on the Book of
Mormon, ed. Bruce A. Van Orden and Brent L. Top (Salt
Lake City: Deseret Book, 1992, 2)

Daily Living

AS YOU ARE FAITHFUL AND DILIGENT, GIVING HEED TO THE WORD OF GOD,
YOU SHALL BE DIRECTED IN ALL THINGS.

- The word of God will tell you all things to do—2 Nephi 32:3

- The word of God will keep you in a strait course—1 Nephi
  15:24–25

- The word of God has the power to help you change your life—
  Alma 31:5

- The word of God shall divide asunder all the cunning of the
  devil—Helaman 3:29

OUR DUTY

*And now, my son, see that ye take care of these sacred things,
yea, see that ye look to God and live. Go unto this people and
declare the word, and be sober. My son, farewell.*
ALMA 37:47

The field is white, all ready to harvest, but the time is so short and
the laborers are so few as we seek to share the gospel with our Father's
other children in all parts of the world. We ask our Heavenly Father
to give you power to extend your knowledge to the people in your
neighborhood who need it and to take the gospel to areas in the
world that need those great blessings now more than ever.

(Spencer W. Kimball, "We Are on the Lord's Errand,"
Ensign, May 1981, 79)

Daily Living

REMEMBER TO BE SERIOUS ABOUT THE WORK.

ଛ Stand as a witness for God at all times and in all places—
Mosiah 18:9

ଛ The gospel must be taken to every nation—Alma 29:9; D&C
90:11

ଛ Go ye into all the world and preach the gospel—Mormon 9:22

ଛ The thing that is of most worth is to declare repentance—
D&C 15:6

ଛ Many are kept from the truth for they know not where to find
it—D&C 123:12

ଛ Warn your neighbor—D&C 88:81

JOY OF PARENTS

*I say unto you, my son, that I have had great joy in thee already,
because of thy faithfulness and thy diligence, and thy patience
and thy long-suffering among the people of the Zoramites.*
ALMA 38:3

"Our home joys are the most delightful earth affords, and the joy of parents in their children is the most holy joy of humanity. It makes their hearts pure and good, it lifts them up to their Father in Heaven."

You and I well understand that this great, superior joy lies well within the realm of every set of parents.

(Spencer W. Kimball, "Seeking Eternal Riches,"
Ensign, May 1976, 108)

Daily Living

REMEMBER, THE JOY AND REJOICING OF PARENTS IS IN THE RIGHTEOUSNESS
OF THEIR CHILDREN—JUST AS IT IS WITH HEAVENLY FATHER.

- ❧ Parents seek joy in their posterity—2 Nephi 1:21; Alma 38:2

- ❧ Remember that our Heavenly Father's purpose is our immortality and eternal life so, likewise, this should be the purpose for parents—Moses 1 :39

- ❧ Happy are the parents that know their children walk in truth— 3 John 1:4

- ❧ Remember that your children are literally investigators when they come to you—D&C 18:10–16

ONLY WAY TO BE SAVED

And now, my son, I have told you this that ye may learn wisdom,
that ye may learn of me that there is no other way or means
whereby man can be saved, only in and through Christ. Behold,
he is the life and the light of the world. Behold, he is the word
of truth and righteousness.

ALMA 38:9

I know that "there is no other way nor means whereby man can be saved, only through the atoning blood of Jesus Christ" [Hel. 5:9] . . . I testify that except for the Atonement of the Holy Redeemer, the demands of justice would prevent every soul born on earth from returning to the presence of God, to partake of His glory and exaltation [see John Taylor, *The Mediation and the Atonement* (1882), 179–83; see also Rev. 3:21; 21:7].

(Richard G. Scott, "Jesus Christ, Our Redeemer,"
Ensign, May 1997, 53)

Daily Living

YOU MUST BE WISE AND LOOK TO CHRIST FOR ALL THINGS INCLUDING
EVERLASTING LIFE.

- ᴇ᷄ Without the Atonement you would perish—Mosiah 13:28

- ᴇ᷄ The only way you can be saved is through the atoning blood of the Lord Jesus Christ—Helaman 5:9

- ᴇ᷄ Your strength is in the Lord—2 Nephi 22:2; Alma 20:4; 26:12; Ether 12:27

- ᴇ᷄ The Lord is your light—3 Nephi 18:16, 24

- ᴇ᷄ The Lord is your great example—2 Nephi 31:16; 3 Nephi 12:48; 18:6; 27:27

CAUTION TO THE WISE

See that ye are not lifted up unto pride; yea, see that ye do not boast in your own wisdom, nor of your much strength.
ALMA 38:11

In an early revelation the Lord warned Oliver: "Behold, thou art blessed, and art under no condemnation. But beware of pride, lest thou shouldst enter into temptation" [D&C 23:1]. Oliver had great intellect and enjoyed marvelous spiritual blessings. However, over time he forgot the Lords warning, and pride entered into his heart. Brigham Young later said of this pride: "I have seen men who belonged to this kingdom, and who really thought that if they were not associated with it, it could not progress" [in *Journal of Discourses,* 11:252].

(James E. Faust, "The Prophetic Voice," *Ensign,* May 1996, 5)

Daily Living

REMEMBER, EVERY PROPHET TEACHES YOU TO BEWARE OF PRIDE.

- ଧ The reward for pride is destruction—2 Nephi 26:10

- ଧ Pride can destroy your soul—Jacob 2:16

- ଧ Are you lifted up with pride because of costly apparel?—4 Nephi 1:24

- ଧ Prophets seek to pull down pride by the power of the word of God—Alma 4:19

- ଧ You suffer from pride if you boast of your own wisdom or strength—Alma 38:11

- ଧ Beware of riches, for pride can enter your heart—Helaman 4:12

ADVICE FOR THOSE WHO TEACH

Use boldness, but not overbearance; and also see that ye bridle all your passions, that ye may be filled with love; see that ye refrain from idleness.
ALMA 38:12

First, you can stand up for the truth wherever you are, at all times, and in all places. Sometimes our members are fearful to speak up for the truth in clubs, associations, or even, at times, among members of the Church. As the Lord has said, it should be done with boldness but not overbearance. Speak out for the Lord and for his prophet on the vital issues of the day.

(Gene R. Cook, "Are You a Member Missionary?"
Ensign, May 1976, 103)

Daily Living

STAND UP FOR TRUTH IN MEEKNESS AND IN LOVE.

- ∞ Be temperate in all things—Alma 7:23

- ∞ Be true to whatever you are entrusted—Alma 53:20

- ∞ Pray with all the energy of heart that you might be filled with the love of Christ—Moroni 7:48

- ∞ Remember that perfect love casteth out all fear—Moroni 8:16

PARENTAL RESPONSIBILITY

*And now the Spirit of the Lord doth say unto me: Command
thy children to do good, lest they lead away the hearts of many
people to destruction; therefore I command you, my son, in the
fear of God, that ye refrain from your iniquities;
That ye turn to the Lord with all your mind, might, and
strength; that ye lead away the hearts of no more to do wickedly;
but rather return unto them, and acknowledge your faults and
that wrong which ye have done.*
ALMA 39:12–13

Homes should be an anchor, a safe harbor, a place of refuge, a happy
place where families dwell together, a place where children are loved.
In the home, parents should teach their children the great lessons of
life. Home should be the center of one's earthly experience, where
love and mutual respect are appropriately blended.

(L. Tom Perry, "Called of God," *Ensign,* November 2002, 9)

Daily Living
TEACH YOUR CHILDREN THROUGH YOUR EXAMPLE.

- Teach your children to love one another and serve one another—
  Mosiah 4:15

- You as parent are responsible to teach your children and the
  children's responsibility is to honor and obey—Mosiah 4:15;
  D&C 68:25–28; Mosiah 13:20

- A poor example causes people to lose confidence in you—Jacob
  2:35

- Teachers should walk in the ways of the Lord—Mosiah 23:14

WORLDLY TREASURES

Seek not after riches nor the vain things of this world; for behold, you cannot carry them with you.
ALMA 39:14

Recently, two young people and one older man have come to me and explained that, although they are successful in a material way, they are unhappy and confused. Each asked my advice as to how he could remedy his situation.

I told them that the Lord had already answered that question when he said:

Seek not for riches but for wisdom, and behold, the mysteries of God shall be unfolded unto you. . . . I suggested that they probably needed to change their priorities in life and seek after wisdom rather than after so many material things and pleasures.

(Franklin D. Richards, "Seek Not for Riches But for Wisdom," *Ensign,* May 1976, 35)

Daily Living

GAIN ALL THE INTELLIGENCE YOU CAN, AND FULFILL YOUR COVENANTS.

- ❧ As you gain knowledge and intelligence through your diligence and obedience you will have a greater advantage in the world to come—D&C 130:18–19

- ❧ The sociality that exists on earth exists in the hereafter—D&C 130:2

- ❧ The power of godliness is manifested through the ordinances of the priesthood—D&C 84:20–21

- ❧ The covenants the Eternal Father has made with Israel will be fulfilled—Moroni 10:31

BLESSINGS OF RIGHTEOUSNESS

*And then shall it come to pass, that the spirits of those who are
righteous are received into a state of happiness, which is called
paradise, a state of rest, a state of peace, where they shall rest
from all their troubles and from all care, and sorrow.*
ALMA 40:12

The spirits of all men, as soon as they depart from this mortal body,
whether they are good or evil, we are told in the Book of Mormon, are
taken home to that God who gave them life, where there is a separa-
tion, a partial judgment, and the spirits of those who are righteous are
received into a state of happiness which is called paradise, a state of rest,
a state of peace, where they expand in wisdom, where they have respite
from all their troubles, and where care and sorrow do not annoy.

(Joseph F. Smith, *Gospel Doctrine: Selections from the Sermons
and Writings of Joseph F. Smith,* comp. John A. Widtsoe
[Salt Lake City: Deseret Book, 1939], 448)

Daily Living

THINK OF THE JOY IN THE SPIRIT WORLD FOR CHOOSING RIGHTEOUSNESS.

- Ω You shall have a perfect knowledge of your righteousness—2 Nephi 9:14

- Ω The righteous shall inherit the kingdom of God—2 Nephi 9:18

- Ω The righteous shall be righteous still; the happy shall be happy still—Mormon 9:14

- Ω You shall rest in the paradise of God—Moroni 10:34

FATE OF THE WICKED

*The spirits of the wicked, yea, who are evil—for behold, they
have no part nor portion of the Spirit of the Lord; for behold,
they chose evil works rather than good; . . . shall be cast out into
outer darkness; there shall be weeping, and wailing, and gnashing
of teeth, and this because of their own iniquity, being led captive
by the will of the devil.
Now this is the state of the souls of the wicked . . . until the
time of their resurrection.*
Alma 40:13–14

If we have not kept the commandments of the Lord, if we have been
unjust, and lovers of sin and our hearts have been set upon evil, then
we shall die and shall not live again until the thousand years [of the
millennium] are ended. It is decreed that the unrighteous shall have
to spend their time during this thousand years in the prison house
prepared for them where they can repent and cleanse themselves.

(Joseph Fielding Smith, *Doctrines of Salvation,* comp. Bruce
R. McConkie [Salt Lake City: Bookcraft, 1956], 3:59–60)

Daily Living

THOSE WHO CHOOSE EVIL ARE IN SPIRIT PRISON UNTIL THE
RESURRECTION.

- ཝ At the time of the Resurrection, those who are dead as to the things
  of the spirit shall be delivered from death and hell—2 Nephi 9:12

- ཝ The gospel preached in spirit prison—D&C 76:73; 1 Peter
  3:19; 4:6

- ཝ The Lord sends messengers to spirit prison—D&C 138:29–30

JUDGMENT

And it is requisite with the justice of God that men should be judged according to their works; and if their works were good in this life, and the desires of their hearts were good, that they should also, at the last day, be restored unto that which is good.
ALMA 41:3

Another unchanging principle, brothers and sisters, is that of your eventual judgment. Each of you will be judged according to your individual works and the desires of your hearts [see D&C 137:9]. You will not be required to pay the debt of any other. Your eventual placement in the celestial, terrestrial, or telestial kingdom will not be determined by chance. The Lord has prescribed unchanging requirements for each. You can know what the scriptures teach, and pattern your lives accordingly [see John 14:2; 1 Cor. 15:40–41; D&C 76:50–119; 98:18].

(Russell M. Nelson, "Constancy Amid Change,"
Ensign, November 1993, 35)

Daily Living

WE MUST CONSTANTLY WATCH OUR THOUGHTS, OUR WORDS, AND OUR
DEEDS.

- ဢ Judged according to your works—1 Nephi 15:32–33; Alma 12:12; 3 Nephi 26:4

- ဢ Judged according to the word of God—2 Nephi 33:14

- ဢ Judged out of the books which are written and shall be written—3 Nephi 27:26

- ဢ Judged according to your works and desires of your hearts—D&C 137:9

HAPPINESS

Do not suppose, because it has been spoken concerning restoration, that ye shall be restored from sin to happiness. Behold, I say unto you, wickedness never was happiness.

ALMA 41:10

It is not God who has given us the spirit of fear; this comes from the adversary. So many of us are fearful of what our peers will say, that we will be looked upon with disdain and criticized if we stand for what is right. But I remind you that "wickedness never was happiness" (Alma 41:10). Evil never was happiness. Sin never was happiness. Happiness lies in the power and the love and the sweet simplicity of the gospel of Jesus Christ.

(Gordon B. Hinckley, "Converts and Young Men," *Ensign*, May 1997, 49)

Daily Living

KEEP THE COMMANDMENTS AND LOOK FORWARD TO ETERNAL JOY.

- ༂ There is opposition in all things but remember that there can be no happiness without righteousness—2 Nephi 2:13; Alma 40:11,15,17

- ༂ If you keep the commandments you can dwell with God in a state of never ending happiness—Mosiah 2:41

- ༂ Good works will help you be resurrected to endless life and happiness—Mosiah 16:11

- ༂ You receive happiness or misery according to the spirit you listed to obey—Alma 3:26

- ༂ Remember that through the love of God you can be happy— 4 Nephi 1:15–16

MERCY AND JUSTICE

*See that you are merciful unto your brethren; . . . yea, [and] ye
shall have mercy restored unto you again; ye shall have justice
restored unto you again; ye shall have a righteous judgment
restored unto you again; and ye shall have good rewarded
unto you again.*
*For that which ye do send out shall return unto you again, and
be restored; therefore, the word restoration more fully condemneth
the sinner, and justifieth him not at all.*

ALMA 41:14–15

The gospel, in fact, gives us glimpses of the far horizon, revealing a
glow from the lights of the City of God. It is a place of happy countenances, where justice and mercy as well as righteousness and truth are
constant companions. Herein gentleness and generosity prevail, "without compulsory means" (D&C 121:46). Coarseness and selfishness are
unknown, belonging to a previous and primitive place. Here envy
would be a sure embarrassment. Neighbors are esteemed as self.

(Neal A. Maxwell, "Called and Prepared from the
Foundation of the World," *Ensign,* May 1986, 35–36)

Daily Living

REMEMBER, JUSTICE REQUIRES RIGHTEOUSNESS.

- ∞ Repent and claim mercy through the Lord Jesus Christ—Alma
  12:33; Ether 11:8

- ∞ Pray for mercy and apply the atoning blood of the Lord Jesus
  Christ—Mosiah 4:2

- ∞ If you are merciful you can obtain mercy—3 Nephi 12:7

PLAN OF MERCY

And thus we see that all mankind were fallen, and they were in the grasp of justice . . . forever to be cut off from his presence. And now, the plan of mercy could not be brought about except an atonement should be made; therefore God himself atoneth for the sins of the world, to bring about the plan of mercy.

ALMA 42:14–15

But through the gracious act of Jehovah, the most beloved son of God, all our promised progress became possible. He expressed his own complete willingness to become a vicarious offering for us, first to break the grip of sin, and then to overcome death and bring about a glorious resurrection of our bodies. So it is that through his grace we can rise above our fallen state, receive redemption from the grave, and move into eternity, there to continue to work toward becoming like our Heavenly Father.

(Mark E. Petersen, "Sacred, Set Prayers," in *Prayer* [Salt Lake City: Deseret Book, 1977], 58)

Daily Living

NEVER FORGET YOU ARE IN A FALLEN STATE AND NEED THE GRACE OF GOD.

- ✤ It is by the grace of God that you are saved after all you can do—2 Nephi 25:23

- ✤ Remember that in the fallen state you are cut off from the presence of God thus there must needs be an infinite atonement else you could not return—2 Nephi 9:6–7

- ✤ You can be brought from a fallen state to a state of righteousness—Mosiah 27:25

- ✤ You merit nothing of yourself but through the Atonement of the Lord—Alma 22:14; 34:9

LAW AND JUSTICE

*But God ceaseth not to be God, and mercy claimeth the penitent,
and mercy cometh because of the atonement; and the atonement
bringeth to pass the resurrection of the dead; and the resurrection
of the dead bringeth back men into the presence of God; and
thus they are restored into his presence, to be judged according to
their works, according to the law and justice.*

ALMA 42:23

Gratitude is also the foundation upon which repentance is built.
The Atonement brought mercy through repentance to balance justice.
How thankful I am for the doctrine of repentance. Repentance is
essential to salvation. We are mortal—we are not perfect—we will
make mistakes. When we make mistakes and do not repent, we suffer.

(Robert D. Hales, "Gratitude for the Goodness of God,"
Ensign, May 1992, 63–64)

Daily Living

COME UNTO CHRIST IN ALL YOU DO AND CLAIM THE BLESSINGS OF MERCY.

- ༀ Mercy is granted as you repent and come unto Christ—2 Nephi 28:32

- ༀ Repent and be received of the Lord through His mercy—Alma 5:32–33

- ༀ Repent and claim mercy through the Lord Jesus Christ—Alma 12:33; Ether 11:8

- ༀ Mercy satisfies justice if you have faith unto repentance—Alma 34:16

- ༀ Mercy is obtained through repentance and the plan of redemption—Alma 42:13–22

LIVE FOR ETERNITY

And now, my son, I desire that ye should let these things trouble you no more, and only let your sins trouble you, with that trouble which shall bring you down unto repentance.

<small>ALMA 42:29</small>

My son, let these things trouble you no more, and only let your sins trouble you . . . Alma ended his instructions and his explanations of God's justice and mercy to Corianton with an exhortation that his son would no more harrow up his soul with thoughts of divine injustice. But instead, live so that past sins shall be forgiven. Worry only about the sins you have committed, not about the administration of justice in return for good or evil.

(George Reynolds and Janne M. Sjodahl, Commentary on the Book of Mormon, comp. Philip C. Reynolds [Salt Lake City: Deseret Book, 1955–1961], 4:228)

Daily Living

YOU MUST NEVER JUSTIFY YOUR BEHAVIOR FOR SOME OBSCURE QUESTION OR SITUATION; YOU ARE ACCOUNTABLE FOR YOUR SINS.

- ☞ Remember your words, works and thoughts will condemn you—Alma 12:14

- ☞ You are accountable for your sins—D&C 101:78; Article of Faith 2

- ☞ You are responsible to magnify your own calling—Jacob 2:2

- ☞ You must labor and do your best whilst in the tabernacle of clay—Moroni 9:6

BEWARE OF RICHES LEST YE FORGET GOD

*But they grew proud, being lifted up in their hearts, because of
their exceedingly great riches . . . and would not give heed to
their words, to walk uprightly before God.*
ALMA 45:24

The acquisition of wealth often demands complete devotion. Such
devotion creates the danger of shifting what we "seek first." Priorities
can become centered on those things that can be seen and owned in
this world rather than on kingdoms and riches visible only to the eye
of faith. People can forget God or perhaps even unconsciously place
his work further down on their list of priorities as they race to acquire
more and more possessions. Samuel the Lamanite reprimanded
Nephites who were similarly off course: "Ye do not remember the
Lord your God in the things with which he hath blessed you, but ye
do always remember your riches" (Hel. 13:22).

(Dennis L. Largey, *Doctrines of the Book of Mormon: The 1991
Sperry Symposium* [Salt Lake City: Deseret Book, 1992], 64)

Daily Living

REMEMBER HIM ALWAYS AS THE GIVER OF ALL THINGS LEST WE SUFFER
FROM PRIDE.

- ❧ If you forget the Lord you will be led away by the devil—Alma
  46:8

- ❧ If you seek the things of the world you will forget God—
  Helaman 7:20–21

- ❧ As you forget the Lord you will wax strong in iniquity—
  Helaman 11:36–37

- ❧ You may forget the Lord due to the ease of the way and your
  prosperity—Helaman 12:2

TITLE OF LIBERTY

*And it came to pass that he rent his coat; and he took a piece
thereof, and wrote upon it—In memory of our God, our religion,
and freedom, and our peace, our wives, and our children—and
he fastened it upon the end of a pole.*
ALMA 46:12

The ability to stand by one's principles, to live with integrity and faith
according to one's belief—that is what matters. That devotion to true
principle—in our individual lives, in our homes and families, and in
all places that we meet and influence other people—that devotion is
what God is ultimately requesting of us. It requires commitment—
whole-souled, deeply held, eternally cherished commitment to the
principles we know to be true in the commandments God has given.
(Howard W. Hunter, "The Great Symbol of Our
Membership," *Ensign,* October 1994, 5)

Daily Living
STAND FOR WHAT YOU BELIEVE IN.

80 Live by the word of God—D&C 84:43–46

80 Follow Christ and do the things that He has done—2 Nephi
31:12

80 Act with no hypocrisy but with real intent—2 Nephi 31:13

80 Be true to whatever you have been entrusted—Alma 53:20

80 If you have faith you will have power to do all things—Moroni
7:33

MORONI, A MAN OF GOD

*Yea, verily, verily I say unto you, if all men had been, and were,
and ever would be, like unto Moroni, behold, the very powers of
hell would have been shaken forever; yea, the devil would never
have power over the hearts of the children of men.*
ALMA 48:17

To make this desire meaningful and practical, we must first relate it
to the principles of the gospel. To incorporate gospel principles into
our daily lives, we must follow the lives of great men and women in
the Church. Their examples are specific and concrete, reducing
abstractions to believable, practical principles we can follow.

(Joseph B. Wirthlin, *Finding Peace in Our Lives* [Salt Lake
City: Deseret Book, 1995], 139)

Daily Living

PATTERN YOUR LIFE AFTER GREAT EXAMPLES.

- Become a person of understanding by knowing the prophecies of the Lord—Mosiah 1:2

- Be full of gratitude and thanksgiving—Alma 7:23; 26:9; 34:38; 37:37

- Serve others—Mosiah 2:17; 4:15–16; 18:8

- Be firm in your faith—Helaman 3:35

- In righteousness Satan has no power—1 Nephi 22:26

HUMBLED BY THE PREACHING OF THE WORD

*And thus they went forth, and the people did humble themselves
because of their words, insomuch that they were highly favored
of the Lord, and thus they were free from wars and contentions
among themselves, yea, even for the space of four years.*
ALMA 48:20

To pray sincerely in public and in private is often a great test. You
will often feel tempted not to do so, and you will often feel no great
need to do so. Your circumstances may be such that, if you are really
honest with yourself, you don't feel a need for God. You aren't forced
to be humble—you will have to be humbled because of the word—
the word of God. (See Alma 32:13–15.) This is why you must stay
very close to the scriptures and let the words of the Lord flow continuously over your mind.

(Stephen R. Covey, *Spiritual Roots of Human Relations,*
2nd ed. [Salt Lake City: Deseret Book, 1993], 291)

Daily Living

STRIVE TO STAY CLOSE TO THE LORD THROUGH THE SCRIPTURES.

- Be humble and put your trust in God as you receive the word
  of God—Alma 5:13

- Remember that the word has the greatest power to cause
  change—Alma 31:5

- When you are humble you are in preparation to hear the word
  of God—Alma 32:6

- You are more blessed when you are humbled by the word—
  Alma 32:14–16

OBTAINING PEACE AND PROSPERITY

*Yea, and there was continual peace among them, and exceedingly
great prosperity in the church because of their heed and diligence
which they gave unto the word of God, which was declared unto
them . . . by all those who had been ordained by the holy order
of God, being baptized unto repentance, and sent forth to preach
among the people.*

ALMA 49:30

As people heed the words of the prophets, the Lord blesses them. When
they disregard His word, however, distress and suffering often follow.
Over and over, the Book of Mormon teaches this great lesson. In its
pages we read of the ancient inhabitants of the American continent
who, because of their righteousness, were blessed of the Lord and
became prosperous. Yet often this prosperity turned into a curse in that
it caused them to "harden their hearts, and . . . forget the Lord their
God" [Hel. 12:2].

(Joseph B. Wirthlin, "Journey to Higher Ground," *Ensign,*
November 2005, 76)

Daily Living

GIVE HEED TO AND LIVE THE WORD OF GOD AND YE SHALL HAVE PEACE IN
YOUR SOUL.

- ଇଠ As you give heed to the word of God you will have the peace of
  God—Alma 7:26–27

- ଇଠ You will be zealous in keeping the commandments—Alma 21:23

- ଇଠ As you give heed to the word you will be pointed in a straight
  course—Alma 37:44

- ଇଠ Listen to the Lord's words, and walk in meekness—D&C 19:23

SONS OF HELAMAN

And they were all young men, and they were exceedingly valiant for courage, and also for strength and activity; but behold, this was not all—they were men who were true at all times in whatsoever thing they were entrusted.

ALMA 53:20

Run from the tide of sleaze that would overcome you. Flee the evils of the world. Be loyal to your better self. Be loyal to the best that is in you. Be faithful and true to the covenants that are associated with the priesthood of God. You cannot wallow about in lasciviousness, you cannot lie, you cannot cheat, you cannot take advantage of others in unrighteousness without denying that touch of divinity with which each of us came into this life. I would pray with all of my strength, brethren, that we would rise above it and be loyal to our best selves.

(Gordon B. Hinckley, "Loyalty," *Ensign,* May 2003, 59)

Daily Living

BE COURAGEOUS IN DEFENDING TRUTH AND RIGHTEOUSNESS.

- ∞ Remember you have entered into a covenant to serve the Lord through out your life—Mosiah 18:13

- ∞ Repent and you become the covenant people of the Lord—2 Nephi 30:2; 1 Nephi 22:9

- ∞ Be faithful in keeping the commandments—1 Nephi 4:1

- ∞ Defend your values in all things—Alma 48:13

THE POWER OF WONDERFUL TEACHERS

_Yea, they were men of truth and soberness, for they had been
taught to keep the commandments of God and to walk
uprightly before him._
ALMA 53:21

"The first and foremost opportunity for teaching in the Church lies
in the home," observed President David O. McKay. "A true Mormon
home is one in which if Christ should chance to enter, he would be
pleased to linger and to rest."
What are we doing to ensure that our homes meet this description?
It isn't enough for parents alone to have strong testimonies. Children
can ride only so long on the coattails of a parents conviction.
(Thomas S. Monson, "If Ye Are Prepared Ye Shall Not Fear,"
Ensign, November 2004, 115)

Daily Living
STRIVE TO TEACH YOUR CHILDREN CORRECT PRINCIPLES BY YOUR EXAMPLE.

- Set a good example so your children will not lose confidence in you—Jacob 2:35; 3:10

- Good fathers teach their children—1 Nephi 1:1; Enos 1:1

- Teach them to walk uprightly before the Lord—Mosiah 4:15–16

- Pray in your families—3 Nephi 18:21

- Parents are responsible to teach their children—D&C 68:25–28

THE DIFFERENCE

Now they never had fought, yet they did not fear death; and they did think more upon the liberty of their fathers than they did upon their lives; yea, they had been taught by their mothers, that if they did not doubt, God would deliver them.

ALMA 56:47

Thanks be to God that He gauges the offerings and sacrifices of His children by the standard of their physical ability and honest intent rather than by the gradation of His exalted station. Verily He is God with us; and He both understands and accepts our motives and righteous desires. Our need to serve God is incalculably greater than His need for our service.

(James E. Talmage, *The Parables of James E. Talmage* [Salt Lake City: Deseret Book, 1973], 39)

Daily Living

WHEN RIGHTEOUS MOTIVES ARE COUPLED WITH FAITH, THERE IS POWER IN YOUR ACTIONS.

- True love will motivate you to righteousness—Mosiah 28:3

- When you desire joy for others you will seek to bring them joy—Alma 36:24

- When caring for others you will pray with faith—Mosiah 27:14

- You will always pray to help others come to Christ—Alma 6:6; 31:34–35

- Love your enemies and those who persecute you—3 Nephi 12:44

MOTHERS ARE MAGNIFICENT TEACHERS

Yea, and they did obey and observe to perform every word of command with exactness; yea, and even according to their faith it was done unto them; and I did remember the words which they said unto me that their mothers had taught them.

ALMA 57:21

Mothers, take time to teach your children. Catch the teaching moments. This can be done anytime during the day—at mealtimes, in casual settings, or at special sit-down times together, at the foot of the bed at the end of the day, or during an early morning walk together. Mothers, you are your children's best teacher. Don't shift this precious responsibility to day-care centers or baby-sitters. A mother's love and prayerful concern for her children are her most important ingredients in teaching her own.

(Ezra Taft Benson, *Come, Listen to a Prophet's Voice* [Salt Lake City: Deseret Book, 1990], 34)

Daily Living

APPLY THE TEACHINGS TO YOUR LIFE. FAITH PROVIDES THE POWER, AND COUPLED WITH EXACT OBEDIENCE, IT RESULTS IN SUCCESS.

∞ Mothers are wonderful teachers. Never doubt your power to bless—Alma 56:47–48

∞ When your faith is unshaken you are endowed with power—Jacob 4:6

∞ If you have faith in the Lord you have power to do all things—Moroni 7:33

PRAY FOR STRENGTH AND DELIVERANCE

Therefore we did pour out our souls in prayer to God, that he would strengthen us and deliver us out of the hands of our enemies, yea, and also give us strength. . . .
Yea, and it came to pass that the Lord our God did visit us with assurances that he would deliver us; yea, insomuch that he did speak peace to our souls.
ALMA 58:10–11

Why do some of these thoughts attack our minds like a relentless enemy? How do we fight against them? The mind is always working; it never stops. Let us guard against the subtle inroads today that can become embedded habits of negativism tomorrow. We will find our strength and our peace when we study and pray and ponder and meditate, and when we strive to listen to the whisperings of the Spirit.

(Ardeth Greene Kapp, *My Neighbor, My Sister, My Friend*
[Salt Lake City: Deseret Book, 1990], 17–18)

Daily Living

PRAY FOR STRENGTH AND DELIVERANCE. THE LORD IS MIGHTY TO SAVE.

- ✂ Pray for strength in all things—1 Nephi 7:17

- ✂ Pray for strength according to your faith in the Lord to be delivered—Alma 14:26

- ✂ Pray for strength to bear your afflictions and infirmities—Alma 31:30–33

- ✂ You can receive comfort to your souls—Alma 31:32

ALWAYS CHARITABLE

And now, in your epistle you have censured me, but it mattereth
not; I am not angry, but do rejoice in the greatness of your
heart. . . . My soul standeth fast in that liberty in the which
God hath made us free.
ALMA 61:9

We have not the right to hate any of the creatures of God, but we have been commanded to love them, and also to forgive them if they have offended us. I believe that you can put this down as a principle, that to start with there are very few offenders who willfully intend to offend, not having given full thought to their acts. They do something that offends us, and we at once feel offended and angry and, perhaps, we let it grow to that greater amount of anger that we call hatred. This should not be. Perhaps if we had spoken to our brother at once we would have learned that he did not really mean what we thought he did, and that we have become offended too hastily. Let us have enough charity for one another that we will not allow anything to be an offense to cause us hardness of heart.

(Anthon H. Lund, Conference Report, October 1920, 13)

Daily Living

SHOW FORTH CHARITY AND THE BLESSINGS OF THE LORD ARE YOURS.

- ঞ Charity suffereth long and is patient—Moroni 7:45

- ঞ Charity is not easily provoked and thinketh no evil—Moroni 7:45

- ঞ Judge not that ye be not judged—3 Nephi 14:1–2

ATTITUDE MAKES THE DIFFERENCE

But behold, because of the exceedingly great length of the war
between the Nephites and the Lamanites many had become
hardened, because of the exceedingly great length of the war;
and many were softened because of their afflictions, insomuch
that they did humble themselves before God, even in the depth
of humility.

ALMA 62:41

Attitude can make a greater difference than all else. . . . It troubles
me to see the uncalled-for divisiveness between people of this state.
There is no need for it. There is no factual basis for it. It comes of
prejudice and negativism.

(Gordon B. Hinckley, quoted in "Attitude Can Make 'Great
Difference,'" *Church News,* Sept. 17, 1988)

Daily Living

YOUR ATTITUDE AND DESIRE WILL MAKE A DIFFERENCE IN YOUR ACTIONS.

⟋ Do you have a desire for the welfare of your own soul and the
souls of others?—Enos 1:4, 9, 11

⟋ What is your disposition towards good and evil?—Mosiah 5:2

⟋ Are your thoughts directed to the Lord?—Alma 37:36

⟋ What are your desires towards true happiness?—Alma 41:5;
27:18

⟋ What are your motives in regard to giving?—Moroni 7:6

AUGUST

෨

And behold, the people did rejoice and glorify God, and the whole face of the land was filled with rejoicing; and they did no more seek to destroy Nephi, but they did esteem him as a great prophet, and a man of God, having great power and authority given unto him from God.

—HELAMAN 11:18

TEACH THE WORD WITH POWER

Therefore, Helaman and his brethren went forth, and did declare the word of God with much power unto the convincing of many people of their wickedness, which did cause them to repent of their sins and to be baptized unto the Lord their God.
ALMA 62:45

There is an interesting conceptual chain related to the "power of the word" that flows through this section of the Book of Mormon. As the account of the mission of the sons of Mosiah begins, Alma testifies that through personal preparation, including scripture study, fasting, and prayer, these brethren were able to teach the word "with power and authority of God" (Alma 17:3).

(Gerald N. Lund, *Selected Writings of Gerald N. Lund: Gospel Scholars Series* [Salt Lake City: Deseret Book, 1999], 118)

Daily Living

TEACH BY THE SPIRIT; THE POWER OF THE WORD CAN CONVINCE PEOPLE TO CHANGE.

- ဆ Remember the power of the word has the greatest power to change lives—Alma 31:5

- ဆ The Spirit can carry the words unto their hearts—2 Nephi 33:1

- ဆ Always teach in the nurture and admonition of the Lord—Enos 1:1

- ဆ Teach in the ways of the Lord—Jarom 1:7

- ဆ Live righteously and teach others to keep the commandments—Mosiah 2:4

- ဆ Prepare well so you can teach with the power and authority of God—Alma 17:2–3

PRIDE IS A CHOICE

But notwithstanding their riches, or their strength, or their
prosperity, they were not lifted up in the pride of their eyes; neither
were they slow to remember the Lord their God; but they did
humble themselves exceedingly before him.
ALMA 62:49

The scriptures abound with condemnations and cautions about pride. . . .

It is significant that this important prophecy includes both those who do wickedly and those who think wickedly (pride). . . . The Savior taught that pride was one of the things that comes from "within" that "defile the man" (Mark 7:22–23).

(Dallin H. Oaks, *Pure in Heart* [Salt Lake City: Bookcraft, 1988], 90)

Daily Living

REMEMBER THAT PRIDE IS A CONDITION OF THE HEART, AS IS HUMILITY.

৪০ Don't become puffed up with pride when you become wise, learned, or rich as to the things of the world—2 Nephi 28:15

৪০ Remember that pride is a condition of your heart—Jacob 2:16

৪০ Let the word of God keep you humble—Alma 48:20

৪০ Fast and pray to be strong in your humility—Helaman 3:35

LAY HOLD UPON THE WORD

Yea, we see that whosoever will may lay hold upon the word of God, which is quick and powerful, which shall divide asunder all the cunning and the snares and the wiles of the devil, and lead the man of Christ in a strait and narrow course across that everlasting gulf of misery which is prepared to engulf the wicked.
HELAMAN 3:29

The spiritually submissive will make it through. The word of God will lead the man and the woman of Christ "in a strait and narrow course across that everlasting gulf of misery" (Helaman 3:29) and land their souls at the right hand of God in the kingdom of heaven, "to sit down with Abraham, Isaac, and Jacob, and the holy prophets who have been ever since the world began" (Alma 7:25; see also Ether 12:4).

(Neal A. Maxwell, "For I Will Lead You Along,"
Ensign, May 1988, 9)

Daily Living
YOU MUST CLEAVE TO THE WORD OF GOD.

- ∞ Remember the word of God will show you all things to do—2 Nephi 32:3

- ∞ Hold to the word of God for it will protect you—1 Nephi 15:24–25

- ∞ Remember the word of God has great power to change your soul—Alma 31:5

- ∞ Live by every word that proceedeth forth from the mouth of God—D&C 84:43–46

- ∞ Remember to liken the word of God to your life—1 Nephi 19:23

BEING STRONG IN HUMILITY AND FIRM IN FAITH

*Nevertheless they did fast and pray oft, and did wax stronger
and stronger in their humility, and firmer and firmer in the
faith of Christ, unto the filling their souls with joy and consolation,
yea, even to the purifying and the sanctification of their hearts,
which sanctification cometh because of their yielding their
hearts unto God.*

HELAMAN 3:35

Mormon's account in Helaman chapter 3 clarifies that sanctification is a distinct process and that through prayer and fasting we wax strong in humility and firm in our faith in Christ. Sanctification occurs in our lives as we purge from the natural man carnal tendencies and proclivities by yielding our heart unto God. Developing the ability to allow our personal desires to be subordinated to the will of the Father creates a transformation and softening of our hearts.

(Ralph W. Pew, in *Helaman through 3 Nephi 8: According to
Thy Word,* ed. Monte S. Nyman and Charles D. Tate Jr.
[Provo, UT: Religious Studies Center, 1992], 222)

Daily Living

THROUGH FASTING AND PRAYER YOU CAN ACQUIRE CHRIST-LIKE QUALITIES
THAT WILL PURIFY AND SANCTIFY YOUR HEART BECAUSE YOU YIELD YOUR
HEART TO GOD.

- ঙ Fast and pray and offer your whole soul to the Lord—Omni 1:26

- ঙ Pray with all the energy of your heart that you might be filled with charity—Moroni 7:48

- ঙ Fast and pray that you might teach with the power and authority of God—Alma 17:3

- ঙ You become sanctified through the Savior by the Holy Ghost—Alma 13:11–12

BEWARE LEST YOU SUCCUMB TO INIQUITY

And it was because of the pride of their hearts, because of their exceeding riches, yea, it was because of their oppression to the poor, withholding their food from the hungry . . . smiting their humble brethren upon the cheek, making a mock of that which was sacred, denying the spirit of prophecy . . . rising up in great contentions.
HELAMAN 4:12

Contentions result from the prideful power struggle that comes from pitting ourselves—our possessions or our intellect against others. The proud are easily offended, hold grudges, withhold forgiveness, and will not receive counsel or correction. All of these internal traits become a fertile seedbed for the external manifestation of contention. The Savior warned of the evil of contention (see 3 Nephi 11:28–29), because it repels the Spirit of the Lord and opens the door to other "fiery darts" of the adversary.

(Joseph Fielding McConkie and Robert L. Millet, *Doctrinal Commentary on the Book of Mormon* [Salt Lake City: Bookcraft, 1987–1992], 3:347–348)

Daily Living

PRIDE FOSTERS AN UNRIGHTEOUS ATTITUDE, AND UNRIGHTEOUS BEHAVIOR FOLLOWS IT.

- ∞ When one boasts of his own strength, he's left to himself—Helaman 4:13

- ∞ Don't forget God and harden your heart—Helaman 12:1–7

- ∞ Reject the word of God and you stand before the bar of God in shame—Jacob 6:8–9

- ∞ Study the scriptures that you might be wise—1 Nephi 19:23; Jacob 6:12; Alma 37:35

AN AWAKENING

*Yea, they began to remember the prophecies of Alma, and
also the words of Mosiah; and they saw that they had been a
stiffnecked people, and that they had set at naught the
commandments of God.*

HELAMAN 4:21

Our trust is increased through our studying the scriptures and remembering the instruction from our Savior, he who marked the path and led the way. We remember him when we feast, study, and ponder upon his words daily. . . . We remember him when we partake . . . sacred emblems that remind us of our covenants. We remember him in the springtime, in the miracles of rebirth, new life, new promise of the resurrection. We remember him in the summer, for he is the light and the life. We remember him in the fall, when the blossoms are gone and the roots of the trees reach deep into the soil in preparation for another season. We remember him in the winter, when we walk by faith, knowing that there will be yet another spring.

(Ardeth Greene Kapp, *Rejoice! His Promises Are Sure* [Salt
Lake City: Deseret Book, 1997], 8)

Daily Living

REALIZE THAT GOD IS OVER ALL AND REMEMBER ALL HE HAS DONE FOR YOU.

- ✪ Ponder on the goodness and mercy of God—Moroni 10:4

- ✪ As you partake of the sacrament remember your covenants—Moroni 4:3; 5:2

- ✪ In forgetting the Lord you can be quick to do iniquity—Alma 46:8

- ✪ Keep in remembrance the words of the prophets—2 Nephi 1:12,16

WHEN THE WICKED OUTNUMBER
THE RIGHTEOUS

For as their laws and their governments were established by the
voice of the people, and they who chose evil were more numerous
than they who chose good, therefore they were ripening for
destruction, for the laws had become corrupted.
HELAMAN 5:2

Lacking the Spirit in their lives and rejecting the teachings and mores of their parents, they were in a "carnal and sinful state" (v 4). Early in Mosiah's reign, these wicked people, who had not been "half so numerous" as the faithful, became more numerous "because of the dissensions among the brethren" (v 5). With flattering words the wicked enticed many Church members to abandon their standards and join with them in their sins.

(Monte S. Nyman and Charles D. Tate Jr., eds., *Mosiah:*
Salvation Only through Christ [Provo, UT: Religious
Studies Center, 1991], 212)

Daily Living

YOU MUST ALWAYS BE INVOLVED IN CIVIC AFFAIRS LEST THE IMMORAL
MINORITY OR SEEMING MAJORITY CAUSE THE BREAKDOWN OF A MORAL AND
CIVIL SOCIETY.

- Regardless of the situation, do your very best lest you be condemned—Moroni 9:6

- The prayers of the righteous can preserve a people—Alma 10:22–23

- When laws and standards of a nation are upheld there can be peace—Alma 1:33

- It doesn't take long for a people to be without civilization—Moroni 9:7–11

ONLY THE "WORD" CAN SAVE MANKIND

And it came to pass that Nephi had become weary because of
their iniquity; and he yielded up the judgment-seat, and took it
upon him to preach the word of God all the remainder of his
days, and his brother Lehi also, all the remainder of his days.
HELAMAN 5:4

Several years before Christ came to the American continent, the Lamanites exercised such great faith and courage that they completely destroyed the influence of the Gadianton robbers in their society by "preach[ing] the word of God among . . . them" [Hel. 6:37]. Brethren, we are now in a similar position to "stand as witnesses of God" by setting an example, keeping Church standards, and sharing our testimony with those around us.

(M. Russell Ballard, "Standing for Truth and Right,"
Ensign, November 1997, 38)

Daily Living
LIVE AND TEACH THE WORD BY PRECEPT AND EXAMPLE.

- ෨ The word is Jesus Christ—John 1:1,14; Revelations 19:13

- ෨ You must live by His word—D&C 84:43–46

- ෨ By holding to the iron rod, the word of God, you can partake of the tree of life and enjoy happiness—1 Nephi 1:19; 1 Nephi 8:10

- ෨ Remember that the word will tell you all things to do—2 Nephi 32:3

- ෨ You must teach those within your stewardship the word of God else you become responsible for their sins—Jacob 1:19

REMEMBER

Behold, my sons, I desire that ye should remember to keep the commandments of God; and I would that ye should declare unto the people these words. Behold, I have given unto you the names of our first parents who came out of the land of Jerusalem; and this I have done that when you remember your names ye may remember them; and when ye remember them ye may remember their works; and when ye remember their works ye may know how that it is said, and also written, that they were good.

HELAMAN 5:6

When you look in the dictionary for the most important word, do you know what it is? . . . "Remember" is the word.

(Spencer W. Kimball, quoted in *Studies in Scripture Vol. 8: Alma 30 to Moroni,* ed. Kent P. Jackson [Salt Lake City: Deseret Book, 1988], 286)

Daily Living

MAKE A LIST OF THE THINGS THAT WILL HELP YOU TO KEEP THE COMMANDMENTS.

- ৪০ Remember to pray—Alma 13:28
- ৪০ Remember to search the scriptures diligently—Mosiah 1:7; Alma 17:2
- ৪০ Remember the Savior and to keep His commandments—Moroni 4:3; 5:2
- ৪০ Remember the poor and the needy—Alma 34:28
- ৪০ Remember, without charity you are nothing—Moroni 7:44

SEEK ETERNAL THINGS

And now my sons, behold I have somewhat more to desire of you, which desire is, that ye may not do these things that ye may boast, but that ye may do these things to lay up for yourselves a treasure in heaven, yea, which is eternal, and which fadeth not away; yea, that ye may have that precious gift of eternal life, which we have reason to suppose hath been given to our fathers.
HELAMAN 5:8

Nephi's example teaches us that the blessings of the scriptures are far more valuable than property and other worldly things. Pursuing the things of the world can sometimes give us momentary pleasures but not lasting joy and happiness. When we seek after the things of the Spirit, the rewards are eternal and will bring us the satisfaction we seek through this mortal experience.

(L. Tom Perry, "Blessings Resulting from Reading the Book of Mormon," *Ensign,* October 2005, 83)

Daily Living

LAY UP FOR YOURSELF TREASURES IN HEAVEN; EVERYTHING ELSE WILL FADE AWAY.

- ༃ Let your good works glorify God—3 Nephi 12:16

- ༃ Seek to bless and serve others—Mosiah 2:17

- ༃ Always abound in good works—Mosiah 5:15

- ༃ Remember, your joy is helping others come unto Christ—Alma 29:9–10; 36:24

THE ONLY WAY TO BE SAVED

O remember, remember, my sons, the words which king Benjamin spake unto his people; yea, remember that there is no other way nor means whereby man can be saved, only through the atoning blood of Jesus Christ, who shall come; yea, remember that he cometh to redeem the world.

HELAMAN 5:9

The truth was spoken by Nephi . . . "We are saved [by grace], after all we can do" (2 Ne. 25:23).

It will require maximum effort for us to bring ourselves within the reach of the atoning blood of Jesus Christ so that we can be saved. There will be no government dole which can get us through the pearly gates. Nor will anyone go through those gates who wants to go through on the efforts of another.

(Marion G. Romney, "Fundamental Welfare Services,"
Ensign, May 1979, 94)

Daily Living

REMEMBERING AND ACTING UPON THE ATONEMENT IS
THE WAY TO EXALTATION.

ଛ   The gospel is centered in the Lord's atoning sacrifice—3 Nephi 27:13–14

ଛ   The principles and ordinances of the gospel are essential to exaltation—3 Nephi 27:19–22

ଛ   Without the Atonement you would perish and be subject to the devil—2 Nephi 9:8

ଛ   The only name whereby you can be saved is the Lord Jesus Christ—2 Nephi 25:20; 31:21; Mosiah 5:8

CHRIST, THE SURE FOUNDATION

And now, my sons, remember, remember that it is upon the rock of our Redeemer, who is Christ, the Son of God, that ye must build your foundation; that when the devil shall send forth his mighty winds, yea, his shafts in the whirlwind, yea, when all his hail and his mighty storm shall beat upon you, it shall have no power over you to drag you down to the gulf of misery and endless wo, because of the rock upon which ye are built, which is a sure foundation, a foundation whereon if men build they cannot fall.
HELAMAN 5:12

I pray, brothers and sisters, that all of us, especially those who are coming into manhood and womanhood, may give sober thought to these glorious principles and be able to build our lives upon the sure foundation of the gospel of Jesus Christ, "whereon if men build they cannot fall."

(Elray L. Christiansen, Conference Report, April 1958, 7)

Daily Living

YOU MUST BUILD YOUR FOUNDATION UPON THE SAVIOR OF THE WORLD; IF YOU DO YOU CANNOT FALL.

- ଞ You can be saved only through the atoning blood of Jesus Christ—Helaman 5:8

- ଞ Come unto Him through repentance and baptism—3 Nephi 11:32–34

- ଞ Recognize that your strength is in the Lord—Alma 26:11–12

- ଞ You can do all things through faith in the Lord Jesus Christ—Moroni 10:23

REMEMBER THE WORDS OF ETERNAL LIFE

And they did remember his words; and therefore they went forth, keeping the commandments of God, to teach the word of God among all the people of Nephi, beginning at the city Bountiful.
HELAMAN 5:14

Live by Every Word of God. Addressing priesthood bearers, the Lord says, "For you shall live by every word that proceedeth forth from the mouth of God" (D&C 84:44). This statement reinforces the need for obedience. It also suggests the need to know the word of the Lord.

Words of eternal life come from one source: God. They are made available to us through the fountain of the holy scriptures and the fountain of living prophets and reconfirmed by personal revelation through the power of the Holy Ghost.

(Carlos E. Asay, "The Oath and Covenant of the Priesthood," *Ensign,* November 1985, 44)

Daily Living

SEARCH THE SCRIPTURES THAT YOU MIGHT REMEMBER
THE WORDS OF THE PROPHETS.

ৰ Hearken to the word and come to know of the greatness of our Savior—2 Nephi 9:40

ৰ Hearken to the words of the prophets and come unto Christ—2 Nephi 9:51

ৰ Feast upon the word of Christ and endure to the end—2 Nephi 31:20

ৰ Hearken to the words of our Savior and His servants—3 Nephi 28:34–35

GIVEN THE WORDS

And it came to pass that Nephi and Lehi did preach unto the Lamanites with such great power and authority, for they had power and authority given unto them that they might speak, and they also had what they should speak given unto them—
HELAMAN 5:18

It is the duty of the Elders to constantly study the revelations which the Lord has given to his children in all ages, and to make themselves thoroughly familiar with all the doctrines and principles of the Church, and to store their minds with all the direct or indirect proofs, whether from sacred or profane history of the truths they are advocating. Then, they may with confidence, ask and expect the Spirit of the Lord to aid them in selecting and bringing forth . . . those truths which are best adapted to the wants and circumstances of the people they are addressing.

(George Q. Cannon, in *Latter-day Prophets and the Doctrine and Covenants,* comp. Roy. W. Doxey [Salt Lake City: Deseret Book, 1978], 3:99–100)

Daily Living

STRIVE TO PREACH AND TEACH BY THE AUTHORITY YOU
HAVE BEEN GIVEN AND BY THE SPIRIT.

- ❧ You are called to preach by those in authority—2 Nephi 6:2; Alma 6:8

- ❧ You can speak whatsoever the Lord shall put into your heart— Helaman 13:4–5

- ❧ The Lord will give to you the words to say—D&C 84:85–88; 100:5–6

- ❧ You can speak as you are moved upon by the power of the Holy Ghost—D&C 68:3–7

HEARTS UPON THEIR RICHES

For behold, the Lord had blessed them so long with the riches of the world that they had not been stirred up to anger, to wars, nor to bloodshed; therefore they began to set their hearts upon their riches; yea, they began to seek to get gain that they might be lifted up one above another.

HELAMAN 6:17

Humility is a state of mind, and not a condition, necessarily, of finances. It is too often true that people who gain financial prosperity are led away by pride of the heart and the desire for the things of this world. As I read history there has been no nation that has ever fallen because of prevailing humility among the people. But there are many instances of downfall due to pride. So long as nations have maintained a humble spirit they have been able to endure and to grow; but whenever they have become steeped in pride, they have been led to destruction.

(Sylvester Q. Cannon, Conference Report,
April 1931, 16–17)

Daily Living

BEWARE OF THE THINGS OF THE WORLD LEST THEY BECOME
THE TREASURES OF YOUR HEART.

- The Lord despiseth those who are puffed up because of learning and riches—2 Nephi 9:42

- Never compare yourself to another as to the things of the world for you will suffer from pride—Jacob 2:13

- When your heart is on your riches you will commit sins—Mosiah 11:14; 12:29

- Don't set your heart upon riches and you will be liberal to all those in need—Alma 1:30

SATAN CAN GET HOLD OF YOUR HEART

And thus we see that the Nephites did begin to dwindle in unbelief, and grow in wickedness and abominations, while the Lamanites began to grow exceedingly in the knowledge of their God; yea, they did begin to keep his statutes and commandments, and to walk in truth and uprightness before him.

HELAMAN 6:34

Nephi saw most clearly these things which threaten the world, and the dangers that threaten the Church. I see no dark clouds gathering against the Church, but I do see most clearly that which Nephi declared, that in this day Satan would stir up the hearts of men, and he would rage in their hearts against the truth, and he would seek to gain power and control over the kingdoms of this world.

(Melvin J. Ballard, Conference Report, April 1928, 114)

Daily Living

AVOID SATAN AND THE THINGS OF THE WORLD AT ALL COSTS.

- ༀ Watch and pray that you might be delivered from Satan—Alma 15:17; 3 Nephi 18:18

- ༀ Satan has the power to stir up contention—Helaman 6:21; 3 Nephi 11:28–29

- ༀ Satan is real and seeks to lead you away from the Savior—3 Nephi 2:2–3; 6:16

- ༀ The Devil seeks that all might be miserable like unto himself— 2 Nephi 2:27

- ༀ You can lose the Spirit because of yielding to the Devil—Alma 34:35; Helaman 6:35

WHEN YOU PUT THE WORLD FIRST

*O, how could you have forgotten your God in the very day that
he has delivered you?
But behold, it is to get gain, to be praised of men. . . . And ye have
set your hearts upon the riches and the vain things of this world,
for the which ye do murder, and plunder, and steal, and bear false
witness against your neighbor, and do all manner of iniquity.*
HELAMAN 7:20–21

There is a constant battle between the things of the flesh and the
things of God—the desire for peace and the attractions of the flesh.
It is also a well-known fact that in times of prosperity man is often
tempted to forget God, but in days of trial and sorrow he prays unto
the Lord that his countenance may smile upon him and that the
Lord will remember him.

(Joseph Anderson, "Strength of the Spirit,"
Ensign, May 1974, 9)

Daily Living

YOU FORGET GOD WHENEVER YOU PUT THE THINGS OF THE WORLD FIRST
AND LIFT YOURSELF ABOVE OTHERS.

- ၹ If you believe the words of the wicked you can easily forget
  God—Alma 46:7–8

- ၹ In sin you can become impenitent and forget the Lord—Alma
  47:36

- ၹ Due to the ease of the way and in prosperity you can forget
  God—Helaman 12:2–3

- ၹ Be careful lest in seeking gain you set aside your values and
  sin—Alma 11:20

- ၹ Don't turn aside the just for a thing of naught, for you will
  perish—2 Nephi 28:16

THE JUDGMENT DAY

But behold, ye have rejected the truth, and rebelled against your holy God; and even at this time, instead of laying up for yourselves treasures in heaven, where nothing doth corrupt, and where nothing can come which is unclean, ye are heaping up for yourselves wrath against the day of judgment.

HELAMAN 8:24–25

The gospel is "to prepare the saints for the hour of judgment which is to come; That their souls may escape the wrath of God, the desolation of abomination which awaits the wicked, both in this world and in the world to come" (D&C 88:84–85).

(Bruce R. McConkie, *Doctrinal New Testament Commentary*
[Salt Lake City: Bookcraft, 1965–1973], 3:44)

Daily Living

SUBMIT TO THE LORD'S WILL IN ALL THINGS.

- ᨠ Exhort everyone to remember to keep His commandments in all things—1 Nephi 15:25

- ᨠ You must be obedient to the commandments of God—1 Nephi 22:30–31

- ᨠ You must endure to the end in all things to prepare for the justice and judgment of God—3 Nephi 27:16–17

- ᨠ The atonement will satisfy the demands of justice if you repent—D&C 19:15–19

POWER OF TESTIMONY

And there were some of the Nephites who believed on the words of Nephi; and there were some also, who believed because of the testimony of the five, for they had been converted while they were in prison.

HELAMAN 9:39

Even while facing the task of building a city, the Mormons did not neglect the preaching of the gospel. During the summer of 1839, seven members of the Council of the Twelve Apostles left Nauvoo for England.

These men were powerful missionaries. The trials through which they had passed had strengthened their convictions concerning the cause with which they were associated, and they won hundreds of converts through the powerful testimonies which they bore.

(Gordon B. Hinckley, *What of the Mormons?* [Salt Lake City: Deseret Book, 1947], 127–128)

Daily Living

PURE TESTIMONY IS ALWAYS BORN BY THE SPIRIT AND
HAS POWER TO TOUCH LIVES.

- ৪৩ You should stand as a witness at all times—Mosiah 18:9

- ৪৩ Fast and pray to know the truth by the Spirit of revelation—Alma 5:45–46

- ৪৩ What testimony of Christ is in you?—Alma 7:10–13

- ৪৩ All things testify that there is a God in the Heavens—Alma 30:41,44

- ৪৩ You can know the truth of all things by the power of the Holy Ghost—Moroni 10:5–7

RIGHTEOUSNESS BRINGS BLESSINGS

Blessed art thou, Nephi, for those things which thou hast done. . . .
And now, because thou hast done this with such unwearyingness,
behold, I will bless thee forever; and I will make thee mighty in
word and in deed, in faith and in works; yea, even that all
things shall be done unto thee according to thy word, for thou
shalt not ask that which is contrary to my will.
HELAMAN 10:4–5

We could follow the example of Nephi, a son of Helaman, who after laboring diligently to teach and live righteously, had decided to give up and return home because the people refused to accept his counsel and to repent. As he approached his home, the voice of the Lord came to him. The Lord reminded Nephi of the blessings that would result from the unwearyingness with which he had labored and taught the people and with which he had kept the commandments of God. With renewed vigor and determination, Nephi turned from his home and returned to his labors to continue as he had commenced (see Hel. 10:2–12).

(Rex D. Pinegar, "We Need to Continue in Righteousness,"
Ensign, November 1974, 44)

Daily Living

DILIGENTLY SEEK TO DO THE LORD'S WILL AND STAY THE COURSE.

- As you do the will of God He doth bless you—Alma 10:11

- As you give all to bless others the Lord doth bless you—Alma 48;11–13

- Serve the Lord with all diligence and He will deliver you—Mosiah 7:33

WHY YOU FORGET GOD

Yea, and we may see at the very time when he doth prosper his people . . . sparing their lives, and delivering them out of the hands of their enemies; . . . yea, and in fine, doing all things for the welfare and happiness of his people; yea, then is the time that they do harden their hearts, and do forget the Lord their God . . . yea, and this because of their ease, and . . . great prosperity.
HELAMAN 12:2

We do not all of us sufficiently comprehend the great blessings that God has conferred upon us. We forget, sometimes, that we are the Saints of God. . . . We forget, sometimes, that we are engaged . . . in . . . planting the kingdom of God upon the earth; and we condescend to little meannesses. . . . Many of us give way to temptation . . . and lose the Spirit of the Lord. We forget that God and angels are looking . . . forward for the establishment of the kingdom of God upon the earth . . . and that our acts are open to the inspection of all the authorized agencies of the invisible world.

(John Taylor, *The Gospel Kingdom: Selections from the Writings and Discourses of John Taylor,* sel. G. Homer Durham [Salt Lake City: Bookcraft, 1987], 179)

Daily Living

NEVER FORGET THE LORD AND HIS GOODNESS.

- ஐ You are slow to remember when your heart is past feeling—1 Nephi 17:45

- ஐ In forgetting the Lord you can be quick to do iniquity—Alma 46:8

- ஐ The word will help you remember—Alma 4:19

CHASTENING OF THE LORD

And thus we see that except the Lord doth chasten his people
with many afflictions, yea, except he doth visit them with death
and with terror . . . they will not remember him.
HELAMAN 12:3

Even when righteously chastised or rebuked, we need not faint, for in the correcting is renewing love: "My son, despise not thou the chastening of the Lord, nor faint when thou art rebuked of him: For whom the Lord loveth he chasteneth" (Heb. 12:5–8).

One's life, therefore, cannot be both faith-filled and stress-free. President Wilford Woodruff counseled us all about the mercy that is inherent in some adversity: "The chastisements we have had from time to time have been for our good, and are essential to learn wisdom, and carry us through a school of experience we never could have passed through without" (In Journal of Discourses, 2:198).

(Neal A. Maxwell, "Lest Ye Be Wearied and Faint in Your
Minds," *Ensign,* May 1991, 88)

Daily Living

REMEMBER HE LOVES YOU. YOU ARE CHASTENED
SO YOU WON'T FORGET HIM.

🙵 Chastening of the Lord can bring repentance—1 Nephi 16:39

🙵 In chastening your patience and faith are tested—Mosiah 23:21

🙵 Chastening helps you remember the Lord—Helaman 12:3

🙵 Remember, whom the Lord chastens He loves—D&C 95:1–2

LESS THAN THE DUST

Behold, they do not desire that the Lord their God, who hath created them, should rule and reign over them; notwithstanding his great goodness and his mercy towards them, they do set at naught his counsels, and they will not that he should be their guide.
O how great is the nothingness of the children of men; yea, even they are less than the dust of the earth.
For behold, the dust of the earth moveth hither and thither, to the dividing asunder, at the command of our great and everlasting God.
HELAMAN 12:6–8

Here Mormon explains another way in which the children of men are less than the dust of the earth—the inanimate dust of the earth obeys when God speaks, whereas the highest of the animate creation, man, so often fails to hearken to and obey the word of the Lord.
(Joseph Fielding McConkie and Robert L. Millet, *Doctrinal Commentary on the Book of Mormon* [Salt Lake City: Bookcraft, 1987–1992], 3:397)

Daily Living

EVEN THE CREATIONS HONOR GOD WITH THEIR OBEDIENCE; YOU SHOULD DO LIKEWISE.

- ෨ The Lord will provide a way to keep the commandments—1 Nephi 3:7

- ෨ Have the attitude that if the Lord commands you will obey—2 Nephi 33:15

- ෨ You will prosper as you keep the commandments—Mosiah 2:22

- ෨ When you love the Lord you will keep the commandments—John 14:15

JOY AND GLORY OF GOD

Therefore, blessed are they who will repent and hearken unto the voice of the Lord their God; for these are they that shall be saved.
HELAMAN 12:23

That great truth ought to fill us all with hope, as long as we are quick to remember that the effect of grace in our lives is conditioned upon repenting of our sins.

Therefore, blessed are they who will repent . . . [Hel. 12:23–24].

A repentant heart and good works are the very conditions required to have grace restored to us. When someone pleads fervently in prayer for an answer, the answer may be more conditioned on repentance of personal sins than on any other factor (see D&C 101:7–8; Mosiah 11:23–24).

(Gene R. Cook, "Receiving Divine Assistance through the Grace of the Lord," *Ensign,* May 1993, 80)

Daily Living

REPENT, AND THROUGH YOUR GOOD WORKS VALIDATE YOUR REPENTANCE AND BLESS OTHERS THAT THEY TOO MIGHT REPENT. THIS IS THE WAY BACK TO THE PRESENCE OF GOD.

ဆ The Lord has great joy over the soul that repenteth—D&C 18:13

ဆ The desire to do good always follows true repentance—Enos 1:9, 11; Mosiah 28:3

ဆ You bring forth good works as you follow Christ—Alma 5:41

ဆ As you repent, exercise faith and perform good works you can bring many others to repentance—Alma 26:22

RESULTS OF A HARDENED HEART

*Therefore, thus saith the Lord: Because of the hardness of the
hearts of the people of the Nephites, except they repent I will
take away my word from them, and I will withdraw my Spirit
from them, and I will suffer them no longer, and I will turn the
hearts of their brethren against them.*

HELAMAN 13:8

When the light of the Spirit, because of transgression and hardness
of heart, departs from the soul of the transgressor, he is left to himself to grope through the darkness of temptation and evil. Therefore,
he does not reason righteously nor act according to principles of
honesty, truthfulness, or morality.

(Delbert L. Stapley, Conference Report, April 1963, 34)

Daily Living

WHEN YOU ALLOW YOUR HEARTS TO BE HARDENED AND CHOOSE TO NOT
REPENT YOU LOSE THE POWER OF THE WORD IN YOUR LIVES AND THE
BLESSINGS OF THE HOLY SPIRIT.

- Remember that the temptations of the devil can harden your heart—1 Nephi 12:17

- If you harden your heart against the Spirit it has no place in you and you will not receive the word of God—2 Nephi 33:2; Moroni 9:4

- Through unbelief you cannot understand the word and your heart hardens—Mosiah 26:3

- If you harden your heart you receive a lesser portion of the word—Alma 12:10–11

- If you harden not your heart the great plan of redemption can be yours—Alma 34:31

FOLLOW THE PROPHET WITH EXACTNESS

Behold ye are worse than they; for as the Lord liveth, if a prophet come among you and declareth unto you the word of the Lord, which testifieth of your sins and iniquities, ye are angry with him, . . . and seek all manner of ways to destroy him . . . because he testifieth that your deeds are evil.

HELAMAN 13:26

I thought how true, and how serious when we begin to choose which of the covenants, which of the commandments we will keep and follow. When we decide that there are some of them that we will not keep or follow, we are taking the law of the Lord into our own hands and become our own prophets, and believe me, we will be led astray, because we are false prophets to ourselves when we do not follow the Prophet of God. No, we should never discriminate between these commandments, as to those we should and should not keep.

(N. Eldon Tanner, Conference Report, October 1966, 98)

Daily Living

SEEK TO UNDERSTAND AND APPRECIATE THE WORDS OF OUR PROPHETS. DON'T FIND FAULT WITH THEIR WORDS OR KEEP ONLY THE "CONVENIENT" COMMANDMENTS.

- Prophets teach us the consequences of sin—2 Nephi 9:48

- Prophets and leaders speak the words given to them by the Spirit— Helaman 5:18; D&C 84:88; 100:5–6

- The Lord will put into the prophet's hearts the words to say— Helaman 13:4–5

- Hearken to the Lord's prophets or you stand under condemnation—3 Nephi 28:34–35

NOW IS THE TIME

But behold, your days of probation are past; ye have procrastinated the day of your salvation until it is everlastingly too late, and your destruction is made sure; yea, for ye have sought all the days of your lives for that which ye could not obtain; and ye have sought for happiness in doing iniquity, which thing is contrary to the nature of that righteousness which is in our great and Eternal Head.

HELAMAN 13:38

Such indulgence in premeditated sin shows pitiful misunderstanding of repentance. As Amulek warned, we must not procrastinate the day of our repentance until the end. (See Alma 34:32–35.) Judgment for us could be today or tomorrow. We must not risk our opportunity to repent. Salvation is not just an escape from the penalty of sin but deliverance from sinfulness. The truly penitent not only seek forgiveness for past sins but plead for the Savior to purge their hearts of the desire or appetite for sin.

(J. Richard Clarke, "The Lord of Life," *Ensign,* May 1993, 10)

Daily Living

YOU MUST NOT PROCRASTINATE YOUR REPENTANCE.

ༀ Do not procrastinate the day of your repentance—Alma 13:27

ༀ Now is the time to prepare to meet God. Repent now—Alma 34:32–35

ༀ The Lord commandeth all to repent or suffer the consequences—2 Nephi 9:23–24

ༀ If you repent you are redeemed of the Lord and born of the Spirit—Mosiah 27:24

ANGERED IN YOUR WEAKNESS

And now, because I am a Lamanite, and have spoken unto you the words which the Lord hath commanded me, and because it was hard against you, ye are angry with me and do seek to destroy me, and have cast me out from among you.

HELAMAN 14:10

"When a corrupt man is chastened he gets angry and will not endure it," the Prophet explained. Such a course, therefore, was "not calculated to gain the good will of all, but rather the ill will of many." Nevertheless, he concluded: "I frequently rebuke and admonish my brethren, and that because I love them, not because I wish to incur their displeasure, or mar their happiness." When rebukes were given according to righteous principles, they were not only to be made in love, but were to be followed by an increase of love toward the chastened individual.

(Hyrum L. Andrus, *Doctrines of the Kingdom* [Salt Lake City: Bookcraft, 1973], 3:170)

Daily Living

BEWARE LEST YOU SEPARATE YOURSELVES FROM THE LORD'S ANOINTED SERVANTS AND THUS SEPARATE YOURSELVES FROM GOD.

- හ Never be offended by the strictness of the word of God—Alma 35:15

- හ Remember true chastening is motivated by love—D&C 95:1–2

- හ Chastening helps you remember the Lord—Helaman 12:3

- හ If you lose the Spirit you can be angered by the messenger or by the word—Moroni 9:4

CONSEQUENCES OF FAILING TO REPENT

Therefore repent ye, repent ye, lest by knowing these things and not doing them ye shall suffer yourselves to come under condemnation, and ye are brought down unto this second death.

HELAMAN 14:19

The Lord sent prophets to urge his chosen people to repent, return to spiritual and moral fidelity, and fulfill their covenants with God; to warn the Israelites and others of the consequences of failing to repent; to remind people that the Lord does not forsake them, though they sometimes forsake him; to let future generations of Israel and others know that if they are faithful to the true and living God, he will fulfill his covenant promises.

(Ellis T. Rasmussen, *A Latter-day Saint Commentary on the Old Testament* [Salt Lake City: Deseret Book, 1993], 628)

Daily Living

IF YOU FAIL TO REPENT YOU BRING UPON YOURSELVES THE SECOND DEATH—SPIRITUAL DEATH—OR BEING CAST OUT OF THE PRESENCE OF GOD, DEAD AS TO THINGS OF THE SPIRIT.

- ଊ The second death results from failure to repent and follow the prophets—Jacob 3:11

- ଊ Bring forth fruit of repentance and partake not of the second death—Alma 12:15–17

- ଊ The wrath of the Lord comes to those who will not repent— Alma 13:30

- ଊ Remember you must suffer for sins not repented of—D&C 19:15–19

RESPONSIBLE AND ACCOUNTABLE

*And now remember, remember, my brethren, that whosoever
perisheth, <u>perisheth unto himself</u>; and whosoever doeth iniquity,
doeth it unto himself; for behold, <u>ye are free</u>; ye are permitted to
<u>act for yourselves</u>; for behold, God hath given unto you a
knowledge and <u>he hath made you free</u>.
He hath given unto you that ye might know good from evil, and
he hath given unto you that ye might <u>choose life or death</u>.*
HELAMAN 14:30–31

Why run against the laws of life? Why run headlong into ill health and
unhappiness? Why live contrary to conscience? Think of the heart-
break and waste and regret that could be prevented by living as we
ought to live. No one can set aside consequences. As Cecil B. DeMille
said: "<u>We cannot break the</u> . . . Commandments. We can only break
<u>ourselves against them</u>."

(Richard L. Evans, "Where Are You Really Going?"
Ensign, June 1971, 74)

Daily Living

DON'T BREAK YOURSELVES AGAINST THE COMMANDMENTS. CHOOSE TO OBEY.

- ∞ You have the gift of moral agency—2 Nephi 2:27

- ∞ You have the light of Christ to know right from wrong—
  Moroni 7:15–17

- ∞ Remember you are free to act for yourselves—2 Nephi 10:23

- ∞ Remember that you will be punished for your own sins—
  Article of Faith 2

FEEDING THE LOST SHEEP

Yea, I say unto you, that the more part of them are doing this, and they are striving with unwearied diligence that they may bring the remainder of their brethren to the knowledge of the truth; therefore there are many who do add to their numbers daily.

HELAMAN 15:6

Finding lost sheep and loving them back into full fellowship with the Saints must, therefore, be seen as an intrinsic, eternal part of the shepherd's role. Faithful shepherds for all seasons understand that winter or summer, year in and year out, finding, bringing back, and tenderly caring for the sheep are among the tasks the Lord expects His undershepherds to carry out.

(Alexander B. Morrison, *Feed My Sheep: Leadership Ideas for Latter-day Shepherds* [Salt Lake City: Deseret Book, 1992], 29)

Daily Living

YOU SHOULD DO ALL IN YOUR POWER TO BRING THE LOST SHEEP AND THOSE STRUGGLING BACK.

- ೮ Remember that all mankind is lost in a fallen sate and needs redemption—1 Nephi 10:6

- ೮ Desire to help all come unto Christ—Mosiah 28:1–3

- ೮ Souls are precious . . . seek to help them return—Alma 31:34–35

- ೮ Have the desire to help others taste of the joy that you taste in the gospel—Alma 36:24

- ೮ Lift up the hands that hang down and strengthen the feeble knees—D&C 81:5

- ೮ Strengthen your brothers and sister in all your doings—D&C 108:7

SEPTEMBER

&

*And they did rejoice and cry again
with one voice, saying: May the God
of Abraham, and the God of Isaac,
and the God of Jacob, protect this
people in righteousness, so long as
they shall call on the name of their
God for protection.*

—3 Nephi 4:30

TRULY BELIEVE

And now, because of their steadfastness when they do believe in that thing which they do believe, for because of their firmness when they are once enlightened, behold, the Lord shall bless them and prolong their days, notwithstanding their iniquity.
HELAMAN 15:10

With all my soul I appeal to the youth of Zion:
Believe with all your heart in the restored gospel as given us through the Prophet Joseph Smith. Believe that this restored gospel is the way of truth and joy.
Know that wickedness never was happiness, but that obedience and chastity lead to the abundant life. Know that virtue is a vital part of the restored gospel and can never be separated from it.
(Mark E. Petersen, Conference Report, April 1965, 37)

Daily Living
SEEK TO BELIEVE WITH ALL YOUR HEART.

- ☞ Through true belief you can behold the things of God—1 Nephi 11:3–6

- ☞ If you believe and endure well you shall inherit the kingdom of God—2 Nephi 9:18

- ☞ If you believe in Christ and you can have the manifestations of the Spirit—2 Nephi 26:13

- ☞ If you truly believe see that you keep the commandments—Mosiah 4:9–10

- ☞ When you believe and know of surety and truth of the word of God you will have no disposition to do evil but to do good continually—Mosiah 5:1–2

THE FAULTY REASONING OF MAN

And they began to reason and to contend among themselves, saying:
That it is not reasonable that such a being as a Christ shall
come. . . .
But behold, we know that this is a wicked tradition, which has
been handed down unto us by our fathers, to cause us that we
should believe in some great and marvelous thing which should
come to pass . . . for we cannot witness with our own eyes that they
are true.
HELAMAN 16:17–18, 20

The world worships the learning of man . . . To them, men's reasoning is greater than God's revelations. The precepts of man have gone so far in subverting our educational system that in many cases a higher degree today, in the so-called social sciences, can be tantamount to a major investment in error. . . . President Joseph F. Smith was right when he said that false educational ideas would be one of the three threats to the Church within (*Gospel Doctrine,* pp. 312–313).

(Ezra Taft Benson, Conference Report, April 1969, 12–13)

Daily Living

BEWARE LEST THE FINITE REASONING OF MAN DEMEAN THE POWER AND
GOODNESS OF GOD.

- ଽ To be learned is good only if you hearken to the counsels of God—2 Nephi 9:28–29

- ଽ Beware of being puffed up in your learning—2 Nephi 9:42

- ଽ Unto such shall the mysteries of God be unfolded—Alma 26:22

- ଽ Learn wisdom in your youth to keep the commandments of God—Alma 37:35

GOODNESS OF GOD

And their hearts were swollen with joy, unto the gushing out of many tears, because of the great goodness of God in delivering them out of the hands of their enemies; and they knew it was because of their repentance and their humility that they had been delivered from an everlasting destruction.

3 NEPHI 4:33

When the people heard Benjamin's discourse and asked him how they could "apply the atoning blood of Christ . . ." (Mosiah 4:2), Benjamin told them they (1) must believe in the goodness of God and in the Atonement of Jesus Christ, (2) must repent of their sins and forsake them, and (3) must humble themselves before God and ask . . . for forgiveness (Mosiah 4:6–10).

(Daniel H. Ludlow, *A Companion to Your Study of the Book of Mormon* [Salt Lake City: Deseret Book, 1976], 180)

Daily Living

STRIVE TO REPENT AND FORSAKE YOUR SINS.

- ∞ The great plan of redemption prepares a way to escape death and hell—2 Nephi 9:10

- ∞ If you don't partake of the goodness of God His words will condemn you at the last day—2 Nephi 33:14

- ∞ Always retain in remembrance the goodness of God—Mosiah 4:11

- ∞ Remember this is the time to repent and serve God—Alma 42:4

DISCIPLE OF CHRIST

Behold, I am a disciple of Jesus Christ, the Son of God. I have been called of him to declare his word among his people, that they might have everlasting life.

3 NEPHI 5:13

First, we should exercise our faith and pray individually and as families, asking for help in finding ways to share the restored gospel of Jesus Christ. Ask the Lord to open the way. Prayerfully set a date with your family to have someone in your home for the missionaries to teach. Remember, brothers and sisters, this is the Lord's Church. Let Him guide you through constant prayer. With a prayer in your heart, talk to everyone you can. Don't prejudge. Don't withhold the good news from anyone. . . . Over time, the Lord will put into your path those who are seeking the truth. He is the Good Shepherd. He knows His sheep, and they will know His voice, spoken through you, and they will follow Him (see John 10).

(M. Russell Ballard, "The Essential Role of Member Missionary Work," *Ensign,* May 2003, 38)

Daily Living

PRAY TO KNOW WITH WHOM YOU CAN SHARE THE GOSPEL.

- ℘ Stand as a witness at all times and places—Mosiah 18:9
- ℘ Pray for all those who know not God—Alma 6:6
- ℘ Seek to be an instrument in the Lord's hands—Alma 29:9–10
- ℘ Open your mouth and preach the gospel everywhere—Alma 26:29
- ℘ Go ye into all the world and preach the gospel to every creature— Mormon 9:22

REALITY OF SATAN

Now the cause of this iniquity of the people was this—Satan had great power, unto the stirring up of the people to do all manner of iniquity, and to the puffing them up with pride, tempting them to seek for power, and authority, and riches, and the vain things of the world.
And thus Satan did lead away the hearts of the people to do all manner of iniquity.
3 NEPHI 6:15–16

Alexander Pope's couplet succinctly sums up the manner in which Satan leads the unwary "carefully down to hell."

Vice is a monster of so frightful mien,
As, to be hated, needs but to be seen;
Yet seen too oft, familiar with her face,
We first endure, then pity, then embrace.

(Rodney Turner, *Woman and the Priesthood* [Salt Lake City: Deseret Book, 1977], 109–110)

Daily Living

KEEP THE SPIRIT WITH YOU THAT YOU MAY AVOID THE ENTICEMENTS OF THE ADVERSARY.

- ଓ Remember you are free to choose eternal life or eternal misery—2 Nephi 2:27

- ଓ The devil will tell you there is no hell—2 Nephi 28:22

- ଓ Remember that all evil cometh of the devil—Omni 1:25

- ଓ You become carnal and devilish when you love Satan more than God—Moses 5:13

THE SAVIOR'S LOVE

O all ye that are spared because ye were more righteous than
they, will ye not now return unto me, and repent of your sins,
and be converted, that I may heal you?
Yea, verily I say unto you, if ye will come unto me ye shall have
eternal life. Behold, mine arm of mercy is extended towards you,
and whosoever will come, him will I receive; and blessed are
those who come unto me.
3 NEPHI 9:13–14

I bear testimony that as we accept the invitation to come unto Christ, we will find that He can heal all wounds. He can lift our burdens and carry them for us, and we can feel "encircled about eternally in the arms of his love" (2 Ne. 1:15).

(Margaret D. Nadauld, "Come unto Christ,"
Ensign, May 1998, 65)

Daily Living

COME UNTO CHRIST AND YOU SHALL BE BLESSED.

- ත Come unto me is the clarion call of the Savior—2 Nephi 26:25–28; Ether 4:13–14,18

- ත The Lord's arm is always lengthened out in mercy if you but repent—2 Nephi 28:32

- ත Imagine the joy at the end of life—Alma 5:16

- ත The Lord promises many blessings as you come unto Him— 3 Nephi 12:3, 19, 20

- ත Be reconciled to your brother and then come unto Him— 3 Nephi 12:23–24

OUR SACRIFICE

And ye shall offer for a sacrifice unto me a broken heart and a contrite spirit. And whoso cometh unto me with a broken heart and a contrite spirit, him will I baptize with fire and with the Holy Ghost, even as the Lamanites, because of their faith in me at the time of their conversion, were baptized with fire and with the Holy Ghost, and they knew it not.

3 NEPHI 9:20

The gift or sacrifice He will accept now is a broken heart and a contrite spirit. As you seek the blessing of conversion, you can offer the Lord the gift of your broken, or repentant, heart and your contrite, or obedient, spirit. In reality, it is the gift of yourself—what you are and what you are becoming.

(D. Todd Christofferson, "When Thou Art Converted,"
Ensign, May 2004, 12)

Daily Living

HUMBLY SUBMIT TO HIS WILL, TAKE HIS NAME UPON YOU, AND RECEIVE THE HOLY GHOST.

- ∞ The Atonement is an exalting blessing—2 Nephi 2:7; D&C 97:8

- ∞ Call upon Heavenly Father with a broken heart and contrite spirit—Ether 4:15

- ∞ In order to rightfully come unto Christ through repentance and baptism you must come with a broken heart and contrite spirit—Moroni 6:4; D&C 20:37

- ∞ The Lord is always near you if you have a broken heart and contrite spirit—Psalm 34:18

LIGHT AND LIFE OF THE WORLD

*And behold, I am the light and the life of the world; and I have
drunk out of that bitter cup which the Father hath given me,
and have glorified the Father in taking upon me the sins of the
world, in the which I have suffered the will of the Father in all
things from the beginning.*

3 Nephi 11:11

"Jesus is the Living Christ, the immortal Son of God. He is the great
King Immanuel, who stands today on the right hand of His Father. . . .
His way is the path that leads to happiness in this life and eternal life in
the world to come. God be thanked for the matchless gift of His divine
Son" ["The Living Christ: The Testimony of the Apostles"].
Jesus, the very thought of Thee fills my heart with inexpressible joy.
It controls every part of my being. My life, my loves, my ambitions
are molded, enlivened, and given purpose because I know that Thou
art the Christ, the Holy One.

(Keith B. McMullin, "Jesus, the Very Thought of Thee,"
Ensign, May 2004, 3)

Daily Living

You should seek to emulate His life.

- Seek only the will of Heavenly Father—Helaman 10:4–5

- By the light of the Lord can your soul cast out all darkness—
  Alma 19:6

- Let your light shine that you might glorify God—3 Nephi 12:16

- Let your eye be single to the glory of the Father—3 Nephi 13:22

- Remember that Christ is the light that you hold up—3 Nephi
  18:24

CONTENTION

For verily, verily I say unto you, he that hath the spirit of contention is not of me, but is of the devil, who is the father of contention. . . . Behold, this is not my doctrine, to stir up the hearts of men with anger, one against another; but this is my doctrine, that such things should be done away.

3 NEPHI 11:29–30

Through love of God, the pain caused by the fiery canker of contention will be extinguished from the soul. This healing begins with a personal vow: "Let there be peace on earth, and let it begin with me" ("Let There Be Peace on Earth," Sy Miller and Jill Jackson; Jan-Lee Music, Beverly Hills, Calif., 1972). This commitment will then spread to family and friends and will bring peace to neighborhoods and nations.

Shun contention. Seek godliness. Be enlightened by eternal truth. Be like-minded with the Lord in love and united with Him in faith.

(Russell M. Nelson, "The Canker of Contention," *Ensign*, May 1989, 71)

Daily Living

BE LOVING AND SEEK PEACE YET STAND FOR TRUTH AND RIGHTEOUSNESS.

- ɞ When you contend with another you list to obey the evil spirit—Mosiah 2:32

- ɞ Let your hearts should be knit together in unity and love—Mosiah 18:21

- ɞ When contentions arise on a large scale, war is the result—Helaman 11:1

- ɞ When people possess the love of God there will be no contentions—4 Nephi 1:15–16

HOW HAPPY YOU WILL BE

Blessed are ye if ye shall give heed unto the words of these twelve whom I have chosen from among you to minister unto you, and to be your servants; and unto them I have given power that they may baptize you with water; and after that ye are baptized with water, behold, I will baptize you with fire and with the Holy Ghost; therefore blessed are ye if ye shall believe in me and be baptized, after that ye have seen me and know that I am.

3 NEPHI 12:1

Fathers and mothers and children, wherever you are, I want you to know that I know we have a Father in heaven, and I want you to know that his Son Jesus is the Christ; and I want you to know that I know he established his kingdom on the earth for our blessing and for our benefit. I testify that there is a prophet on the earth, and I testify that we will be happy if we follow his teachings.

(H. Burke Peterson, "Harmony in the Home," *Ensign,* January 1973, 115)

Daily Living

YOUR HAPPINESS IS DETERMINED BY YOUR WILLINGNESS
TO HEARKEN TO THE PROPHETS.

- ☙ If we fail to heed the words of the prophets there will be dissension—Alma 45:23

- ☙ Remember the prophets purpose is to help save your soul—2 Nephi 2:30

- ☙ The prophets all testify of Christ—2 Nephi 25:26; 3 Nephi 23:5

- ☙ Heed the words of the prophets—3 Nephi 28:34–35

- ☙ All the words of the prophets will be fulfilled—3 Nephi 29:2

HOW HAPPY ARE THE POOR IN SPIRIT

Yea, blessed are the poor in spirit who come unto me, for theirs is the kingdom of heaven.
3 NEPHI 12:3

All men and women, if they are to achieve true happiness, must come unto Christ and be perfected in Him. To achieve such supernal joy requires a life of dedication and devotion to duty and Deity, a life of service and sacrifice, a life of keeping the commandments. Such a life is characterized by partaking of holy ordinances and by making and keeping sacred covenants, those solemn, celestial agreements between man and God.

(Alexander B. Morrison, *Feed My Sheep: Leadership Ideas for Latter-day Shepherds* [Salt Lake City: Deseret Book, 1992], 61)

Daily Living

WHEN YOU HUMBLE YOURSELVES AND COME UNTO CHRIST YOU CAN INHERIT THE KINGDOM OF HEAVEN.

- ᏹ The prophets labor diligently that they might persuade all to come unto Christ—Jacob 1:7

- ᏹ You come unto Christ as you offer your whole soul and endure to the end—Omni 1:26

- ᏹ The Lord invites us to come unto Him and partake of the tree of life—Alma 5:34–35

- ᏹ The Lord's arm of mercy is always extended towards us—3 Nephi 9:14; 12:19–20, 23–24

- ᏹ Come with full purpose of heart that the Lord may heal you—3 Nephi 18:32

- ᏹ Come unto Christ and be perfected in Him—Moroni 10:32

HOW HAPPY ARE THOSE WHO MOURN

And again, blessed are all they that mourn, for they
shall be comforted.
3 NEPHI 12:4

The mourner shall be comforted when he sees the divine purpose in his grief. The Lord has told us: "Come unto me, all ye that labour and are heavy laden, and I will give you rest" (Matt. 11:28). . . . We must not allow ourselves to become embittered in times of mourning and sorrow. We must keep faith and seek comfort from the Lord through prayer. We have his promise that we shall be blessed. Those who are burdened shall be made happy when they learn the real comfort of the gospel through their faith and through their works.

(O. Leslie Stone, "The Beatitudes," *Ensign,*
November 1974, 31–32)

Daily Living

WHETHER IT IS GODLY SORROW UNTO REPENTANCE, SORROW FOR OTHERS,
OR PERSONAL TRIALS . . . THE LORD WILL COMFORT YOU IN PEACE.

- ๛ Often an emissary of the Lord will be an instrument in His hands to comfort you and likewise you can comfort others— Mosiah 18:9

- ๛ The Lord is always there to nurture and bless you—Alma 7:11–12

- ๛ Pray for comfort in your sorrows and for success in helping others—Alma 31:32–35

- ๛ Charity causes one to mourn for others and their iniquity— Alma 62:2

HOW HAPPY ARE THE MEEK

And blessed are the meek, for they shall inherit the earth.
3 NEPHI 12:5

And what of the meek? In a world too preoccupied with winning through intimidation and seeking to be number one, no large crowd of folk is standing in line to buy books that call for mere meekness. But the meek shall inherit the earth, a pretty impressive corporate takeover—and done without intimidation! Sooner or later, and we pray sooner than later, everyone will acknowledge that Christ's way is not only the right way, but ultimately the only way to hope and joy. Every knee shall bow and every tongue will confess that gentleness is better than brutality, that kindness is greater than coercion, that the soft voice turneth away wrath. In the end, and sooner than that whenever possible, we must be more like him. "To those who fall, how kind thou art! How good to those who seek!"

(Howard W. Hunter, "Jesus, the Very Thought of Thee,"
Ensign, May 1993, 64–65)

Daily Living

BE SUBMISSIVE, HUMBLE, GOD FEARING, AND SEEK ONLY RIGHTEOUSNESS.

- ❧ The meek find joy in the Lord—2 Nephi 27:30

- ❧ You can become a saint through the Atonement of Christ—Mosiah 3:19

- ❧ Through humility and prayer you won't be tempted above what you can bear—Alma 13:28

- ❧ Be meek and lowly of heart and you will rest for your soul—Alma 37:33–34

HOW HAPPY ARE THOSE WHO SEEK RIGHTEOUSNESS

And blessed are all they who do hunger and thirst after righteousness, for they shall be filled with the Holy Ghost.
3 NEPHI 12:6

All around us we have the good examples of those who seek permanent treasures—those who "hunger and thirst after righteousness" (Matt. 5:6) and put the kingdom of God first in their lives. Among the most visible such examples are the men and women who set aside their worldly pursuits and even say good-bye to their families to serve missions for the Lord. Tens of thousands of these are young missionaries. . . . Their remarkable service evidences their priorities, and their impressive example is a guide to their families and to all who know them.

(Dallin H. Oaks, "Focus and Priorities," *Ensign,* May 2001, 84)

Daily Living

HUNGER FOR THE THINGS OF GOD AND HIS RIGHTEOUSNESS
AND YOU WILL BE FILLED.

- ✇ The righteous are justified according to the truth—1 Nephi 16:2

- ✇ Remember the righteous are favored of the Lord—1 Nephi 17:35

- ✇ The Lord writes His law in the hearts of the righteous—2 Nephi 8:7

- ✇ The righteous shall be clothed in purity and inherit the kingdom—2 Nephi 9:14, 16, 18

- ✇ Remember that the if you obey the evil spirit the Lord has no place in you—Mosiah 2:37

- ✇ Seek the works of righteousness—Alma 5:35–36

HOW HAPPY ARE THE MERCIFUL

And blessed are the merciful, for they shall obtain mercy.
3 NEPHI 12:7

How godlike a quality is mercy. It cannot be legislated. It must come from the heart. It must be stirred up from within. It is part of the endowment each of us receives as a son or daughter of God and partaker of a divine birthright. I plead for an effort among all of us to give greater expression and wider latitude to this instinct which lies within us. I am convinced that there comes a time, possibly many times, within our lives when we might cry out for mercy on the part of others. How can we expect it unless we have been merciful ourselves?

(Gordon B. Hinckley, "Blessed Are the Merciful,"
Ensign, May 1990, 68)

Daily Living

SEEK TO OBTAIN FORGIVENESS AND MERCY BY BEING MERCIFUL.

- ☙ Seek mercy through the Atonement of Christ—Mosiah 4:2

- ☙ Mercy given to those who love God and keep the commandments—Mosiah 13:14

- ☙ The doctrine of restoration teaches that the merciful are restored to mercy—Alma 41:13–14

- ☙ Be forgiving else suffer condemnation—Mosiah 25:29–31

- ☙ As you forgive your Heavenly Father will forgive you—3 Nephi 13:14–15

HOW HAPPY ARE THE PURE IN HEART

And blessed are all the pure in heart, for they shall see God.
3 Nephi 12:8

When He [Christ] spoke of being without guile, He referred to something far deeper than outward appearance. He was reaching into the soul, to the very heart of righteousness. He was touching the key to goodness and to the Christlike life.

To be without guile is to be pure in heart an essential virtue of those who would be counted among true followers of Christ. . . . He revealed to the Prophet Joseph Smith that Zion is the pure in heart (see D&C 97:21) and that a house is to be built in Zion in which the pure in heart shall see God (see D&C 97:10–16).

(Joseph B. Wirthlin, "Without Guile,"
Ensign, May 1988, 80)

Daily Living

When you have an eye single to His glory and have righteous motives for your actions you will have a pure heart and you shall see God.

     You worship Heavenly Father with a pure heart and clean hands—2 Nephi 25:16

     The pure in heart will be blessed and receive the pleasing word of God—Jacob 3:1–2

     Wo unto those who are not pure in heart unless they repent—Jacob 3:3

     If your eye be single to the glory of God your whole body will be filled with light—3 Nephi 13:22

HOW HAPPY ARE THE PEACEMAKERS

*And blessed are all the peacemakers, for they shall be called
the children of God.*
3 NEPHI 12:9

"To err is human, to forgive divine" (Alexander Pope, *An Essay on
Criticism,* 2:1711). There is no peace in harboring old grudges. There
is no peace in reflecting on the pain of old wounds. There is peace
only in repentance and forgiveness. This is the sweet peace of the
Christ, who said, "Blessed are the peacemakers; for they shall be called
the children of God" (Matt. 5:9).

(Gordon B. Hinckley, "Of You It Is Required to Forgive,"
Ensign, November 1980, 63)

Daily Living

YOU BECOME PEACEMAKERS WHEN YOU HELP OTHERS RECEIVE THE GOSPEL
THAT BRINGS PEACE. THIS APPLIES TO CONTENTION AS WELL AS CONVERSION.

- ஐ As you publish peace you assist in bringing forth Zion—1 Nephi
  13:37

- ஐ You can enjoy peace in the land as everyone keeps the commandments—Mosiah 2:4

- ஐ As you are filled with the love of God you shall not have a desire
  to injure one another—Mosiah 4:12–13

- ஐ As you are taught of the Lord you shall enjoy peace and righteousness—3 Nephi 22:13–14

BLESSED ARE THE PERSECUTED

And blessed are all they who are persecuted for my name's sake,
for theirs is the kingdom of heaven.
And blessed are ye when men shall revile you and persecute, and
shall say all manner of evil against you falsely, for my sake;
For ye shall have great joy and be exceedingly glad, for great
shall be your reward in heaven.
3 NEPHI 12:10–12

We are to love the Lord, our God, with all our hearts and our neighbors as ourselves. We are even to love our enemies, to bless them that curse us, do good to them that hate us and pray for them which despitefully use us, and persecute us, following the example of Jesus who, when being persecuted to the death, prayed to the Father to forgive his persecutors. This represents the true spirit of Christ which should motivate all our life's actions.

(George F. Richards, Conference Report, October 1947, 55)

Daily Living

AS YOU ENDURE TRIALS AND TRIBULATIONS FOR THE LORD YOU SHALL
RECEIVE REWARDS.

- ❧ Remember to always praise the Lord in your afflictions—1 Nephi 18:11, 16

- ❧ In persecution look forward to Christ and you shall not perish—2 Nephi 26:8

- ❧ Be courageous in defending righteousness—Mosiah 17:10

- ❧ Pray for them that despitefully use you and persecute you—3 Nephi 12:44

SALT OF THE EARTH

*Verily, verily, I say unto you, I give unto you to be the salt of the
earth; but if the salt shall lose its savor wherewith shall the earth
be salted? The salt shall be thenceforth good for nothing, but to
be cast out and to be trodden under foot of men.*
*Verily, verily, I say unto you, I give unto you to be the light of
this people. A city that is set on a hill cannot be hid.*
*Therefore let your light so shine before this people, that they may
see your good works and glorify your Father who is in heaven.*
3 NEPHI 12:13–14, 16

Those then who are the "salt of the earth" are also the light of the world,
and the radiance of that light, shining through their good works to
mankind, glorifies our Eternal Father and strengthens his work and
kingdom on the earth.

[Being the salt of the earth] suggests unquestioned Christlike character
and conduct, uprightness, honesty, spirituality, sincerity of purpose,
dignity, and other noble character virtues and qualities patterned after
the divine nature of our Heavenly Father.

(Delbert L. Stapley, Conference Report, October 1964, 65)

Daily Living

LET YOUR LIGHT (THE LORD JESUS CHRIST) SHINE TO ALL.

- As a disciple of Christ you are a light unto the people—3 Nephi
  15:12

- Remember the light you hold up is the Lord Jesus Christ—
  3 Nephi 18:24

- You are accounted as the salt of the earth—D&C 101:39–40

OVERCOMING ANGER

*But I say unto you, that whosoever is angry with his brother shall
be in danger of his judgment. And whosoever shall say to his
brother, Raca, shall be in danger of the council; and whosoever
shall say, Thou fool, shall be in danger of hell fire.
Therefore, if ye shall come unto me, or shall desire to come unto
me, and rememberest that thy brother hath aught against thee—
Go thy way unto thy brother, and first be reconciled to thy
brother, and then come unto me with full purpose of heart, and
I will receive you.*
3 NEPHI 12:22–24

One chief purpose of life is to overcome evil tendencies, to govern our
appetites, to control our passions—anger, hatred, jealousy, immorality.
We have to overcome them; we have to subject them, conquer them,
because God has said: "My spirit will not dwell in unclean tabernacles,
nor will it always strive with man."

(David O. Mckay, Conference Report, October 1950, 163)

Daily Living

SEEK TO BE RECONCILED WITH YOUR BROTHER; THEN YOU ARE WORTHY TO
COME UNTO CHRIST.

- ဆ Pray to not have anger against your enemies—2 Nephi 4:29

- ဆ The devil seeks to stir you up to contention and anger—3 Nephi
  11:29

- ဆ The Lord's doctrine is not to stir people up to anger one with
  another—3 Nephi 11:30

- ဆ Be slow to anger—Psalm 103:8; Proverbs 15:18; 16:32

LUST

*But I say unto you, that whosoever looketh on a woman, to lust
after her, hath committed adultery already in his heart.
Behold, I give unto you a commandment, that ye suffer none of
these things to enter into your heart;
For it is better that ye should deny yourselves of these things,
wherein ye will take up your cross, than that ye should be
cast into hell.*

3 NEPHI 12:28–30

We covenant to live the law of chastity. The law of chastity is virtue
and sexual purity. This law places us under covenant to live this
commandment strictly. "Thou shalt love thy wife with all thy heart,
and shalt cleave unto her and none else. And he that looketh upon
a woman to lust after her shall deny the faith, and shall not have the
Spirit; and if he repents not he shall be cast out" (D&C 42:22–24).

(Ezra Taft Benson, *The Teachings of Ezra Taft Benson*
[Salt Lake City: Bookcraft, 1988], 278)

Daily Living

SEEK TO OVERCOME ANY FORM OF LUST.

- ∞ Learn to bridle your passions—Alma 38:12

- ∞ Deny yourself forsake lustful thoughts else you cannot inherit
the kingdom—Alma 39:9

- ∞ Possess the love of God and you will have no manner of lasciviousness—4 Nephi 1:16

- ∞ Be wise and seek to control your passions by praying to avoid
temptation—Mormon 9:28

THE CELESTIAL LAW

And behold, it is written, an eye for an eye, and a tooth for a tooth;
But I say unto you, that ye shall not resist evil, but whosoever
shall smite thee on thy right cheek, turn to him the other also;
And if any man will sue thee at the law and take away thy
coat, let him have thy cloak also;
And whosoever shall compel thee to go a mile, go with him twain.
Give to him that asketh thee, and from him that would borrow
of thee turn thou not away.
3 NEPHI 12:38–42

This attitude of hate, this spirit of revenge is not in harmony with the teachings of the gospel of Christ. The gospel is a message of love and tolerance and does not foster the spirit of hate or intolerance.
(Clifford E. Young, Conference Report, April 1949, 73)

Daily Living

SEEK NOT REVENGE, SUBMIT IN HUMILITY YET DEFEND THE TRUTH, GO THE EXTRA MILE, AND GIVE FREELY OF YOUR POSSESSIONS.

- Remember to love your neighbor as yourself—Mosiah 23:15
- Attributes and behaviors that will help you abound in good works—Alma 7:23–24
- The pure love of Christ is perfect love and endureth all things—Moroni 7:44–48
- Meekness, which follows repentance, will bring the blessings of the Spirit—Moroni 8:26

LOVE EVERYONE

And behold it is written also, that thou shalt love thy neighbor
and hate thine enemy;
But behold I say unto you, love your enemies, bless them that
curse you, do good to them that hate you, and pray for them
who despitefully use you and persecute you.

3 NEPHI 12:43–44

Imagine for a moment the result if everyone were to love one another as Jesus loves his disciples. We would have no bickering, quarreling, strife, or contention in our homes. We would not offend or insult one another either verbally or in any other way. We would not have unnecessary litigation over small matters. War would be impossible, especially war waged in the name of religion.

(Joseph B. Wirthlin, "Our Lord and Savior,"
Ensign, November 1993, 7)

Daily Living

EARNESTLY STRIVE TO HAVE THE PURE LOVE OF CHRIST THAT YOU MIGHT
LOVE EVERYONE WITH THAT ULTIMATE CONCERN THAT BRINGS ABOUT
RIGHTEOUS SERVICE.

- ᘓ Disciples of Christ love one another—John 13:34–35
- ᘓ Be filled with love towards God and all men—Mosiah 2:4
- ᘓ Remember as you serve you are expressing love—D&C 42:29
- ᘓ The pure love of Christ has all the facets of love—Moroni 7:44–47
- ᘓ Pray with all the energy of your heart to be filled with charity—Moroni 7:48

PERFECTION

*Therefore I would that ye should be perfect even as I, or your
Father who is in heaven is perfect.*
3 NEPHI 12:48

I would emphasize that the teachings of Christ that we should become perfect were not mere rhetoric. He meant literally that it is the right of mankind to become like the Father and like the Son, having overcome human weaknesses and developed attributes of divinity.

Because many individuals do not fully use the capacity that is in them does nothing to negate the truth that they have the power to become Christlike. It is the man and woman who use the power who prove its existence; neglect cannot prove its absence.

Working toward perfection is not a one-time decision but a process to be pursued throughout ones lifetime.

(Spencer W. Kimball, "Hold Fast to the Iron Rod,"
Ensign, November 1978, 5)

Daily Living

SEEK TO BECOME EVEN AS HE IS.

- ༀ Seek to become even as the Lord Jesus Christ—3 Nephi 27:27

- ༀ As you come unto Christ you can be perfected in Him through the grace of God—Moroni 19:32

- ༀ Just men and women are made perfect—D&C 76:69

GIVE WITH A PURE HEART

Take heed that ye do not your alms before men to be seen of them;
otherwise ye have no reward of your Father who is in heaven.
Therefore, when ye shall do your alms do not sound a trumpet
before you, as will hypocrites do in the synagogues and in the
streets, that they may have glory of men. . . .
But when thou doest alms let not thy left hand know what thy
right hand doeth;
That thine alms may be in secret; and thy Father who seeth in
secret, himself shall reward thee openly.

3 NEPHI 13:1–4

In his teachings to the people of both the Old World and the New, the Savior stressed that those who give to the poor "to be seen of men" have acted to obtain an earthly reward and will receive no reward in heaven: Clearly, unless motivated by pure love, even the most generous gifts of earthly treasures "profiteth . . . nothing."

(Dallin H. Oaks, *Pure in Heart* [Salt Lake City:
Bookcraft, 1988], 22–23)

Daily Living

AS YOU GIVE, OFFER GLORY TO GOD FOR THE OPPORTUNITY.

- ࢯ Think of others like unto yourselves and be free with your substance—Jacob 2:17

- ࢯ Give according to your ability to give, but always give—Mosiah 4:26; 18:27

- ࢯ Remember you prayers are vain if you fail to give to the needy—Alma 34:28

- ࢯ Visit the poor and administer to their relief—D&C 44:6

PRAY WITH A PURE HEART

*And when thou prayest thou shalt not do as the hypocrites, for
they love to pray, standing in the synagogues and in the corners
of the streets, that they may be seen of men. . . .
But thou, when thou prayest, enter into thy closet, and when
thou hast shut thy door, pray to thy Father who is in secret; and
thy Father, who seeth in secret, shall reward thee openly.*
3 NEPHI 13:6–7

Joseph Smith . . . believed in the promise he read in the book of
James. He went to the grove with faith that his prayer would be
answered. . . . He was submissive enough to be ready to do whatever
he was told to do. So he prayed, as we must, already committed to
obey.
What he was told to do required his whole soul and finally his life.
He endured during the 24 years that followed by continuing to pray
with that childlike faith and humility. We can teach those we love to
pray with the intent to obey.

(Henry B. Eyring, "An Enduring Testimony of the Mission
of the Prophet Joseph," *Ensign,* November 2003, 90)

Daily Living
PRAY WITH REAL INTENT HAVING FAITH FROM THE HEART.

ꝏ Pray with faith and a believing heart—1 Nephi 15:11

ꝏ Pray in "mighty prayer" for the welfare of your own soul—Enos 1:4

ꝏ Pray with faith believing that you will receive and you will receive
hope—Alma 22:16

ꝏ Pray to know the truth of all things—Moroni 10:4–5

FORGIVING IS THE KEY TO FORGIVENESS

*For, if ye forgive men their trespasses your heavenly Father will
also forgive you;
But if ye forgive not men their trespasses neither will your
Father forgive your trespasses.*
3 Nephi 13:14–15

Closely related to our own obligation to repent is the generosity of
letting others do the same—we are to forgive even as we are forgiven.
In this we participate in the very essence of the Atonement of Jesus
Christ. Surely the most majestic moment of that fateful Friday,
when nature convulsed and the veil of the temple was rent, was that
unspeakably merciful moment when Christ said, "Father, forgive
them; for they know not what they do" [Luke 23:34]. As our advocate with the Father, He is still making that same plea today—in
your behalf and in mine.

(Jeffrey R. Holland, "The Peaceable Things of the
Kingdom," *Ensign,* November 1996, 83)

Daily Living

You should remember that of all the liberating and exalting
doctrines that forgiveness is quintessential. It requires charity.

- ∞ Forgive others and encourage others to pray for forgiveness—
  1 Nephi 7:21

- ∞ Forgiveness comes from faith and repentance through the Lord
  Jesus Christ—Enos 1:5–8

- ∞ Confess and forsake your sins that you might be forgiven—
  Mosiah 26:29

- ∞ Remember that as often as you repent and seek forgiveness with
  real intent you will be forgiven—Moroni 6:8

HYPOCRISY

Moreover, when ye fast be not as the hypocrites, of a sad
countenance, for they disfigure their faces that they may appear
unto men to fast. Verily I say unto you, they have their reward.
But thou, when thou fastest, anoint thy head, and wash thy face;
That thou appear not unto men to fast, but unto thy Father,
who is in secret; and thy Father, who seeth in secret, shall
reward thee openly.
3 NEPHI 13:16–18

Nephi, an early American prophet, admonished his people: "Wherefore, my beloved brethren, I know that if ye shall follow the Son, with full purpose of heart, acting no hypocrisy and no deception before God, but with real intent, repenting of your sins, witnessing unto the Father that ye are willing to take upon you the name of Christ, by baptism . . . then shall ye receive the Holy Ghost . . . and then can ye speak with the tongue of angels, and shout praises unto the Holy One of Israel" (2 Ne. 31:13).

(Delbert L. Stapley, Conference Report, October 1968, 28)

Daily Living

STRIVE NOT TO BE SEEN OF THE WORLD OR EVEN SINGLED OUT BUT TO DO
GOOD SILENTLY.

- ୨ If you fail to help others after praying to so do your prayers are in vain—Alma 34:28

- ୨ Don't pray to be heard of men or to flaunt your wisdom—Alma 38:13

- ୨ Hypocrites tend to judge when they have beams in their own eye—3 Nephi 14:1–5

- ୨ Giving is righteous when done with real intent—Moroni 7:6

TREASURES AND YOUR HEART

*But lay up for yourselves treasures in heaven, where neither
moth nor rust doth corrupt, and where thieves do not break
through nor steal.
For where your treasure is, there will your heart be also.*
3 NEPHI 13:20–21

The Apostle Paul counseled young Timothy, "Charge them that are
rich in this world, that they be not highminded, nor trust in uncertain
riches, but in the living God, who giveth us richly all things to enjoy"
(1 Tim. 6:17). . . .
If allowed to become an object of worship or priority, money can
make us selfish and prideful, "puffed up in the vain things of the
world" (Alma 5:37).

(Dallin H. Oaks, "Spirituality," *Ensign,*
November 1985, 62–63)

Daily Living

YOU WILL KNOW WHAT YOUR TREASURE IS BY THE TIME, ATTENTION, AND
EFFORT YOU GIVE IT.

- ཞ Never despise others for their lack of material things—2 Nephi 9:30

- ཞ Remember to always seek the kingdom of God first—Jacob 2:18

- ཞ Remember you can't carry your riches with you in the hereafter—
  Alma 39:14

- ཞ Don't set your heart upon the vain things of the world—
  Helaman 7:21

- ཞ Rebel against God, and you will have no heavenly treasures—
  Helaman 8:25

POWER OF LIGHT

The light of the body is the eye; if, therefore, thine eye be single,
thy whole body shall be full of light.
But if thine eye be evil, thy whole body shall be full of darkness.
If, therefore, the light that is in thee be darkness, how great is
that darkness!

3 Nephi 13:22–23

To love God more than anything else impels us to take control of our priorities and order our lives so as to be in accord with Him. We come to love all of God's creations, including our fellowman. Placing God first in all things kindles greater love and devotion between husband and wife, parents and children. In Zion, we find "every man seeking the interest of his neighbor, and doing all things with an eye single to the glory of God" [D&C 82:19].

(Keith B. McMullin, "Come to Zion! Come to Zion!"
Ensign, November 2002, 94)

Daily Living

REMEMBER YOUR EYE ALLOWS THE LIGHT TO ENTER YOUR MIND AND YOUR VERY SOUL, HENCE IF IT IS SINGLE TO THE GLORY OF GOD YOUR WHOLE BODY WILL BE FILLED WITH LIGHT AND YOU WILL COMPREHEND ALL THINGS. IF NOT, YOU ARE LEFT IN DARKNESS.

- ✠ In unity you can look forward with one eye, being knit together—Mosiah 18:21

- ✠ Light is given to you from God if your eye is single to His glory—Mormon 8:15

- ✠ Let your light shine that others may glorify your Father in Heaven—3 Nephi 12:14–16

- ✠ Remember as disciples you are a light to others—3 Nephi 15:12

OCTOBER

ɞ

*And now, because of stiffneckedness
and unbelief they understood not my
word; therefore I was commanded to
say no more of the Father concerning
this thing unto them.*

—3 Nephi 15:18

SERVING GOD

No man can serve two masters; for either he will hate the one and love the other, or else he will hold to the one and despise the other. Ye cannot serve God and Mammon.

3 Nephi 13:24

The exact opposite of such vacillating is the life and character of the one to whom we should hold fast as the very ideal of integrity—Jesus Christ, the Savior, who taught that man cannot live a divided life, that he cannot serve both God and mammon, and that he cannot serve two masters. Not only were Christ's teachings directed to a oneness of purpose, but his own life was the personification of integrity. This virtue is one of our greatest needs today.

(N. Eldon Tanner, "Integrity," *Ensign,* May 1977, 15)

Daily Living

Your desires should be to God and He will prosper you according to your efforts. You do know right from wrong and need not make this the great debate.

- As you serve others you are serving God—Mosiah 2:16–18
- You cannot know the Lord unless you serve Him—Mosiah 5:13
- Choose ye this day, whom ye shall serve—Alma 30:8
- Your covenant of baptism suggests the determination to serve God—Moroni 6:3
- Serve God with all your heart, might, mind, and strength—D&C 4:2

THE KINGDOM OF GOD

But seek ye first the kingdom of God and his righteousness, and all these things shall be added unto you.

3 NEPHI 13:33

The youngest and the newest member can seek to build up the kingdom of God. . . . Even the smallest act to build faith in another person or in a family qualifies us for the gift and power of the Holy Ghost. The Holy Ghost testifies of truth. Therefore, in our service, our faith increases that Jesus is the Christ, that our Heavenly Father lives and loves us, and that Joseph was Their prophet. You can expect that, every time you go to a home to build faith, as a home teacher or a visiting teacher or a friend.

(Henry B. Eyring, "An Enduring Testimony of the Mission of the Prophet Joseph," *Ensign,* November 2003, 91)

Daily Living

SEEK TO BUILD UP THE KINGDOM OF GOD AND HIS RIGHTEOUSNESS AND ALL THE BLESSINGS OF GOD ARE YOURS.

- Saints who have believed and endured well shall inherit the kingdom—2 Nephi 9:18

- The doctrine of Christ is the way to eternal life—2 Nephi 31:20–21

- Seek for the kingdom of God before you seek for the riches of the world—Jacob 2:18

- Prophets and teachers teach things pertaining to the kingdom of God—Mosiah 18:18

- Help others as well as yourselves to repent that all might partake—Alma 9:12; 29:15–17

AS YE JUDGE

Jesus . . . did open his mouth unto them again, saying: Verily,
verily, I say unto you, Judge not, that ye be not judged.
For with what judgment ye judge, ye shall be judged; and with
what measure ye mete, it shall be measured to you again.
3 NEPHI 14:1–2

Coupled with such underlying philosophies, he (President Faust) knew that, although it was his job to argue a particular position, "not everything in life is black or white. There are other colors and shades of black or white. It is important that we not judge. I have learned in my many years in the arena of life that we don't always have all the facts, and that being slow to judge will save us from the effects of the principle enunciated by the Savior: 'Judge not, that ye be not judged.'"

(James P. Bell, *In the Strength of the Lord: The Life and Teachings of James E. Faust* [Salt Lake City: Deseret Book, 1999], 74)

Daily Living

BE EMPATHETIC, SLOW TO FIND FAULT—SIMPLY PUT, DON'T JUDGE ANYONE, AND REMEMBER THAT IF YOU DO JUDGE HARSHLY IT IS THE WAY THAT YOU WILL BE JUDGED.

- ‍ Remember that all are judged by God—1 Nephi 15:32–33

- ‍ Don't condemn or judge others for their poverty—Mosiah 4:22

- ‍ It is given to you the way to judge—Moroni 7:16

- ‍ Trust in the Spirit and you will judge righteously—Alma 41:14; D&C 11:12–13

SEE CLEARLY

And why beholdest thou the mote that is in thy brother's eye,
but considerest not the beam that is in thine own eye?
Or how wilt thou say to thy brother: Let me pull the mote out
of thine eye—and behold, a beam is in thine own eye?
Thou hypocrite, first cast the beam out of thine own eye; and
then shalt thou see clearly to cast the mote out of thy brother's eye.
3 Nephi 14:3–5

The discerning realize that it is not realistic to expect perfection in others when none of us is perfect. . . .

Meaningful progress can be made only when all of us can cast the motes out of our own eyes, leave judgment to our Father in Heaven, and lose ourselves in righteous living.

(Marvin J. Ashton, "Pure Religion," *Ensign,*
November 1982, 63–64)

Daily Living

As you seek to help another in a corrective manner be sure your heart is pure.

- ৪০ Reprove only when moved upon by the Holy Ghost—D&C 121:41–44

- ৪০ Never take offense when misjudged—Alma 61:9

- ৪০ Never judge without correct and true information—Alma 61:9

- ৪০ Judge not that ye be not judged—3 Nephi 14:1–2

- ৪০ Never judge rashly; remember, judgment is the Lord's—Mormon 8:19–20

ASK WITH EFFORT

Ask, and it shall be given unto you; seek, and ye shall find;
knock, and it shall be opened unto you.
For every one that asketh, receiveth; and he that seeketh, findeth;
and to him that knocketh, it shall be opened.

3 NEPHI 14:7–8

Wisdom comes through effort. All good things require effort. That which is worth having will cost part of your physical being, your intellectual power and your soul power. . . . But you have to seek, you have to knock. . . . Truth and wisdom are gained only by seeking, by prayer, and by effort.

(David O. Mckay, Conference Report, October 1965, 145)

Daily Living

DILIGENTLY DO YOUR PART TO BRING ABOUT YOUR REQUEST.

- ଔ Pray in faith believing that you will receive—Alma 22:16

- ଔ Pray in the name of Jesus Christ for that which is good with faith believing that you will receive and it will be done unto you—Moroni 7:26

- ଔ Pray with a sincere heart, with real intent having faith in Christ and it will be manifest unto you by the power of the Holy Ghost—Moroni 10:4

- ଔ Remember you must do more than simply ask—D&C 9:7–9

THE GOLDEN RULE

Therefore, all things whatsoever ye would that men should do to you, do ye even so to them, for this is the law and the prophets.
3 NEPHI 14:12

Wherever it is found and however it is expressed, the Golden Rule encompasses the moral code of the kingdom of God. It forbids interference by one with the rights of another. It is equally binding upon nations, associations, and individuals. With compassion and forbearance, it replaces the retaliatory reactions of an "eye for an eye, and a tooth for a tooth" [Matt. 5:38; see also Exodus 21:24–27; Leviticus 24:20]. If we were to stay on that old and unproductive path, we would be but blind and toothless [see Joseph Stein, *Fiddler on the Roof* (1964), 142].

(Russell M. Nelson, "Blessed Are the Peacemakers," *Ensign,* November 2002, 39)

Daily Living

SEEK TO LOVE OTHERS AS YOU WOULD BE LOVED.

- ꝏ Deal justly one to another and do good continually—Alma 41:14; 4 Nephi 1:2

- ꝏ Remember to love your enemies and those who seemingly persecute you—3 Nephi 12:44

- ꝏ Think of others like unto yourself—Jacob 2:17

- ꝏ Love and esteem your neighbor as yourself—Mosiah 23:15; 27:4

ACTIONS SPEAK

Wherefore, by their fruits ye shall know them.
3 NEPHI 14:20

The Savior gave the criteria for His friendship in the 15th chapter of John, in which He states, "Ye are my friends, if ye do whatsoever I command you" (v.14). He further gave the acid test when He said, "Ye shall know them by their fruits (vv. 7:16; see also 7:17–18, 20). This is how we will all be judged—by our fruits, good or bad. In the final judgment, if our fruits so warrant, we will be invited to sit on the right hand of God. There I believe will be His friends.

(Richard C. Edgley, "A Disciple, a Friend,"
Ensign, May 1998, 12)

Daily Living

ALL THAT YOU DO AND SAY REPRESENTS YOUR VALUE SYSTEM AND BELIEFS.

- ∞ Remember when you let your light shine and people see your good works it is for the purpose of glorifying Heavenly Father— 3 Nephi 12:16

- ∞ You will reap your reward according to your good works— Alma 9:28

- ∞ Seek to help others come unto Christ for in that labor you shall have much fruit—Alma 26:30–31

- ∞ Where is your joy and glory?—Alma 29:9–10; 31:34–35; 36:24

KNOWING GOD AND CHRIST

Not every one that saith unto me, Lord, Lord, shall enter into the kingdom of heaven; but he that doeth the will of my Father who is in heaven.

3 NEPHI 14:21

True disciples are those who go beyond simply believing. They act out their belief. Said the Savior, "If any man will do his will, he shall know of the doctrine, whether it be of God, or whether I speak of myself." (John 7:17). Disciples follow the Divine Master. Their actions speak in symphonic harmony with their beliefs. They know who they are. They know what God expects of them.

(James E. Faust, "The Resurrection," *Ensign,* May 1985, 30)

Daily Living

REMEMBER THAT DOING HIS WILL IS ABSOLUTELY ESSENTIAL TO KNOWING GOD.

- ✿ The scriptures help us know Heavenly Father and Jesus Christ—Jacob 4:4

- ✿ You come to know God as you repent—Alma 26:35; D&C 93:1

- ✿ All things testify that there is a God—Alma 30:44

- ✿ To know God, put away your fears and humble yourself—D&C 67:10

- ✿ The pure in heart see God in His holy temple—D&C 97:16

- ✿ Abide the law, stay on the strait and narrow path—D&C 132:21–24

- ✿ It is life eternal to know Heavenly Father and Jesus Christ—John 17:3

BE WISE

Therefore, whoso heareth these sayings of mine and doeth them, I will liken him unto a wise man, who built his house upon a rock.
3 NEPHI 14:24

If a person is humble, sincere, pure of heart, unselfish, and earnestly seeking to know and do God's will, surely the Lord will be inclined to hearken to his desire and respond to his faith. Contrariwise, God cannot be expected to inspire men who are out of harmony with his holy purposes and his own divine attributes.

(Lowell L. Bennion, *An Introduction to the Gospel* [Salt Lake City: The Deseret Sunday School Union Board, 1955], 88)

Daily Living

WHEN YOU HEARKEN (HEAR AND DO) AS THE SAVIOR TAUGHT IN THE SERMON AT THE TEMPLE YOU WILL BE WISE AND BUILD UPON THE LORD.

- "Be wise; what can I say more?"—Jacob 6:12

- Be wise in the days of your probation and serve God—Mormon 9:28

- Hearken to the word of God and avoid temptation—D&C 15:24

- Hearken to the voice of the Lord—Alma 5:37–38, 60

- If you fail to hearken to the words of Christ you stand under condemnation—D&C 28:34–35

REMEMBER THE WORDS OF CHRIST

*And now it came to pass that when Jesus had ended these sayings
he cast his eyes round about on the multitude, and said unto
them: Behold, ye have heard the things which I taught before I
ascended to my Father; therefore, whoso remembereth these sayings of mine and doeth them, him will I raise up at the last day.*
3 NEPHI 15:1

Nephi taught his brothers, "Whoso would hearken unto the word of
God, and would hold fast unto it, they would never perish; neither
could the temptations and the fiery darts of the adversary overpower
them unto blindness, to lead them away to destruction" (1 Nephi 15:24).
Then he gave this example of how to teach: "I did exhort them with
all the energies of my soul, and with all the faculty which I possessed,
that they would give heed to the word of God and remember to keep
his commandments always in all things" (v. 25).

(Richard G. Scott, "To Help a Loved One in Need,"
Ensign, May 1988, 60)

Daily Living

STRIVE TO DO AS YOU HAVE BEEN COMMANDED.

- ᔆ The prophets admonish you to give heed to the word—1 Nephi 15:25; Alma 46:23

- ᔆ As you keep the commandments you shall prosper—Alma 50:20

- ᔆ It is upon the rock of our Redeemer that you must build your foundation—Helaman 5:12

- ᔆ As you remember Jesus Christ you can have His Spirit to be with you—Moroni 4:3; 5:2

THE LAW AND THE LIGHT

*Behold, I am the law, and the light. Look unto me, and endure
to the end, and ye shall live; for unto him that endureth to the
end will I give eternal life.*

3 NEPHI 15:9

Let us try to live our religion, and try to be friends of God; and let us
make war against the works of the devil. Let us seek to overcome ourselves, and all our evil impressions, and bring our bodies in subjection
to the law of Christ, that we may walk in the light of the Lord, gain
power with him, and assist in sanctifying the earth and in building up
temples, and in attending to the ordinances of the house of God, that
we may be saviors of men, both of the living and the dead. These are
our privileges, and the blessings which the God of heaven has put into
our hands.

(Wilford Woodruff, quoted in Heber J. Grant,
Conference Report, April 1933, 13)

Daily Living

SEEK TO KEEP THE COMMANDMENTS AND ENDURE TO THE END.

- ಲ Look to Christ, hearken to His commandments, and be faithful—
2 Nephi 2:28

- ಲ Press forward with a steadfastness in Christ with hope and the
love of God always feasting upon His words and you shall have
eternal life—2 Nephi 31:20

- ಲ Look to the Lord, keep the commandments and endure to the
end—Alma 38:2

- ಲ Remember that Christ is the light and life of the world—Alma
38:9

- ಲ The Lord leadeth you to do good—Ether 4:12

SEEK TO UNDERSTAND

Therefore, go ye unto your homes, and ponder upon the things which I have said, and ask of the Father, in my name, that ye may understand, and prepare your minds for the morrow, and I come unto you again.

3 NEPHI 17:3

Pondering is more than reading words; it is searching for meanings that will help us as we relate to one another and as we make choices in our lives. It is allowing the word to move from our minds to our hearts. The Spirit bears witness to our hearts as we prayerfully seek to know the things of our Heavenly Father. When we have that witness and knowledge, we think and live and relate to each other in more Christlike ways.

(Anne G. Wirthlin, "Teaching Our Children to Love the Scriptures," *Ensign,* May 1998, 10)

Daily Living

WHEN YOU PONDER THE THINGS OF GOD AND SEEK TO UNDERSTAND THEM YOU WILL PRAY WITH FAITH.

- Ponder in your heart, seeking to understand—1 Nephi 11:1

- Ponder the scriptures for your profit and learning—1 Nephi 19:23; 2 Nephi 4:15–16

- Ponder upon the things the Lord has taught you—Helaman 10:2–5

- Ponder the goodness and mercy of God in your hearts—Moroni 10:3

- The eyes of your understanding can be opened—D&C 138:1, 11

JOY OF THE SAVIOR

And they arose from the earth, and he said unto them: Blessed
are ye because of your faith. And now behold, my joy is full.
3 Nephi 17:20

There are both tears of sorrow and tears of joy (D&C 128:23).
When the heart is touched with feelings of tenderness, compassion,
and love, tears of joy may flow. The resurrected Lord, ministering
among the Nephites, beholding their supreme faith and devotion,
said: "Blessed are ye because of your faith. And now behold, my joy
is full. And when he had said these words, I wept, and the multitude
bare record of it" (3 Ne. 17:20–21).

(Bruce R. McConkie, *Mormon Doctrine,* 2nd ed. [Salt Lake
City: Bookcraft, 1966], 833)

Daily Living

FAITH ALWAYS MOVES YOU TO ACTION, ESPECIALLY TO REPENTANCE.

- ‽ The joy of your Savior is great over a soul that repenteth—
  D&C 18:13

- ‽ You can experience the joy of helping others come unto Christ—
  Alma 26:11, 16, 30; Alma 29:9–10

- ‽ Remember the work and glory of your Heavenly Father and
  Savior is your immortality and eternal life—Moses 1:39

- ‽ Faith will always move you to repentance—Alma 34:15–17

- ‽ It is impossible to please God without faith—Hebrews 11:6

THE SACRAMENT

And this shall ye do in remembrance of my body, which I have shown unto you. And it shall be a testimony unto the Father that ye do always remember me. And if ye do always remember me ye shall have my Spirit to be with you.
3 NEPHI 18:7

And we are not only to partake of the emblems of the sacrament in remembrance of the Redeemer, testifying that we do always remember him, but we are also thereby to witness unto the Father that we are willing to take upon us the name of his Son and that we will keep his commandments. This amounts to a virtual renewal of the covenant of baptism, for you will recall that candidates for baptism are, among other things, to ". . . witness before the church that they . . . are willing to take upon them the name of Jesus Christ, having a determination to serve him to the end" (D&C 20:37).
(Marion G. Romney, Conference Report, April 1946, 40)

Daily Living

PARTAKE OF THE BREAD OR WATER, AND COVENANT TO ALWAYS REMEMBER OUR SAVIOR.

- ဢ Always be worthy to partake of the sacrament—3 Nephi 18:29

- ဢ You renew your covenants as you partake of the sacrament—Moroni 4:3; 5:2

- ဢ Ponder your baptismal covenants—Moroni 6:1–4; Mosiah 18:8–9; D&C 20:37

- ဢ You partake of the sacrament to help you remember your covenants—Moroni 6:6

AVOIDING TEMPTATION

Behold, verily, verily, I say unto you, ye must watch and pray always lest ye enter into temptation; for Satan desireth to have you, that he may sift you as wheat.
3 NEPHI 18:18

Prayer is one of the greatest blessings we have while here on earth. Through prayer we can communicate with our Heavenly Father and seek His guidance daily. Jesus taught, "Ye must always pray unto the Father in my name" (3 Ne. 18:19). We should pray each day that we will have the power to resist temptation. Amulek teaches us that we should pray "morning, mid-day, and evening" and that our hearts should "be full, drawn out in prayer unto [God] continually" (Alma 34:21, 27). Our daily prayers influence our thoughts, our words, and our actions. In order to retain a remission of our sins, it is essential that we ask our Heavenly Father each day for strength to stay in the straight and narrow way.

(Keith Crockett, "Retaining a Remission of Sin," *Ensign,* November 2000, 78)

Daily Living

WATCH AND PRAY TO OVERCOME TEMPTATION.

- ༇ The Lord can strengthen you as you hold fast to the word of God—1 Nephi 15:24; Helaman 3:29

- ༇ The Lord will nurture you in all your trials and afflictions—Alma 7:11–12

- ༇ Humble yourself and pray to not be tempted above that which you can bear—Alma 13:28

- ༇ Be wise in your probation; be firm and unshaken—Mormon 9:28

FAMILY PRAYER

*Pray in your families unto the Father, always in my name, that
your wives and your children may be blessed.*
3 Nephi 18:21

Be consistent in holding daily family prayer and weekly family home
evenings. Both of these invite the Lord's Spirit, which provides the
help and power we need as parents and family leaders. The Church
curriculum and magazines have many good ideas for family home
evening. Also consider holding a family testimony meeting where
parents and children can express their beliefs and feelings to each
other in a private and personal setting.

(M. Russell Ballard, "What Matters Most Is What Lasts
Longest," *Ensign,* November 2005, 43)

Daily Living

GATHER YOUR CHILDREN AROUND YOU AND KNEEL TOGETHER IN PRAYER.

- ❧ Parents should teach their children to pray and to walk uprightly
  before the Lord—D&C 68:28

- ❧ The scriptures continually admonish you to pray—Mosiah 4:11

- ❧ The prayers of the family and others call down the blessings of
  Heaven—Mosiah 27:14

- ❧ Establish a house of prayer—D&C 88:119

INVITE ALL TO COME UNTO CHRIST

And behold, ye shall meet together oft; and ye shall not forbid any man from coming unto you when ye shall meet together, but suffer them that they may come unto you and forbid them not; But ye shall pray for them, and shall not cast them out; and if it so be that they come unto you oft ye shall pray for them unto the Father, in my name.

3 Nephi 18:22–23

Make friends with your neighbors, watch out for each other, and help build a spirit of unity, peace, and love among them. These may seem like small things, but I assure you, if we do these kinds of things, they may be every bit as effective in keeping people away from evil and crime as whittling and whistling were in the days of Nauvoo. True friendship may well be the best thing that we can do to help reach those who may be drifting toward unsafe and morally damaging activities and counterfeit forms of belonging.

(M. Russell Ballard, "Standing for Truth and Right," *Ensign,* November 1997, 39)

Daily Living

REACH OUT TO ALL, AND PRAY THAT THEY MIGHT COME UNTO HIM.

- Fast and pray for all those who know not God—Alma 6:6
- The Lord invites all to come unto Him—2 Nephi 26:25, 33; 3 Nephi 18:25
- The prophets and the scriptures persuade all to come unto Christ—1 Nephi 6:4; Jacob 1:7
- Work with all your heart to help those who are struggling to return—Alma 31:34–35
- You never know when someone might repent and return to the fold—3 Nephi 18:32

CHRIST IS THE LIGHT

Therefore, hold up your light that it may shine unto the world.
Behold I am the light which ye shall hold up—that which ye
have seen me do. Behold ye see that I have prayed unto the
Father, and ye all have witnessed.
3 Nephi 18:24

Young women, mothers, leaders, let us all be filled—filled with the light, the strength, the faith that comes from prayer, scripture study, and obedience to Gods commandments each day of our lives. Let us stand united together, shoulder to shoulder, heart to heart, and hand in hand, bonded together by that light that never grows dim. We'll hold our torches high that Christ's true light through us will shine, His name to glorify.

(Ardeth G. Kapp, "Stand for Truth and Righteousness,"
Ensign, November 1988, 95)

Daily Living

You must pray to be an instrument in the Lord's hands.

- ৪ Let your light shine that it may glorify your Heavenly Father—3 Nephi 12:16

- ৪ Remember that you, as a disciple of Christ, are a light to the world—3 Nephi 15:12

- ৪ The Lord is the light and life of the world—Ether 4:12

- ৪ Remember that your eye must always be single to the glory of God and your whole body will be filled with light and you can comprehend all things—D&C 88:67

PARTAKING OF THE SACRAMENT UNWORTHILY

*And now behold, this is the commandment which I give unto
you, that ye shall not suffer any one knowingly to partake of my
flesh and blood unworthily, when ye shall minister it;
For whoso eateth and drinketh my flesh and blood unworthily
eateth and drinketh damnation to his soul; therefore if ye know
that a man is unworthy to eat and drink of my flesh and blood
ye shall forbid him.*

3 NEPHI 18:28–29

When you were baptized, you became participants in the first great
hope, the Atonement of Christ. Every time you worthily partake of
the sacrament, you have the opportunity to begin again and do a little better. It is like burying the old, unworthy part of yourself and
starting over with a new life.

(Julie B. Beck, "There Is Hope Smiling Brightly before Us,"
Ensign, May 2003, 103)

Daily Living

PARTAKING OF THE SACRAMENT IS A COVENANT-MAKING AND
STRENGTHENING EXPERIENCE.

- ∞ Repent and be worthy to renew your covenants—2 Nephi 30:2;
  Alma 7:15

- ∞ Worthily partake of the sacrament in the name of Jesus Christ—
  Mormon 9:29

- ∞ Do not partake of the sacrament unworthily—1 Corinthians
  11:27–29

- ∞ To be worthy you should have a godly walk—D&C 20:68–69

TEACH THE WORDS OF CHRIST

And when they had ministered those same words which Jesus had spoken—nothing varying from the words which Jesus had spoken—behold, they knelt again and prayed to the Father in the name of Jesus.

3 NEPHI 19:8

The power of the Holy Ghost will then enable us to "speak with the tongue of angels," which, . . . is to speak under the influence of the Holy Ghost, to teach correctly the words of Christ, and to "shout praises unto the Holy One of Israel" (2 Ne. 31:13; 32:2).

(Bruce A. Van Orden, in *Doctrines of the Book of Mormon: 1991 Sperry Symposium,* ed. Bruce A. Van Orden and Brent L. Top [Salt Lake City: Deseret Book, 1992], 215)

Daily Living

TEACH THE WORDS OF CHRIST AS DIRECTED BY THE HOLY GHOST; HE WILL SUPPLY THEM WHEN WE NEED THEM.

෨ Speak the words that the Lord will put into your heart— Helaman 13:4–5; D&C 100:5–6

෨ Preach the word that a mighty change may take place—Alma 5:13

෨ Remember that the word has the greatest power to cause change—Alma 31:5

෨ Preach the word according to the spirit of prophecy—Alma 43:1–2

෨ Treasure up the word of God—D&C 84:85

WHAT YOU SHOULD DESIRE MOST

*And they did pray for that which they most desired; and they
desired that the Holy Ghost should be given unto them.*
3 NEPHI 19:9

Now I desire that I may speak under the influence of the Holy Ghost,
because I never feel satisfied in my soul when I am called upon to
address a congregation, unless I can feel that the Spirit of God is with
me. When I do know that, then I feel measurably satisfied, although
I am occasionally somewhat dissatisfied with myself when I sit down;
but when I realize that the Spirit of God has been with me, and particularly when I feel that I was inspired to say the things that came to
my mind, then I am satisfied, and I glorify and praise the Lord.
(Charles W. Penrose, Conference Report, October 1917, 18)

Daily Living

YOU SHOULD PRAY FOR THE BLESSING OF THE HOLY GHOST IN YOUR LIFE
FOR HE SHOWS YOU ALL THINGS WHAT YOU SHOULD DO, COMFORTS,
DIRECTS, TESTIFIES OF THE THINGS OF GOD.

- The Holy Ghost will show you all things to do—2 Nephi 32:5

- You are sanctified by the power of the Holy Ghost—3 Nephi
  27:20

- The Holy Ghost as the Comforter fills you with hope and perfect
  love—Moroni 8:26

- The Holy Ghost makes known the truth of all things—Moroni
  10:5

- Trust in the Spirit which leadeth to do good—D&C 11:12–13

GIFT OF THE HOLY GHOST

Father, I thank thee that thou hast given the Holy Ghost unto these whom I have chosen; and it is because of their belief in me that I have chosen them out of the world.
3 NEPHI 19:20

Heavenly Father has given you the gift of the Holy Ghost to be available to help you whenever you earnestly seek Him. Like Nephi, you can know what to do to build according to the Lord's plan for you. You will want to invite this power to help you navigate through the challenges of mortality until you are safely home.
(Sharon G. Larsen, "Your Celestial Guide,"
Ensign, May 2001, 86)

Daily Living

SEEK THE COMPANIONSHIP OF THE THIRD MEMBER OF THE GODHEAD.

- ∞ The gift of the Holy Ghost is given to those who have faith in Christ—1 Nephi 10:17

- ∞ When you are born of God you can receive the Holy Ghost—Alma 36:24

- ∞ The Holy Ghost will help you conduct your meetings—Moroni 6:9

- ∞ The gifts of the Spirit are many and will bless your life—Moroni 10:4–25

PURIFIED

Father, I thank thee that thou hast purified those whom I have chosen, because of their faith, and I pray for them, and also for them who shall believe on their words, that they may be purified in me, through faith on their words, even as they are purified in me.

3 Nephi 19:28

That is what it means in Moroni when it says, "Relying alone upon the merits of Christ, who was the author and the finisher of their faith" (6:4). It is the Savior who made possible our being purified through His Atonement and our obedience to His commandments. And it is the Savior who will nourish those who go down in faith into the waters of baptism and receive the gift of the Holy Ghost. When they always remember Him, and when they continue in childlike obedience, it is He who will assure that they have His Spirit always to be with them.

(Henry B. Eyring, "Feed My Lambs,"
Ensign, November 1997, 84)

Daily Living

REMEMBER HIM THROUGH OBEDIENCE AND SEEK TO BE PURE BEFORE HIM.

- ଚ You can be purified as you are forgiven through the Atonement of the Lord Jesus Christ—Mosiah 4:2

- ଚ You are cleansed through the Atonement of the Lord Jesus Christ as you repent and are baptized you become sanctified by the Holy Ghost—3 Nephi 27:19–20

- ଚ You can become pure even as the Lord Jesus Christ as you pray for charity—Moroni 7:48

- ଚ Deny yourself of all ungodliness and become perfected in Christ—Moroni 10:32–33

GREAT FAITH

So great faith have I never seen among all the Jews; wherefore I could not show unto them so great miracles, because of their unbelief.
Verily I say unto you, there are none of them that have seen so great things as ye have seen; neither have they heard so great things as ye have heard.
3 NEPHI 19:35–36

Wilford Woodruff claimed the Book of Mormon promise that "God has provided a means that man, through faith, might work mighty miracles; therefore he becometh a great benefit to his fellow beings" [Mosiah 8:18]. My young brethren of the Aaronic Priesthood, I would remind you that our Father in Heaven not only wants you to be good, but to be good for something, to serve and bless the lives of others, and to become a benefit to your fellow beings.

(Spencer J. Condie, "Becoming a Great Benefit to Our Fellow Beings," *Ensign,* May 2002, 44)

Daily Living

FAITH CANNOT BE PASSIVE OR CASUAL; IF IT IS ACCOMPANIED BY REAL INTENT AND ACTION, THEN YOU RECEIVE THE THINGS OF GOD.

- ☙ According to your faith you receive miracles, signs, and wonders—2 Nephi 26:13

- ☙ You can be forgiven and your guilt swept away through faith—Enos 1:8

- ☙ You received additional strength according to your faith—Alma 14:26

- ☙ With faith in the Lord you can do all things that are expedient in Him—Moroni 7:33

PRAYER IN OUR HEARTS

And it came to pass that he commanded the multitude that they should cease to pray, and also his disciples. And he commanded them that they should not cease to pray in their hearts.
3 Nephi 20:1

The Savior has told us that we need not multiply words when we pray. The diligence in prayer which God requires does not take flowery speech nor long hours of solitude. That is taught clearly in Alma in the Book of Mormon: "Yea, and when you do not cry unto the Lord, let your hearts be full, drawn out in prayer unto him continually for your welfare, and also for the welfare of those who are around you" [Alma 34:27]. Our hearts can only be drawn out to God when they are filled with love for Him and trust in His goodness. Joseph Smith, even as a boy, gave us an example of how we can come to pray from a heart filled with the love of God and then pray unceasingly through a life filled with trials and blessings.

(Henry B. Eyring, "Prayer," *Ensign*, November 2001, 16)

Daily Living

YOU CANNOT PRAY VERBALLY THROUGHOUT THE DAY; HOWEVER, WITHIN YOUR HEART SHOULD BE THIS YEARNING PRAYER TO YOUR HEAVENLY FATHER FOR YOUR RIGHTEOUS DESIRES.

- ഇ Remember as you pray verbally pray with all your heart—1 Nephi 1:5

- ഇ Let your heart be drawn out in prayer—Alma 34:27

- ഇ Lift up your heart in faith that you might be delivered—D&C 30:6

- ഇ Remember, the Lord knows your heart—D&C 112:11

FILLED WITH THE SPIRIT

*And he said unto them: He that eateth this bread eateth of my
body to his soul; and he that drinketh of this wine drinketh of
my blood to his soul; and his soul shall never hunger nor thirst,
but shall be filled.*
*Now, when the multitude had all eaten and drunk, behold,
they were filled with the Spirit; and they did cry out with one
voice, and gave glory to Jesus, whom they both saw and heard.*
3 Nephi 20:8–9

I knelt in prayer, asking my Heavenly Father to manifest to me, through
the power of the Holy Ghost, whether or not The Church of Jesus
Christ of Latter-day Saints is the true Church. I made this a matter of
prayer for several days; then I went to a sacrament meeting. As the sacrament was being passed, I was filled with the Spirit of the Lord, and my
bosom burned within me. I knew the Lord had answered my prayers. I
knew this was the restored gospel of Jesus Christ.

(Hartman Rector Jr., and Connie Rector, *No More Strangers*
[Salt Lake City: Bookcraft, 1971–1978], 1:125)

Daily Living

SEEK THE SPIRIT THAT YOU MAY RECEIVE DIRECTION AND COMFORT.

- ‿ According to your faith the Spirit can give you knowledge and
  power—Alma 18:35

- ‿ When you keep His commandments you can have His Spirit
  with you—Moroni 4:3; 5:2

- ‿ The fruits of the Spirit are love, peace, joy, longsuffering, gentleness—Galatians 5:22–2

- ‿ The Holy Ghost is the great Comforter—John 15:26; Acts 9:31;
  Moroni 8:26

COMING OF ELIJAH

And he shall turn the heart of the fathers to the children, and the heart of the children to their fathers, lest I come and smite the earth with a curse.

3 Nephi 25:6

Joseph also unfolded in Nauvoo additional knowledge regarding salvation for the dead and initiated a program of redeeming the dead. Moreover, in the early 1840s he taught distinct doctrines regarding the mission, keys, and sealing power of Elijah and taught the Saints that one of their major responsibilities was to seek after their dead. Every year, between 1840 and 1844, the Prophet delivered major discourses on that theme and before his martyrdom associated Elijah's mission with temple ordinances.

(Milton V. Backman Jr., "Restoration of Tradition of
Temples: A Distinct Contribution of," *LDS Church News,*
11 June 1994)

Daily Living

Seek to bless your family and those who have gone on through temple work.

   ⁖ What you bind on earth shall be bound in Heaven—D&C 128:10

   ⁖ You cannot be perfected without perfecting the dead—D&C 128:15

   ⁖ There must be a welding link between the fathers and the children—D&C 128:18

   ⁖ There must be a record of the dead kept—D&C 128:24

FOUNDATION OF CHURCH . . . THE GOSPEL

*But if it be called in my name then it is my church, if it so be
that they are built upon my gospel.
Verily I say unto you, that ye are built upon my gospel; therefore
ye shall call whatsoever things ye do call, in my name; therefore
if ye call upon the Father, for the church, if it be in my name
the Father will hear you.*

3 Nephi 27:8–9

If we are founded upon a rock, the gates of hell shall not prevail against us. As long as we remain in our house of faith, we shall be preserved when the rains of evil fall, when the winds of false doctrine blow, and when the floods of carnality beat upon us.

Thanks be to God that we, as Latter-day Saints, are founded upon a rock. And so it is that the faithful among us hear a calm voice of quiet certainty saying: "If ye shall build up my church, upon the foundation of my gospel and my rock, the gates of hell shall not prevail against you" [D&C 18:5].

(Bruce R. McConkie, "Upon This Rock,"
Ensign, May 1981, 75)

Daily Living

Seek to do all things in and through Jesus Christ, the gospel's
foundation.

- ৪০ Build up the Lord which is a sure foundation which cannot fall—Helaman 5:12

- ৪০ The Lord is the rock of your salvation—2 Nephi 4:30; 9:45

- ৪০ Build upon the doctrine of Christ, the rock—3 Nephi 11:39–40

- ৪০ Remember the rock, the gospel, is centered in the Atonement—3 Nephi 27:13–14

GOSPEL OF JESUS CHRIST

*Behold I have given unto you my gospel, and this is the gospel
which I have given unto you—that I came into the world to do
the will of my Father, because my Father sent me.
And my Father sent me that I might be lifted up upon the cross;
and after that I had been lifted up upon the cross, that I might
draw all men unto me, that as I have been lifted up by men even
so should men be lifted up by the Father, to stand before me, to be
judged of their works, whether they be good or whether they be evil*

3 NEPHI 27:13–14

Although we can have testimonies of many things as members of the
Church, there are basic truths we need to constantly teach one
another and share with those not of our faith. Testify God is our
Father and Jesus is the Christ. The plan of salvation is centered on
the Savior's Atonement. Joseph Smith restored the fulness of the
everlasting gospel of Jesus Christ, and the Book of Mormon is evidence that our testimony is true.

(M. Russell Ballard, "Pure Testimony," *Ensign,*
November 2004, 41)

Daily Living

REMEMBER THAT THE CORE OF THE GOSPEL IS JESUS CHRIST AND HIS
ATONING SACRIFICE. THROUGH THE POWER OF THE ATONEMENT YOU ARE
DRAWN TO CHRIST.

- ಏ The gospel is "the good news"—Isaiah 52:7; 61:1; Romans 10:15

- ಏ You are drawn to Christ by gratitude for the Atonement—3 Nephi
27:13–14

- ಏ You must repent, be baptized, and receive the Holy Ghost—
3 Nephi 27:19–21

APPLYING THE GOSPEL TO OUR LIVES

Now this is the commandment: Repent, all ye ends of the earth,
and come unto me and be baptized in my name, that ye may be
sanctified by the reception of the Holy Ghost, that ye may stand
spotless before me at the last day.
Verily, verily, I say unto you, this is my gospel; and ye know the
things that ye must do in my church; for the works which ye
have seen me do that shall ye also do; for that which ye have
seen me do even that shall ye do.

3 Nephi 27:20–21

And the life that is to make us happy is the life that conforms to the teachings of the gospel of Jesus Christ, our Lord. Let us see to it that wherever we go we teach by precept the gospel of repentance, and by our conduct live the gospel of repentance and faith in God;

(George Albert Smith, Conference Report,
October 1944, 98)

Daily Living

You must repent and be baptized and do the works of Christ, thus becoming sanctified by the Holy Ghost, becoming clean and pure before the Lord.

- ๛ Be even as the Lord Jesus Christ is—3 Nephi 27:27

- ๛ Seek to become like the Lord and your Heavenly Father—3 Nephi 12:48

- ๛ In JST the prophet notes that the gospel was in fact the word, even the Lord Jesus Christ—JST, John 1:1, 4

- ๛ Apply the gospel as you liken the word of God to your life—1 Nephi 19:23

JUDGMENT

And behold, all things are written by the Father; therefore out of the books which shall be written shall the world be judged.
3 NEPHI 27:26

I thought of the scripture in Revelation in which John saw the books opened, "and the dead were judged out of those things which were written in the books, according to their works" (Rev. 20:12). It was a most sobering experience.

(J. Richard Clarke, "Hold Up Your Light," *Ensign*, May 1985, 74)

Daily Living

YOU MUST SEARCH THE SCRIPTURES THAT YOU MIGHT KNOW ALL THINGS YOU SHOULD DO.

- ఴ You should live by every word that proceedeth forth from the mouth of God—D&C 84:44

- ఴ The word of God will literally be the basis of your judgment— 2 Nephi 25:18

- ఴ You must search and understand the word for it can condemn you at the last day—2 Nephi 33:14

- ఴ You will stand before God and be judged according to your deeds—Alma 5:15

NOVEMBER

☙

Behold, I say unto you that whoso believeth in Christ, doubting nothing, whatsoever he shall ask the Father in the name of Christ it shall be granted him; and this promise is unto all, even unto the ends of the earth.

—MORMON 9:21

HEAVENS REJOICE

*And now, behold, my joy is great, even unto fulness, because of
you, and also this generation; yea, and even the Father rejoiceth,
and also all the holy angels, because of you and this generation;
for none of them are lost.*

3 NEPHI 27:30

Revelations and translations also came regarding God's central purpose
"to bring to pass the immortality and eternal life of man," giving us
divine, succinct reassurances (see Moses 1:39). God's plans for the development of souls have not changed. They were described to ancient
Israel, whose 40 years in the wilderness were "to humble thee, and to
prove thee, to know what was in thine heart, whether thou wouldest
keep his commandments, or no" (Deut. 8:2). Therefore, disciples today
can understand why our faith and patience are tried at times—so that
we can be prepared to go Home (see Mosiah 23:21).

(Neal A. Maxwell, "How Choice a Seer!"
Ensign, November 2003, 100)

Daily Living

REALIZE THAT HEAVENLY FATHER IS GLORIFIED BY YOUR RIGHTEOUS SUCCESS.

- ෨ The work and glory of Heavenly Father is your immortality and
eternal life—Moses 1:39

- ෨ The worth of souls is great in the sight of the Lord—D&C
18:10

- ෨ Heavenly Father's plan is a plan for your happiness—Mosiah
2:41; Alma 42:16

- ෨ If you are true and faithful you receive all the Father has—
D&C 84:38

THE THREE NEPHITES

Ye have desired that ye might bring the souls of men unto me, while the world shall stand.
And for this cause ye shall have fulness of joy; and ye shall sit down in the kingdom of my Father; yea, your joy shall be full, even as the Father hath given me fulness of joy; and ye shall be even as I am, and I am even as the Father; and the Father and I are one.

3 NEPHI 28:9–10

The full-time missionaries and all others engaged in the work of the Lord have answered His call. We are on His errand. We shall succeed in the solemn charge given by Mormon to declare the Lord's word among the people. Wrote Mormon: "Behold, I am a disciple of Jesus Christ, the Son of God. I have been called of him to declare his word among his people, that they might have everlasting life" [3 Ne. 5:13].

(Thomas S. Monson, "Today Determines Tomorrow," *Ensign,* November 1998, 50)

Daily Living

STRIVE TO BRING OTHERS TO KNOW THE SAVIOR.

- Your glory and joy is help souls come unto Christ through repentance—Alma 29:9–10

- You want others to taste of the joy that you feel—Alma 36:24

- Go ye into all the world, and preach the gospel to every creature—Mormon 9:22

- The thing of most worth is to declare repentance—D&C 15:6

- How great will be your joy—D&C 18:13–16

HEED THE WORDS OF OUR PROPHETS

And wo be unto him that will not hearken unto the words of Jesus, and also to them whom he hath chosen and sent among them; for whoso receiveth not the words of Jesus and the words of those whom he hath sent receiveth not him; and therefore he will not receive them at the last day;
And it would be better for them if they had not been born.
3 NEPHI 28:34–35

As people heed the words of the prophets, the Lord blesses them. When they disregard His word, however, distress and suffering often follow. Over and over, the Book of Mormon teaches this great lesson. In its pages we read of the ancient inhabitants of the American continent who, because of their righteousness, were blessed of the Lord and became prosperous. Yet often this prosperity turned into a curse in that it caused them to "harden their hearts, and . . . forget the Lord their God" [Hel. 12:2].

(Joseph B. Wirthlin, "Journey to Higher Ground,"
Ensign, October 2005, 16)

Daily Living

YOU STAND IN JEOPARDY IF YOU FAIL TO HEED THE WORDS OF THE LORD'S SERVANTS.

-   Hearken to the words of the prophets—Jacob 5:2

-   The prophets speak the word of God—Helaman 5:18; D&C 68:3–7

-   Remember that the prophets preach and teach the word of God—Alma 31:5

-   The prophets admonish us with the word of God—Jarom 1:10

-   Beware of rejecting the words of the prophets—Ether 11:13

POWER OF THE LOVE OF GOD

And it came to pass that there was no contention
in the land, because of the love of God which did dwell
in the hearts of the people.
4 NEPHI 1:15

Responding to true love is part of our very being. We innately desire to reconnect here with the love we felt there. Only as we feel God's love and fill our hearts with His love can we be truly happy.

God's love fills the immensity of space; therefore, there is no shortage of love in the universe, only in our willingness to do what is needed to feel it. To do this, Jesus explained we must "love the Lord thy God with all thy heart . . . soul . . . strength, and . . . mind; and thy neighbour as thyself" (Luke 10:27).

The more we obey God, the more we desire to help others. The more we help others, the more we love God and on and on.

(John H. Groberg, "The Power of God's Love,"
Ensign, November 2004, 9)

Daily Living

RECEIVE THE LOVE OF GOD AND HELP OTHERS TO KNOW HE LOVES THEM.

- ෂ You must hold to the iron rod—1 Nephi 11:25

- ෂ Press forward with steadfastness, feasting upon His word—2 Nephi 31:20

- ෂ Remember the goodness and mercy of God—Mosiah 4:12

- ෂ Happiness is always determined by the love of God—4 Nephi 1:15–16

LOSS OF THE HOLY GHOST

And there were no gifts from the Lord, and the Holy Ghost did not come upon any, because of their wickedness and unbelief.
MORMON 1:14

Wickedness invariably leads to a suppression of conscience, until a person could lose all influence of the Lord's Spirit. (See 2 Ne. 26:11; Ether 2:15.) However, a full awareness of sin will smite a person when in the presence of the Lord or his power. (See Alma 12:1; 29:5; 42:18.) Ideally, sinful people will recognize their spiritual shortages and repent so they can regain the Spirit that they enjoyed in their innocence. (See D&C 1:32–34.) Thus, even though a person has been evil, a change of attitude and behavior accompanied by a remission of sins can lead to a restoration of peace and conscience. (See Heb. 9:14; Mosiah 4:3.)

(Victor L. Ludlow, *Principles and Practices of the Restored Gospel* [Salt Lake City: Deseret Book, 1992], 194)

Daily Living

BEWARE LEST YOU LOSE THIS PRECIOUS GIFT.

- ❧ Through wickedness the Spirit will cease to strive with you—2 Nephi 26:10–11

- ❧ If you harden your heart the Spirit has no place in you—2 Nephi 33:2

- ❧ Break the commandments and you withdraw yourself from the Spirit—Mosiah 2:36

- ❧ The Holy Spirit will not dwell in unholy temples—Helaman 4:24

RECOGNIZE THE BLESSINGS OF GOD

And I did cry unto this people, but it was in vain; and they did not realize that it was the Lord that had spared them, and granted unto them a chance for repentance. And behold they did harden their hearts against the Lord their God.
MORMON 3:3

Yes, we need to pause and ponder and meditate upon the glorious privileges and opportunities which are ours. And I say, what is being developed in the way of integrity, thoughtfulness? Are we sharing with others all the glorious principles of the gospel? There is a prayer in my heart this morning: Oh God, always help me to be thankful, and to be mindful of the source of all my blessings, and recognize the privilege which is mine to share with others.

(John Longden, "Are You Doing the Best You Can?" in *BYU Speeches of the Year 1961,* 22 March 1961, 3)

Daily Living

REMEMBER TO ACKNOWLEDGE YOUR HEAVENLY FATHER AND SAVIOR IN ALL THINGS AND YOU WILL BE PRESERVED AND CONTINUALLY BLESSED.

ↈ Delight in the things of the Lord and ponder his goodness— 2 Nephi 4:16

ↈ You can never return enough thanks for you are continually blessed—Mosiah 2:20

ↈ Give thanks in all things—Mosiah 26:39

ↈ Live in thanksgiving daily for His tender mercies—Alma 34:38

BLESSINGS CAN BE WITHHELD

*Behold, I had led them, notwithstanding their wickedness I had
led them many times to battle, and had loved them, according
to the love of God which was in me, with all my heart; and my
soul had been poured out in prayer unto my God all the day
long for them; nevertheless, it was without faith, because of the
hardness of their hearts.*

MORMON 3:12

It is important to remind ourselves that the blessings of eternity are
guaranteed for all who are faithful to the gospel of Jesus Christ,
regardless of their lineage. Furthermore, those blessings are withheld
from anyone who is disobedient and unfaithful, again regardless of
ancestry.

(Daniel H. Ludlow, *Selected Writings of Daniel H. Ludlow*
[Salt Lake City: Deseret Book, 2000], 533)

Daily Living

YOU MUST BE BELIEVING, ACT WITH FAITH, AND HAVE A HUMBLE HEART IN
ORDER TO RECEIVE THE BLESSINGS OF GOD.

- ☙ If you are righteous you are favored of the Lord—1 Nephi 17:35

- ☙ You are blessed if you give heed to the prophets—3 Nephi 12:1

- ☙ As you pay your tithes the windows of heaven are opened and
  shower forth blessings—3 Nephi 24:10

- ☙ Remember that blessings are predicated upon obedience to the
  law—D&C 130:21

A RIGHTEOUS DESIRE

And I would that I could persuade all ye ends of the earth to repent and prepare to stand before the judgment-seat of Christ.
MORMON 3:22

Our mission is to preach "Jesus Christ, and him crucified" (1 Cor. 2:2). Our mission is to proclaim the message of reconciliation to all men. Our mission also is to persuade men to forsake their sins, to "come unto Christ, and be perfected in him," and to deny themselves "of all ungodliness" (Moro. 10:32).

"How great the importance to make these things known unto the inhabitants of the earth, that they may know that there is no flesh that can dwell in the presence of God, save it be through the merits, and mercy, and grace of the Holy Messiah," and then only when they believe and obey his laws (2 Ne. 2:8).

(Bruce R. McConkie, *The Promised Messiah: The First Coming of Christ* [Salt Lake City: Deseret Book, 1978], 262)

Daily Living

SEEK TO BE LIKE MORMON, WHO CARED FOR THE SOULS OF ALL MANKIND.

- ෨ The mission of the prophets is to persuade all to come unto Christ—1 Nephi 6:4; 1 Nephi 19:18, 23

- ෨ The scriptures written to persuade all to believe in Christ—2 Nephi 25:23

- ෨ You are given to know good from evil—Moroni 7:16

YOUR DAY WAS KNOWN BY MORONI

Behold, I speak unto you as if ye were present, and yet ye are not. But behold, Jesus Christ hath shown you unto me, and I know your doing.
And I know that ye do walk in the pride of your hearts; and there are none save a few only who do not lift themselves up in the pride of their hearts, unto the wearing of very fine apparel, unto envying, and strifes, and malice, and persecutions, and all manner of iniquities; and your churches, yea, even every one, have become polluted because of the pride of your hearts.
MORMON 8:35–36

The Doctrine and Covenants tells us that the Book of Mormon is the "record of a fallen people" (D&C 20:9). Why did they fall? . . . Mormon gives the answer in the closing chapters of the book in these words: "Behold, the pride of this nation, or the people of the Nephites, hath proven their destruction" (Moro. 8:27). And then . . . the Lord warns us in the Doctrine and Covenants, "Beware of pride, lest ye become as the Nephites of old" (D&C 38:39).

(Ezra Taft Benson, "Beware of Pride," *Ensign,* May 1989, 4)

Daily Living

HEARKEN TO THE WORDS OF ONE CRYING FROM THE DUST.

- ๗ The pride of your heart can destroy your soul—Jacob 2:16

- ๗ Are you humbly prepared to meet God?—Alma 5:27

- ๗ Fast and pray to be firm in the faith and strong in humility—Helaman 3:35

- ๗ Remember it was the pride of the Nephites that brought their downfall—Moroni 8:27

FAILURE TO CALL UPON THE NAME OF LORD

And for the space of three hours did the Lord talk with the brother of Jared, and chastened him because he remembered not to call upon the name of the Lord.

ETHER 2:14

When God placed man on the earth, prayer became the lifeline between mankind and God. Thus, in Adams generation, men began "to call upon the name of the Lord" [Gen. 4:26]. Through all generations since that time, prayer has filled a very important human need. Each of us has problems that we cannot solve and weaknesses that we cannot conquer without reaching out through prayer to a higher source of strength. That source is the God of heaven to whom we pray in the name of Jesus Christ [see 2 Ne. 32:9; 3 Ne. 20:31]. As we pray we should think of our Father in Heaven as possessing all knowledge, understanding, love, and compassion.

(James E. Faust, "The Lifeline of Prayer,"
Ensign, May 2002, 59)

Daily Living

EXPRESS GRATITUDE AND COUNSEL WITH YOUR FATHER DAILY.

- ೮ Calling upon the Lord is more than just a simple prayer—2 Nephi 22:4

- ೮ When calling upon the Lord, be humble—Alma 13:28

- ೮ Call upon the Lord with all your might with real intent—Alma 19:24; 24:21

AUTHORS NOTE: CALLING UPON THE LORD IN PRAYER INVOLVES ASKING, THANKING, PRAISING, AND THEN DOING AND ENDURING—ACTING IN TRUE DISCIPLESHIP

FAITH TO DO ALL THINGS

*And I know, O Lord, that thou hast all power, and can do
whatsoever thou wilt for the benefit of man; therefore touch
these stones, O Lord, with thy finger, and prepare them that
they may shine forth in darkness; and they shall shine forth unto
us in the vessels which we have prepared, that we may have
light while we shall cross the sea.*

ETHER 3:4

If we have faith, which it is the privilege of all the Saints to have, can
we not exert a powerful influence among the nations of the earth for
our protection and salvation as a people? . . . We can, if we have faith
as we ought to have it, and have that oneness the President spoke of
this morning. If we have this, we can do all things, because faith is
mighty when concentrated in a oneness of action.

(Daniel H. Wells, in *Journal of Discourses,* 7:245)

Daily Living

THE LORD CAN DO ALL THINGS AS YOU EXERCISE FAITH AND ARE OBEDIENT.

- ଛ Your guilt can be swept away through faith on the Lord Jesus
  Christ—Enos 1:8

- ଛ The Lord will give you strength according to your faith—Alma
  14:26

- ଛ Both before and after Christ's mortal ministry, faith has
  wrought miracles and thinned the veil—Ether 12:11–30

- ଛ Exercise your faith do all things that are expedient to the Lord—
  Moroni 7:33

- ଛ With faith you can have the truth of all things manifested unto
  you—Moroni 10:4–5

POWER OF FAITH

And the Lord said unto him: Because of thy faith thou hast seen that I shall take upon me flesh and blood; and never has man come before me with such exceeding faith as thou hast; for were it not so ye could not have seen my finger. Sawest thou more than this?
ETHER 3:9

Motivating faith is centered in trust in the Lord and in His willingness to answer your needs. For "the Lord . . . doth bless and prosper those who put their trust in him" [Hel. 12:1; see also Prov. 3:5–6]. The consistent, willing exercise of faith increases your confidence and ability to employ the power of faith. . . .

With consistent practice, faith will become a vibrant, powerful, uplifting, inspiring force in your life. As you walk to the boundary of your understanding into the twilight of uncertainty, exercising faith, you will be led to find solutions you would not obtain otherwise

(Richard G. Scott, "The Sustaining Power of Faith in Times
of Uncertainty and Testing," *Ensign,* May 2003, 76–77)

Daily Living

BELIEVE THAT BY FAITH WE CAN DO ALL THINGS.

- ✌ You receive no witness until after the trial of your faith—Ether 12:6

- ✌ Miracles can only happen as you exercise your faith—Ether 12:12,16

- ✌ Be humble, exercising faith, and the Lord will strengthen and bless you—Ether 12:27

- ✌ Read the great chapters on faith—Hebrews 11; Alma 32; Ether 12; Moroni 7

RESULTS OF CONTENDING WITH THE WORD

*And he that will contend against the word of the Lord, let him be
accursed; and he that shall deny these things, let him be accursed;
for unto them will I show no greater things, saith Jesus Christ;*
ETHER 4:8

May we avoid contending with the word of God, and, more particularly, may we be free from contending against the words of his
apostles, for these legal administrators are the very channel of light
and truth through which salvation and eternal life will come to any
of us. The Council of the First Presidency and the Quorum of the
Twelve hold the keys to . . . the very covenant-making opportunities
that lead by our obedience to the sacred sanctification process and
to the perfections of Jesus Christ. Having these endowments of
power, we will then be able to allow the Lord to reveal his will to us
in any manner he chooses.

(Kenneth W. Anderson, "The Knowledge Hid Up Because
of Unbelief," in *Fourth Nephi through Moroni: From Zion to
Destruction,* ed. Monte S. Nyman and Charles D. Tate Jr.
[Provo, UT: Religious Studies Center, 1995], 43)

Daily Living

ONLY WITH A WILLING HEART CAN YOU EVER HOPE TO KNOW AND SEE THE
THINGS OF GOD.

- ౭ If you are pure in heart you will receive the pleasing word of
  God—Jacob 3:2

- ౭ Seek to prepare your heart to receive the word of God—Alma
  13:24; 16:16

- ౭ A hardened heart makes you unbelieving—Alma 16:17

- ౭ If your heart is hardened you receive a lesser portion of the
  word—Alma 1210–11

BLESSINGS OF BELIEVING

*But he that believeth these things which I have spoken, him will
I visit with the manifestations of my Spirit, and he shall know
and bear record.*
ETHER 4:11

We entered into covenants with the Lord that we will keep ourselves
pure and unspotted from the world. . . . We cannot neglect, slight,
or depart from the spirit, meaning, intent and purpose, of these
covenants and agreements, that we have entered into with our
Father in heaven, without shearing ourselves of our glory, strength,
right and title to His blessings, and to the gifts and manifestations
of His Spirit.

(N. B. Lundwall, *Temples of the Most High* [Salt Lake City:
Bookcraft 1993], 275–276)

Daily Living

WHEN YOU BELIEVE, YOU WILL BE BLESSED WITH THE SPIRIT; YOU WILL
KNOW THE TRUTH AND HAVE A DESIRE TO DO GOOD, WHICH IS ALWAYS A
SIGN OF THE SPIRIT.

- The Spirit will show you all things to do—2 Nephi 32:5
- The Spirit manifests itself to those who believe—Alma 7:17
- The Lord has promised the Holy Ghost to those who believe—3 Nephi 19:21–22
- As you keep the commandments you'll have the Spirit to be with you—Moroni 4:3; 5:2
- The Spirit manifests the truth of all things—Moroni 10:5
- When you trust in the Spirit you will have a desire to do good—D&C 11:12–13

GOOD COMETH OF GOD

And whatsoever thing persuadeth men to do good is of me; for good cometh of none save it be of me. I am the same that leadeth men to all good; he that will not believe my words will not believe me—that I am; and he that will not believe me will not believe the Father who sent me. For behold, I am the Father, I am the light, and the life, and the truth of the world."
ETHER 4:12

Parents must strengthen their homes and teach their loved ones to distinguish between Satan and our Savior. They must teach their loved ones that "all things which are good cometh of God; and that which is evil cometh of the devil; for the devil is an enemy unto God . . . and inviteth and enticeth to sin, and to do that which is evil continually" (Moroni 7:12).

(David B. Haight, *A Light unto the World* [Salt Lake City: Deseret Book, 1997], 157)

Daily Living

LET GOD PERSUADE, LEAD, AND INSPIRE YOU TO DO GOOD.

- ࢤ Remember whatsoever is good cometh of God—Alma 5:40

- ࢤ If you believe in God you will have hope which cometh of faith and you will abound in good works which will glorify God—Ether 12:4

- ࢤ Remember the devil inviteth and enticeth to do evil continually—Moroni 7:12

- ࢤ Everything which inviteth and enticeth to do good and to love God is inspired of God—Moroni 7:13

COMING FORTH OF THE BOOK OF MORMON

Therefore, when ye shall receive this record ye may know that the work of the Father has commenced upon all the face of the land.
ETHER 4:17

I suppose that this work of restoration among all nations, kindreds, tongues, and people, of which the coming forth of the Book of Mormon was the beginning, embraces activity on both sides of the veil, for the salvation of the race. St. Paul, certainly, had such an application in view, when he wrote to the Saints in Ephesus "That in the dispensation of the fulness of times"—and that is the times of which Nephi speaks—"he might gather together in one all things in Christ, both which are in heaven and which are on earth; even in him" (Eph. 1:10).

(George Reynolds and Janne M. Sjodahl, *Commentary on the Book of Mormon,* comp. Philip C. Reynolds [Salt Lake City: Deseret Book, 1955], 1:421)

Daily Living

WHEN THE BOOK OF MORMON CAME FORTH IT WAS A SIGN THAT THE FINAL DISPENSATION HAD STARTED—THESE ARE THE LAST DAYS.

- ℘ The coming forth of the Book of Mormon was prophesied—3 Nephi 21:1–7

- ℘ When the Book of Mormon comes forth you will know that Israel will be restored to their lands of their inheritance and the words of the Lord will be fulfilled—3 Nephi 29:1–2

- ℘ The Book of Mormon will shine forth out of the darkness—Mormon 8:16

- ℘ The Book of Mormon restored the fullness of the gospel—D&C 20:9; 42:12

LAW OF WITNESSES

*And in the mouth of three witnesses shall these things be
established; and the testimony of three, and this work, in the
which shall be shown forth the power of God and also his word,
of which the Father, and the Son, and the Holy Ghost bear
record—and all this shall stand as a testimony against the world
at the last day.*
ETHER 5:4

The law of witnesses has always been a part of the Lord's work on earth.
This law states that in the mouth of two or three witnesses shall every
word be established" (2 Cor. 13:1; see also Deut. 17:6; 19:15; Matt.
18:15–16; John 8:12–29). This witness confirms that certain events
took place and that God-given doctrine and principles are true.

(Loren C. Dunn, "Witnesses," *Ensign,* November 1995, 28)

Daily Living

TO ESTABLISH TRUTH THE LORD ALWAYS USES THE LAW OF WITNESSES.

- ‿ Out of the mouth of two or three witnesses everything shall be
  established—2 Cor. 13:1

- ‿ The Lord uses witnesses to establish His word—2 Nephi 11:3

- ‿ The testimony of many witnesses gives you hope and your faith
  can become unshaken—Jacob 4:6

- ‿ You are to stand as a witness as well—Mosiah 18:9

- ‿ A continual stream of witnesses testify of all things—Alma
  34:30

THE POWER OF REMEMBERING

And there were no more wars in the days of Shule; and he remembered the great things that the Lord had done for his fathers in bringing them across the great deep into the promised land; wherefore he did execute judgment in righteousness all his days.
ETHER 7:27

As you start to write, you could ask yourself, "How did God bless me today?" If you do that long enough and with faith, you will find yourself remembering blessings. And sometimes, you will have gifts brought to your mind which you failed to notice during the day, but which you will then know were a touch of God's hand in your life.
(Henry B. Eyring, "Remembrance and Gratitude," *Ensign,* November 1989, 13)

Daily Living

WHEN YOU REMEMBER THE GOODNESS OF GOD YOU ARE FILLED WITH.

- ৪৩ Remember the great knowledge the Lord has given you—2 Nephi 10:20

- ৪৩ Remember how the Lord has preserved and delivered His people—Mosiah 27:16

- ৪৩ Remember the Lord has delivered His servants out of their afflictions—Alma 62:50

- ৪৩ You will be humbled as you remember the great things the Lord has done—Ether 6:30

- ৪৩ As you remember the goodness and greatness of God you will have more power of righteousness—Ether 7:27

APATHY TOWARD SIN RESULTS IN DESTRUCTION

And they [secret combinations] have caused the destruction of this people [Jaredites] of whom I am now speaking, and also the destruction of the people of Nephi.
ETHER 8:21

Lawmaking bodies will listen to effectively organized citizens. However, too often the trend is tragically toward citizen apathy and a sense of futility.

And who is to blame? We could conveniently point the accusing finger at public prosecutors who are not vigorously enforcing the law. But we need men and women of courage and conviction in these offices of public trust if the awful tide is to be stemmed.

(David B. Haight, "Personal Morality," *Ensign,* November 1984, 71)

Daily Living

APATHY TOWARD POLITICAL INVOLVEMENT WILL LEAD TO DESTRUCTION OF THE INDIVIDUAL, THE FAMILY, AND THE COMMUNITY.

- When there are strict laws and discipline, you will have peace in the land—Alma 1:33
- Don't be lulled away with carnal security by the devil—2 Nephi 28:21
- Awake and arouse your faculties and be involved in righteousness—Jacob 3:11
- Be sensitive to others and never turn your back on the poor and needy—Alma 5:55
- Now is the time to prepare to meet God; don't procrastinate—Alma 34:32–33
- Remember the Lord rewards your diligence and not your slothfulness—Alma 37:41

AWAKE AND BE INVOLVED

Wherefore, the Lord commandeth you, when ye shall see these things come among you that ye shall awake to a sense of your awful situation, because of this secret combination which shall be among you; or wo be unto it, because of the blood of them who have been slain; for they cry from the dust for vengeance upon it, and also upon those who built it up.
ETHER 8:24

Improve your community by active participation and service. Remember in your civic responsibility that "the only thing necessary for the triumph of evil is for good men to do nothing" (Edmund Burke, in George Seldes, comp., *The Great Thoughts* [New York: Ballantine Books, 1985], 60). Do something meaningful in defense of your God-given freedom and liberty.

(Ezra Taft Benson, "To the Single Adult Brethren of the Church," *Ensign,* May 1988, 51)

Daily Living

EACH DISCIPLE OF CHRIST SHOULD DO ALL THEY CAN TO FIGHT EVIL AND PERSUADE OTHERS TO DO GOOD.

- ဢ You are accountable to do your best for the people you serve—Jacob 1:19

- ဢ You are responsible to magnify your office—Jacob 2:2

- ဢ Help others awaken to the sense of their duties—Alma 7:22

- ဢ Seek to feel like Alma that you might help others come unto Christ—Alma 29:9–10

- ဢ In spite of hardheartedness, you must still do all you can—Moroni 9:6

HEARKEN TO THE VOICE OF THE LORD

And they hearkened not unto the voice of the Lord, because of their wicked combinations; wherefore, there began to be wars and contentions in all the land, and also many famines and pestilences, insomuch that there was a great destruction, such an one as never had been known upon the face of the earth; and all this came to pass in the days of Shiblom.

ETHER 11:7

The blessings of the gospel are universal, and so is the formula for peace: keep the commandments of God. War and conflict are the result of wickedness; peace is the product of righteousness.

(Dallin H. Oaks, "World Peace," *Ensign,* May 1990, 72)

Daily Living

YOU MUST DO ALL IN YOUR POWER TO RESIST EVIL AND FOLLOW THE VOICE OF THE LORD.

- ࢒ If you hearken to the Lord He shall manifest Himself in word, power, and deed—1 Nephi 14:1

- ࢒ Hearken to the word of God and be protected from the adversary—1 Nephi 15:24

- ࢒ When you don't hearken to the Lord and His words the result is contention—Mosiah 7:25

- ࢒ When you don't hearken to the voice of the Lord you cannot be redeemed—Mosiah 16:2

- ࢒ If you hearken to the voice of the Lord you bring forth good works—Alma 5:41

- ࢒ If you hearken not unto the Lord you will be as salt that has lost its savor—3 Nephi 16:15

PLEADINGS OF A PROPHET

For he did cry from the morning, even until the going down of the sun, exhorting the people to believe in God unto repentance lest they should be destroyed, saying unto them that by faith all things are fulfilled.

ETHER 12:3

I plead with men everywhere to "Come, listen to a prophet's voice" and hear the word of God from our living prophet who sits with us here today. I know he is God's recognized prophet. I beg of you to listen and act, in the name of Jesus Christ. Amen.

(Spencer W. Kimball, Conference Report, October 1961, 34)

Daily Living

YOU MUST REPENT AND ACT WITH FAITH IN THE LORD JESUS CHRIST

  The prophets preach and teach faith and repentance—Mosiah 18:7; 25:22

  Remember that salvation cometh only through repentance and faith on the Lord Jesus Christ—Mosiah 3:12

  Mercy can satisfy the demands of justice—Alma 34:15–17

  The prophets admonished those who would preach to teach repentance and faith, to be humble and to withstand temptation with their faith—Alma 37:33

  The teachings of the prophets had a great effect upon those who listened—Helaman 15:7

  Prophets are bold in proclaiming the gospel of repentance—3 Nephi 7:16

BELIEVE IN GOD

Wherefore, whoso believeth in God might with surety hope for a better world, yea, even a place at the right hand of God, which hope cometh of faith, maketh an anchor to the souls of men, which would make them sure and steadfast, always abounding in good works, being led to glorify God.

ETHER 12:4

In the Book of Mormon, in which we find many answers and so much direction in solving problems, there is a scripture that, to me, sheds great light on the matter of a positive, trusting, hopeful attitude of faith as a substitute for facing life's problems with discouragement and despair. Listen to the words of the prophet Ether . . . : "By faith all things are fulfilled—Wherefore, whoso believeth in God might with surety hope for a better world, yea, even a place at the right hand of God, which hope cometh of faith" (Ether 12:3–4).

(Paul H. Dunn, "By Faith and Hope, All Things Are Fulfilled," *Ensign,* May 1987, 74)

Daily Living

FAITH IN GOD EMPOWERS US TO GOOD WORKS AND RIGHTEOUSNESS.

- ༂ Press forward with steadfastness and a perfect brightness of hope—2 Nephi 31:20

- ༂ By searching the words of the prophets your faith becomes unshaken—Jacob 4:6

- ༂ The Comforter even the Holy Ghost filleth you with hope—Moroni 8:26

- ༂ Faith, hope, and charity are necessary for salvation—Moroni 10:20–22

FAITH . . . A DEFINITION

And now, I, Moroni, would speak somewhat concerning these things; I would show unto the world that faith is things which are hoped for and not seen; wherefore, dispute not because ye see not, for ye receive no witness until after the trial of your faith.
ETHER 12:6

Only through our faith can we heed God's counsel to "choose ye this day, whom ye will serve" [Alma 30:8]—"to serve the Lord God who made you" [Moses 6:36]. And only through a trial of our faith can we receive the miraculous blessings we seek for ourselves and our families. "For if there be no faith among the children of men God can do no miracle among them; wherefore, he showed not himself until after their faith" [Ether 12:12].

(Robert D. Hales, "Couple Missionaries: Blessings from Sacrifice and Service," *Ensign,* May 2005, 39)

Daily Living

AS WE EXERCISE THIS FAITH WE WILL GAIN A SURE WITNESS.

- ଚ Exercise your faith as you seek the Lord with lowliness of heart—1 Nephi 2:19

- ଚ Through faith you can receive the power of the Holy Ghost—1 Nephi 10:17

- ଚ Miracles, signs, and wonders come according to your faith—2 Nephi 26:13

- ଚ You can be forgiven and your guilt swept away as you exercise faith—Enos 1:8

- ଚ Your heart can be changed through faith on the Lord Jesus Christ—Mosiah 5:7

- ଚ You can be healed according to your faith—3 Nephi 17:8

GAINING HOPE

Wherefore, ye may also have hope, and be partakers of the gift,
if ye will but have faith.
ETHER 12:9

That kind of redeeming faith, Mormon taught, leads to hope, a special, theological kind of hope. The word is often used to express the most general of aspirations-wishes, if you will. But as used in the Book of Mormon it is very specific and flows naturally from one's faith in Christ. "How is it that ye can attain unto faith, save ye shall [as a consequence] have hope?" Mormon asked [Moroni 7:40]. This is the same faith-leads-to-hope sequence that Moroni used, saying, "Ye may also have hope . . . if ye will but have faith" [Ether 12:9].

(Jeffrey R. Holland, *Christ and the New Covenant: The Messianic Message of the Book of Mormon* [Salt Lake City: Deseret Book, 1997], 334)

Daily Living

AS YOU EXERCISE THIS FAITH YOU CAN ENJOY HOPE, THUS BEING ABLE TO PARTAKE OF THESE HEAVENLY BLESSINGS.

- ❧ Your hope increases as you feast upon the word of God from the prophets and scriptures—Jacob 4:6

- ❧ With faith in the Lord you can have hope of eternal life—Alma 13:29; 25:16

- ❧ Repent, call upon the Lord in humility and you can receive hope—Alma 22:16

- ❧ As you are meek and lowly you have hope through the Atonement—Moroni 7:41–43

FAITH PRECEDES MIRACLES

For if there be no faith among the children of men God can do
no miracle among them; wherefore, he showed not himself until
after their faith.
ETHER 12:12

Miracles are the fruit of faith. Signs follow those who believe. If
there is faith, there will be miracles; if there are no miracles, there is
no faith. The two are inseparably intertwined with each other; they
cannot be separated, and there cannot be one without the other.
Faith and miracles go together, always and everlastingly. And faith
precedes the miracle.

(Bruce R. McConkie, *The Mortal Messiah: From Bethlehem*
to Calvary [Salt Lake City: Deseret Book, 1981],
2:286–287)

Daily Living

DILIGENTLY EXERCISE THE POWER OF FAITH THE BLESSINGS SO THE MIRACLES
OF GOD CAN BE MADE MANIFEST IN YOUR LIFE.

- ❧ Miracles, signs, and wonders are wrought according to your
  faith—2 Nephi 26:13; Alma 37:40

- ❧ Remember that God is a God of miracles according to your
  faith—2 Nephi 27:23

- ❧ When there is unbelief the Lord cannot show so great of miracles—3 Nephi 19:35

- ❧ Remember that all miracles can only be done in the name of
  Jesus Christ—4 Nephi 1:5

EXERCISE FAITH

Behold, it was the faith of Nephi and Lehi that wrought the change upon the Lamanites, that they were baptized with fire and with the Holy Ghost.
ETHER 12:14

How can we build this faith? Through our actions. We must "go and do the things which the Lord hath commanded," [1 Ne. 3:7] just as Nephi counseled. We must trust in the Lord with all our hearts, as my mother so lovingly taught me. Gratefully, many times when we exercise faith to do the Lord's will, we find that we are richly blessed for our obedience.

(David E. Sorensen, "Faith Is the Answer," *Ensign,* May 2005, 73)

Daily Living

YOU CAN BRING GREAT BLESSINGS TO OTHERS AS YOU EXERCISE YOUR FAITH.

- ঙ You receive direction from the Lord according to your faith—1 Nephi 16:28–29

- ঙ As you pray for others with faith they shall be blessed—2 Nephi 33:3; Mosiah 27:14

- ঙ Enos set a good example in praying for others—Enos 1:11–12, 18

- ঙ You can work mighty miracles for your fellow beings through faith—Mosiah 8:18

- ঙ You can bring forth good works according to your faith—Alma 26:22

MIRACLES THROUGH FAITH

Behold, it was the faith of Ammon and his brethren which wrought so great a miracle among the Lamanites. Yea, and even all they who wrought miracles wrought them by faith, even those who were before Christ and also those who were after.

ETHER 12:15–16

My young beloved brethren, I pray that each of us, through our faith, will use our priesthood power to work mighty miracles through sharing the gospel and serving others, thereby becoming a great benefit to our fellow beings, in the name of Jesus Christ, amen.

(Spencer J. Condie, "Becoming a Great Benefit to Our Fellow Beings," *Ensign,* May 2002, 46)

Daily Living

SEEK EARNESTLY FOR THE BEST GIFTS THROUGH FAITH.

- Miracles, signs, and wonders come according to your faith—2 Nephi 26:13
- You can work mighty miracles for your fellow beings through faith—Mosiah 8:18
- The gifts of the Spirit to heal and perform miracles can be yours—D&C 46:20–21

STRENGTH IN HUMILITY

And if men come unto me I will show unto them their weakness.
I give unto men weakness that they may be humble; and my
grace is sufficient for all men that humble themselves before me;
for if they humble themselves before me, and have faith in me,
then will I make weak things become strong unto them.
ETHER 12:27

We should even give thanks for our afflictions because they turn our hearts to God and give us opportunities to prepare for what God would have us become. . . . In the midst of the persecutions the Latter-day Saints were suffering in Missouri, the Lord gave a . . . promise: "Verily I say unto you my friends, fear not, let your hearts be comforted; yea, rejoice evermore, and in everything give thanks; . . . and all things wherewith you have been afflicted shall work together for your good" (D&C 98:1, 3). And to Joseph Smith in the afflictions of Liberty Jail, the Lord said, "Know thou, my son, that all these things shall give thee experience, and shall be for thy good" (D&C 122:7).

(Dallin H. Oaks, "Give Thanks in All Things,"
Ensign, May 2003, 96)

Daily Living

SEEK TO BE HUMBLE AND TEACHABLE IN YOUR WEAKNESSES.

- ଚ Fast and pray for faith and humility—Helaman 3:35
- ଚ In the strength of the Lord you can do all things—Alma 20:4
- ଚ Remember to always call upon the Lord for your strength—Moses 1:20

LOVE OF CHRIST

And again, I remember that thou hast said that thou hast loved the world, even unto the laying down of thy life for the world, that thou mightest take it again to prepare a place for the children of men.
And now I know that this love which thou hast had for the children of men is charity; wherefore, except men shall have charity they cannot inherit that place which thou hast prepared in the mansions of thy Father.
ETHER 12:33–34

The final and crowning virtue of the divine character is charity, or the pure love of Christ (see Moroni 7:47). If we would truly seek to be more like our Savior and Master, then learning to love as He loves should be our highest goal. Mormon called charity "the greatest of all" (Moro. 7:46).

(Ezra Taft Benson, "Godly Characteristics of the Master,"
Ensign, November 1986, 47)

Daily Living
SEEK TO HAVE THIS KIND OF PERFECT LOVE.

- ๛ The Savior doeth nothing save it be a benefit for you—2 Nephi 26:24

- ๛ Like Nephi have charity for all people—2 Nephi 33:7–9

- ๛ Charity has the ultimate attributes of Christ and you should pray with all the energy of your heart to be filled with charity—Moroni 7:44–48

- ๛ Without faith, hope and charity you cannot saved in the kingdom of God—Moroni 10:21

DECEMBER

&

*My beloved son, Moroni, I rejoice
exceedingly that your Lord Jesus Christ
hath been mindful of you, and hath
called you to his ministry, and to
his holy work.*

—MORONI 8:2

SACRAMENTAL PRAYER

O God, the Eternal Father, we ask thee in the name of thy Son,
Jesus Christ, to bless and sanctify this bread to the souls of all
those who partake of it; that they may eat in remembrance of
the body of thy Son, and witness unto thee, O God, the Eternal
Father, that they are willing to take upon them the name of thy
Son, and always remember him, and keep his commandments
which he hath given them, that they may always have his Spirit
to be with them. Amen.

MORONI 4:3 (SEE ALSO 5:2)

As we sincerely listen to the sacrament prayers, phrases such as "always remember him," "keep his commandments," "have his Spirit to be with them" will fill our hearts with an overwhelming desire to be better (see D&C 20:77, 79). Then when we partake of the bread and the water with a broken heart and a contrite spirit, I know we can feel and even hear those most wondrous words "I love you. I love you."

(John H. Groberg, "The Power of God's Love," *Ensign,*
November 2004, 10)

Daily Living

IF YOU ALWAYS REMEMBER HIM, TAKE HIS NAME UPON YOU, AND KEEP HIS COMMANDMENTS YOU WILL ALWAYS HAVE HIS SPIRIT TO BE WITH YOU.

- ℘ You partake of the sacrament that you will always remember— 3 Nephi 18:7

- ℘ Renew your covenants by partaking of the sacrament regularly— 3 Nephi 26:13

- ℘ Be worthy of the sacrament, walking in holiness before God— D&C 20:68–69

QUALIFICATIONS FOR BAPTISM

*Neither did they receive any unto baptism save they came forth
with a broken heart and a contrite spirit, and witnessed unto
the church that they truly repented of all their sins.
And none were received unto baptism save they took upon them the
name of Christ, having a determination to serve him to the end.*
MORONI 6:2–3

As qualifications for baptism into the Church, I will read to you a
paragraph from the Doctrine and Covenants as follows:
"And again, by way of commandment to the Church concerning the
manner of baptism—All those who humble themselves before God . . .
and truly manifest by their works that they have received of the Spirit
of Christ unto the remission of their sins, shall be received by baptism
into the Church" [D&C 20:37].

(George F. Richards, in Conference Report,
October 1924, 39)

Daily Living

RENEW YOUR BAPTISMAL COVENANTS EACH WEEK
BY TAKING THE SACRAMENT.

- ಐ Baptism is an essential ordinance in order to be saved—3 Nephi
11:33

- ಐ To apply the Atonement you must repent and be baptized—
3 Nephi 27:20–21

- ಐ You promise to stand as a witness at all times and places—
Mosiah 18:8–9

- ಐ As you repent and are baptized you are born again—Alma 7:14

- ಐ Be worthy of baptism and of partaking the sacrament—Mormon
9:29

SUPPORTING NEW CONVERTS

And after they had been received unto baptism . . . their names were taken, that they might be remembered and nourished by the good word of God, to keep them in the right way, to keep them continually watchful unto prayer, relying alone upon the merits of Christ, who was the author and the finisher of their faith.

MORONI 6:4

It is not an easy thing to become a member of this Church. In most cases it involves setting aside old habits, leaving old friends and associations, and stepping into a new society which is different and somewhat demanding. With the ever-increasing number of converts, we must make an increasingly substantial effort to assist them as they find their way. Every one of them needs three things: a friend, a responsibility, and nurturing with "the good word of God" (Moro. 6:4). . . . I am hopeful that a great effort will go forward throughout the Church, throughout the world, to retain every convert who comes into the Church.

(Gordon B. Hinckley, "Every Convert Is Precious," *Liahona,* February 1999, 9)

Daily Living

BE EVER CONCERNED WITH HELPING THE NEW CONVERT OR STRUGGLING SAINT.

- ක As a disciple of Christ you should show forth love one to another—John 13:34–35

- ක The word of God for it has the greatest power to change lives—Alma 31:5

- ක All who hold to the word of God can be protected—1 Nephi 15:24; Helaman 3:29

- ක Fast and pray for all those who know not God—Alma 6:6

MEETINGS

And the church did meet together oft, to fast and to pray, and to
speak one with another concerning the welfare of their souls.
And they did meet together oft to partake of bread and wine, in
remembrance of the Lord Jesus.
Moroni 6:5–6

We have experienced another great conference. What remarkable meetings these are. What a great purpose they serve. We gather together in a spirit of worship and with a desire to learn. We renew our relationships as members of this large family of Latter-day Saints who live in many lands, who speak a variety of languages, who come out of difficult cultures, who even look different. And we recognize that we are all one, each a son or daughter of our Father in Heaven.

(Gordon B. Hinckley, "Closing Remarks," *Ensign,*
November 2004, 104)

Daily Living

Utilize meetings to assist you as well as others in growing spiritually. Sacrament meeting in particular is important for renewing your covenants.

- As a church we are to meet together oft—3 Nephi 18:22

- The Church meets together oft to ensure that everyone is doing their duty—D&C 20:55

- When you conduct or take part in a meeting you have a great responsibility—D&C 43:8–10

REPENTANCE AND FORGIVENESS

But as oft as they repented and sought forgiveness, with real intent, they were forgiven.
MORONI 6:8

Many of you are already on this track, and we commend you for your worthiness and determination. For those of you who are not, let tonight be the beginning of your preparation process. If you find yourself wanting in worthiness, resolve to make the appropriate changes—beginning right now. If you think you need to talk to your father and your bishop about any sins you may have committed, don't wait; do it now. They will help you to repent and change so you can take your place as a member of the greatest generation of missionaries.

(M. Russell Ballard, "The Greatest Generation of Missionaries," *Ensign,* November 2002, 47–48)

Daily Living

BEGIN TODAY. START ANEW BY AVAILING YOURSELF OF THE BLESSINGS OF THE ATONEMENT.

෨ If you confess and repent of your sins the Lord will forgive you—Mosiah 26:29

෨ You can be forgiven only as you forgive—D&C 13:14

෨ Your greatest joy can be in helping others repent—Alma 29:9–10; 36:24; D&C 15:6; 18:10–16

෨ Once you forsake your sins the Lord remembers them no more—D&C 58:42–43

CONDUCTING MEETINGS

*And their meetings were conducted by the church after the manner
of the workings of the Spirit, and by the power of the Holy
Ghost; for as the power of the Holy Ghost led them whether to
preach, or to exhort, or to pray, or to supplicate, or to sing, even
so it was done.*
MORONI 6:9

True, we may systematically perform many of the tasks that are
assigned us such as—teach a Sunday School or priesthood lesson,
prepare reports, conduct a meeting—but unless our spirit is in tune
and we speak, teach, and act under the direction of the Holy Spirit,
we accomplish little of an eternal value.

(H. Burke Peterson, "Purify Our Minds and Spirits,"
Ensign, November 1980, 39)

Daily Living

SEEK THE INSPIRATION OF THE HOLY GHOST, FOR HE WILL TELL YOU ALL
THINGS TO DO. THIS CAN BE IN ADVANCE AS WELL AS SPONTANEOUS.

- ❧ The Spirit will show you all things to do—2 Nephi 32:5

- ❧ Teaching requires the Spirit—D&C 42:14

- ❧ All preaching and teaching requires both the teacher and the
  hearer to have the Spirit of truth and thus both can be edified—
  D&C 50:17–22

- ❧ Treasure up the word and it shall be given to you in the very
  hour you need it—D&C 84:85

PEACEABLE FOLLOWERS OF CHRIST

Wherefore, I would speak unto you that are of the church, that are the peaceable followers of Christ, and that have obtained a sufficient hope by which ye can enter into the rest of the Lord, from this time henceforth until ye shall rest with him in heaven.
MORONI 7:3

Missionaries return home with a love for the people they have served and taught. They are true ambassadors spreading goodwill for the peoples in whose countries they have lived and worked. They are not concerned with income levels and have no racial bias. They are not out to build any worldly kingdoms. They are, in the words of Mormon, "the peaceable followers of Christ" (Moro. 7:3). The only kingdom which interests them is the kingdom of our Lord and Savior which He will establish at His return. Their only hope is to prepare us for that great day.

(L. Tom Perry, "The Peaceable Followers of Christ," *Ensign,* November 1989, 71)

Daily Living

AS DISCIPLES YOU SEEK TO FOLLOW CHRIST.

- ಬ Follow the Savior with full purpose of heart—2 Nephi 31:13

- ಬ As a disciple you have the responsibility to be a light to the world—3 Nephi 12:16; 15:12

- ಬ As a disciple hopefully you will declare His word—3 Nephi 5:13

- ಬ Remember that disciples of Christ love one another—John 13:34–35

- ಬ Learn of me, and listen to my words—D&C 19:23

KNOWN BY YOUR WORKS

For I remember the word of God which saith by their works ye shall know them; for if their works be good, then they are good also.
MORONI 7:5

True saints are known by their works! There neither is nor can be any other standard of judgment. "By their fruits ye shall know them" (Matt. 7:20). Unless and until they do the works of righteousness they are members of the Church in name only, and the gospel is not a living thing in their lives. And so too are the ungodly known by their works; until they do good and love their fellowmen, they are "not of God."

(Bruce R. McConkie, *Doctrinal New Testament Commentary*
[Salt Lake City: Bookcraft, 1965–1973], 3:387–388)

Daily Living

WHEN YOU DO GOOD WORKS YOU REFLECT THE GOODNESS OF GOD IN YOUR LIFE.

- ℰ By your fruits you will be known—3 Nephi 14:20
- ℰ Let your light shine that others may glorify your Father in Heaven—3 Nephi 12:16
- ℰ You will be judged by your works—Mosiah 3:24
- ℰ Be steadfast and immovable always abounding in good works—Mosiah 5:15
- ℰ When you do good works you hearken to the voice of the good Shepherd—Alma 5:41
- ℰ With faith and hope you will always abound in good works—Ether 12:4

PURE MOTIVES

*For behold, God hath said a man being evil cannot do that
which is good; for if he offereth a gift, or prayeth unto God,
except he shall do it with real intent it profiteth him nothing.*
MORONI 7:6

Love is the purification of the heart. It strengthens character and
gives a higher motive and a positive aim to every action of life. The
power to love truly and devotedly is the noblest gift with which a
human being can be endowed. True love is eternal and infinite. It is
equal and pure without violent actions and demonstrations which
are so much in evidence today.

(Delbert L. Stapley, Conference Report, October 1970, 45)

Daily Living

SEEK TO SERVE WITH AN EYE SINGLE TO THE GLORY OF GOD.

- Do things with an eye single to the glory of God—Mormon
  8:15; D&C 88:67

- Remember that Heavenly Father and our Savior are always
  motivated by love—John 3:16; 2 Nephi 26:24

- Seek to have a desire for the welfare of others—Enos 1:9;
  Mosiah 28:3

- Do not do your alms to be seen of men—3 Nephi 13:1

THE MEASURE OF GOOD

Wherefore, all things which are good cometh of God; and that which is evil cometh of the devil; for the devil is an enemy unto God, and fighteth against him continually, and inviteth and enticeth to sin, and to do that which is evil continually. But behold, that which is of God inviteth and enticeth to do good continually; wherefore, every thing which inviteth and enticeth to do good, and to love God, and to serve him, is inspired of God.
MORONI 7:12–13

His Spirit will not lead us to do anything that is evil but will encourage us to do good, and by following that persuasion and by maintaining that guidance, we will grow in nearness to the Lord; we will grow in good deeds; and we will overcome the flesh. A man who has the companionship of the Spirit of the Lord is a happy man. He can be a thoughtful and faithful patriarch and leader in his home and family; he is a good neighbor.

(Joseph Anderson, "Being Anxiously Engaged," *Ensign,* May 1978, 69)

Daily Living

SEEK AFTER THAT WHICH IS LOVELY, PRAISEWORTHY OR OF GOOD REPORT.

ဢ   You will have a desire to do good continually with this mighty change—Mosiah 5:2

ဢ   As you hearken to the word of God you will bring forth good works—Alma 5:40–41

ဢ   When you do good you work by the power and gifts of God—Moroni 10:25

JUDGING GOOD AND EVIL

For behold, the Spirit of Christ is given to every man, that he may know good from evil; wherefore, I show unto you the way to judge; for every thing which inviteth to do good, and to persuade to believe in Christ, is sent forth by the power and gift of Christ
MORONI 7:16

I say, all the revelations of God teach simply this. . . . I have caused you to come upon this earth, where misery, and darkness, and every species of unbelief and wickedness reign, to prove you, that you may understand and know the good from the evil, and be capable of judging between these with a righteous judgment.

(Brigham Young, in *Journal of Discourses,* 6:284–285)

Daily Living

SEEK THOSE THINGS THAT INVITE YOU TO DO GOOD OR PERSUADE YOU TO BELIEVE IN CHRIST.

- ❧ Trust in the Spirit; it will help you judge righteously—D&C 11:12

- ❧ You are accountable and have been instructed sufficiently—2 Nephi 2:5

- ❧ The scriptures are written to persuade you to come unto Christ—1 Nephi 6:4; 19:23

- ❧ The prophets persuade you to remember the Lord your Redeemer—1 Nephi 19:18

- ❧ The prophet's labor diligently to teach you to become reconciled to God—2 Nephi 25:23; Jacob 1:7–8

FAITH COMES BY HEARING THE WORD

Wherefore, by the ministering of angels, and by every word which proceeded forth out of the mouth of God, men began to exercise faith in Christ; and thus by faith, they did lay hold upon every good thing; and thus it was until the coming of Christ.
MORONI 7:25

Stated simply, true conversion is the fruit of faith, repentance, and consistent obedience. Faith comes by hearing the word of God. [see Rom. 10:17; Joseph F. Smith, *Gospel Doctrine,* 5th ed. (1939), 99] and responding to it. You will receive from the Holy Ghost a confirming witness of things you accept on faith by willingly doing them [see Ether 12:6]. You will be led to repent of errors resulting from wrong things done or right things not done. As a consequence, your capacity to consistently obey will be strengthened.
(Richard G. Scott, "Full Conversion Brings Happiness,"
Ensign, May 2002, 25)

Daily Living

BY HEARKENING TO THE WORD OF GOD YOUR FAITH WILL INCREASE AND
YOU WILL DO GOOD.

- ❧ With exceeding faith and good works you are called to serve—Alma 13:3

- ❧ As you exercise faith you will bring forth good works—Alma 26:22

- ❧ When you plant the word in your heart it swelleth and beginneth to grow—Alma 32:30

- ❧ If you are humble you can withstand the temptations of the devil—Alma 37:33

- ❧ Your faith will make you sure and steadfast—Ether 12:4

POWER OF CHRIST IN YOUR LIFE

For he hath answered the ends of the law, and he claimeth all those who have faith in him; and they who have faith in him will cleave unto every good thing; wherefore he advocateth the cause of the children of men; and he dwelleth eternally in the heavens.
MORONI 7:28

The Lord has said, "Whom I love I also chasten that their sins may be forgiven, for with the chastisement I prepare a way for their deliverance" [D&C 95:1]. The Lord loves each one of us. He wants us to be happy. This happiness comes by our faith in Jesus Christ, by our sincere and true repentance, by our obedience to His commandments, and by our endurance to the end. . . .

If we daily exercise faith, meekness, charity, and lowliness in heart, confessing that Jesus is the Christ, and accepting His Atonement, we will be blessed with the strength and hope to face and overcome the trials and pains of this life.

(Adhemar Damiani, "Be of Good Cheer and Faithful in Adversity," *Ensign,* May 2005, 95–96)

Daily Living

THE LORD RECEIVES YOU AS YOU EXERCISE YOUR FAITH IN HIM, AS YOU CLEAVE TO RIGHTEOUSNESS.

∞ Christ's Atonement prepares the way for you—Alma 22:14

∞ You are redeemed through repentance and faith—Mosiah 18:7, 20; Alma 9:27

∞ Exercise faith in the redemption of the Lord—Alma 5:15

∞ Mercy will satisfy the demands of justice—Alma 34:16–17

FAITH—ACCORDING TO THE WILL OF GOD

And Christ hath said: If ye will have faith in me ye shall have
power to do whatsoever thing is expedient in me.
MORONI 7:33

That the disciples by faith—for by faith all things are possible and nothing is too hard for the Lord—can do among men what their Master had done is self-evident. The same measure of faith always has borne and always will bear the same fruit. But what of the greater works? Are the disciples to surpass the mighty miracles of their Lord? Yes—in eternity! No ministry shall ever equal his on earth, but that ministry was only a small foretaste of the miraculous powers to be wielded by all the faithful in the oncoming ages yet to be.

(Bruce R. McConkie, *The Mortal Messiah: From Bethlehem*
to Calvary [Salt Lake City: Deseret Book, 1981], 4:73)

Daily Living

WHEN YOU LIVE BY THE SPIRIT YOUR FAITH WILL BE ACCORDING TO HIS WILL AND YOU CAN DO ALL THINGS; ABOVE ALL YOU WILL BE MOVED TO REPENTANCE.

- ৶ Repent in faith and make the Atonement efficacious in your life—Alma 34:14–17

- ৶ The power of God was manifest through the faith of the 2000 stripling warriors—Alma 57:26–27

- ৶ The righteousness of the Lamanite converts was expressed in their faith—Helaman 15:9–10

- ৶ You can do all things that are expedient in the Lord through faith—Moroni 10:23

POWER OF FAITH

For no man can be saved, according to the words of Christ, save they shall have faith in his name; wherefore, if these things have ceased, then has faith ceased also; and awful is the state of man, for they are as though there had been no redemption made.

MORONI 7:38

Are men then to be saved by works? Nay, verily, by grace are ye saved thro' faith, and that not of yourselves, it is the gift of God (Eph. ii, 8). Not of works, lest any man should boast (v. 9). Not by works of righteousness which we have done, but according to his mercy he saved us (Titus iii, 5), and yet faith without works is dead being alone, (James ii, 17).

(Brigham Young and Willard Richards, "Concluded," in *Times and Seasons* 2 [November 1840–October 1841]: 541)

Daily Living

YOU ARE SAVED THROUGH FAITH, BECAUSE FAITH INITIATES THE GRACE OF GOD AND MOVES YOU TO ACTION AND GOOD WORKS.

- ⟡ Remember there is power in faith to do all things—2 Nephi 1:10

- ⟡ You must have perfect faith or you cannot be saved—2 Nephi 9:23

- ⟡ Your faith moves you to action and good works—James 2:18

- ⟡ Faith is the power that motives you to repent and be forgiven—Enos 1:8; Alma 34:15–17

- ⟡ You are saved by faith in the name of the Lord and all things asked with faith, which is good, will be done unto you—Moroni 7:26

FAITH AND HOPE WORK TOGETHER

And again, my beloved brethren, I would speak unto you concerning hope. How is it that ye can attain unto faith, save ye shall have hope?
Wherefore, if a man have faith he must needs have hope; for without faith there cannot be any hope.
MORONI 7:40, 42

As I read and ponder the scriptures, I see that developing faith, hope, and charity within ourselves is a step-by-step process. Faith begets hope, and together they foster charity. We read in Moroni, "Wherefore, there must be faith; and if there must be faith there must also be hope; and if there must be hope there must also be charity." These three virtues may be sequential initially, but once obtained, they become interdependent. Each one is incomplete without the others. They support and reinforce each other.

(Joseph B. Wirthlin, "Cultivating Divine Attributes,"
Ensign, November 1998, 26)

Daily Living

FAITH AND HOPE WORK TOGETHER UNTIL EVENTUALLY YOU ARE FILLED
WITH CHARITY.

෨ With faith you have hope of eternal life—Alma 13:29

෨ Pray with faith believing you shall receive hope—Alma 22:16

෨ You retain your hope through faith—Alma 25:16

෨ Hope comes of faith and makes an anchor for your soul—Ether 12:4

෨ Faith, hope and charity are integrally connected—Moroni 10:22

ATTRIBUTES OF CHARITY

*And charity suffereth long, and is kind, and envieth not, and is not
puffed up, seeketh not her own, is not easily provoked, thinketh
no evil, and rejoiceth not in iniquity but rejoiceth in the truth,
beareth all things, believeth all things, hopeth all things,
endureth all things.*
MORONI 7:45

To partake fully of the tree of life is thus to be given the nature of
Christ. Those so blessed as to receive this bestowal of the Savior's
own character and attributes are filled with charity, because charity
is central to the divine nature. The totality of the blessing, however,
is complete, sanctified perfection: "Yea, come unto Christ, and be
perfected in him. . . . Then are ye sanctified in Christ by the grace
of God" (Moroni 10:32–33).

(Bruce C. Hafen, *The Broken Heart: Applying the
Atonement to Life's Experiences* (Salt Lake City:
DeseretBook, 1989), 196)

Daily Living

CHARITY IS PATIENCE, KINDNESS, HUMILITY, GOOD THOUGHTS, REJOICING
IN RIGHTEOUSNESS, AND BEING ABLE TO HOPE AND ENDURE ALL THINGS.
CHARITY ALSO LACKS ENVY AND IS SLOW TO ANGER.

- ∞ The Lord has commanded everyone to have charity, else you are
  nothing—2 Nephi 26:30

- ∞ Charity combined with faith and hope will help you abound in
  good works—Alma 7:24

- ∞ The process of obtaining charity—2 Peter 1:3–10; D&C 4:6

- ∞ Righteousness is obtained with faith, hope and charity—Ether
  12:28

CHARITY NEVER FAILETH

Wherefore, my beloved brethren, if ye have not charity, ye are
nothing, for charity never faileth. Wherefore, cleave unto charity,
which is the greatest of all, for all things must fail—
But charity is the pure love of Christ, and it endureth forever.
MORONI 7:46–47

The greater definition of "the pure love of Christ," however, is not what we as Christians try but largely fail to demonstrate toward others but rather what Christ totally succeeded in demonstrating toward us. True charity has been known only once. It is shown perfectly and purely in Christ's unfailing, ultimate, and atoning love for us. It is Christ's love for us that "suffereth long, and is kind, and envieth not." It is his love for us that is not "puffed up . . . , not easily provoked, thinketh no evil." It is Christ's love for us that "beareth all things, believeth all things, hopeth all things, endureth all things."

(Jeffrey R. Holland, *Christ and the New Covenant: The*
Messianic Message of the Book of Mormon [Salt Lake City:
Deseret Book, 1997], 336)

Daily Living

REALIZE THAT HE IS ALWAYS THERE TO NURTURE AND BLESS HIS CHILDREN.

- ∞ Charity edifieth the souls—1 Corinthians 8:1

- ∞ If you can do all things and have not charity you are nothing—1 Corinthians 13:2–3

- ∞ All your actions should be done with charity—1 Corinthians 16:14

- ∞ Remember, with faith, hope, and charity you will abound in good works—Alma 7:24

OBTAINING CHARITY

Wherefore, my beloved brethren, pray unto the Father with all the energy of heart, that ye may be filled with this love, which he hath bestowed upon all who are true followers of his Son, Jesus Christ; that ye may become the sons of God; that when he shall appear we shall be like him, for we shall see him as he is; that we may have this hope; that we may be purified even as he is pure. Amen.

MORONI 7:48

As I have thought about this passage and its meaning in my life, I have found two other parts that speak deeply to me. One is the commandment to "cleave unto charity," and the other is the promise that, if we are endowed with charity, "we shall be like" Jesus Christ when he appears, for we "may be purified even as he is pure" (Moroni 7:46, 48).

(Chieko N. Okazaki, *Lighten Up!* [Salt Lake City: Deseret Book, 1993], 118)

Daily Living

FAST AND PRAY WITH ALL THE ENERGY OF YOUR SOUL THAT YOU MIGHT POSSESS CHARITY, THAT WHEN CHRIST APPEARS YOU WILL BE LIKE HIM.

- ɞ Charity comes of a pure heart, a good conscience, and faith unfeigned—1 Timothy 1:5

- ɞ Seek to possess charity for it will cover a multitude of sins—1 Peter 4:8

- ɞ The process of obtaining—2 Peter 1:3–10; D&C 4:6

- ɞ Clothe yourself with charity—D&C 88:125

LOVE AND JOY OF A FATHER

My beloved son, Moroni, I rejoice exceedingly that your Lord Jesus Christ hath been mindful of you, and hath called you to his ministry, and to his holy work.
I am mindful of you always in my prayers, continually praying unto God the Father in the name of his Holy Child, Jesus, that he, through his infinite goodness and grace, will keep you through the endurance of faith on his name to the end.
MORONI 8:2–3

May the virtue of your children's lives sanctify and hallow your old age. May you be led to exclaim with gratitude as did John, "I have no greater joy than to hear that my children walk in truth" (3 Jn. 1:4). For this I pray, and pray most earnestly, in the sacred name of Jesus Christ, amen.

(Gordon B. Hinckley, "Your Greatest Challenge, Mother,"
Ensign, November 2000, 100)

Daily Living

AS PARENTS, YOUR DESIRE, GOAL, AND PRAYER IS FOR EACH CHILD'S HAPPINESS.

ñ Happy is the parent that knows their child walks in the truth— 3 John 1:4

ñ The joy and responsibility as a parent is to teach your children— 1 Nephi 1:1

ñ Teach children to what source they may look for the remission of sins—2 Nephi 25:26

ñ Pray for struggling children in faith—Mosiah 27:14

AUTHORS NOTE: A WAYWARD CHILD IS NOT A FAILING PARENT.
IT IS ONLY WHEN YOU GIVE UP THAT YOU FAIL.

GOD IS CARING AND PERFECT

But little children are alive in Christ, even from the foundation of the world; if not so, God is a partial God, and also a changeable God, and a respecter to persons; for how many little children have died without baptism!
MORONI 8:12

The good habits of a child's early training form the foundation for his future and sustain him in his later life. Parents, remember the Lord by revelation has given assurance that little children are incapable of committing sin, that they are alive in Christ, and that the devil has no power over them until they reach the age of accountability. The first eight years of a child's life are golden years the Lord has given parents to teach and train their children to form good habits and develop noble characters.

(Delbert L. Stapley, "Good Habits Develop Good
Character," *Ensign,* November 1974, 20)

Daily Living

CHILDREN ARE ALIVE IN CHRIST. HE IS NO RESPECTER OF PERSONS; WE
ARE ALL EQUALLY IMPORTANT IN HIS SIGHT.

᠍ Remember that God is the same yesterday, today, and forever—
2 Nephi 29:9

᠍ Children are blessed through the Atonement of Jesus Christ—
Mosiah 3:16

᠍ Children are alive in Christ and need no repentance or baptism—
Moroni 8:11

᠍ Children who die before the years of accountability are saved—
D&C 137:10

REMISSION OF SINS

And the remission of sins bringeth meekness, and lowliness of heart; and . . . the visitation of the Holy Ghost, which Comforter filleth with hope and perfect love.
MORONI 8:26

The cultivation of this daily attitude of a meek and lowly heart following our baptism is "for the sake of retaining a remission of your sins from day to day, that ye may walk guiltless before God" (Mosiah 4:26). And "if ye do this ye shall always rejoice, and be filled with the love of God" (Mosiah 4:12). This describes, in its highest sense, the moment-to-moment conscientiousness of a good mother or father, or any child of God.

(Bruce C. Hafen and Marie K. Hafen, *The Belonging Heart: The Atonement and Relationships with God and Family* [Salt Lake City: Deseret Book, 1994], 97–98)

Daily Living

WHEN YOU REPENT, YOU ARE MEEK AND LOWLY AND THUS ABLE TO RECEIVE THE HOLY GHOST, WHICH WILL FILL YOU WITH HOPE AND PERFECT LOVE.

- Our Savior Jesus Christ is the source you look to for remission of your sins—2 Nephi 26:25

- You must exercise faith to receive the remission of your sins—Enos 1:2–8

- God's love makes the remission of sins possible in your life—Mosiah 4:11–12

- Come humbly and receive the Holy Ghost and the remission of sins—3 Nephi 12:3

LABOR WITHOUT CEASING

And now, my beloved son, notwithstanding their hardness, let us
labor diligently; for if we should cease to labor, we should be
brought under condemnation; for we have a labor to perform
whilst in this tabernacle of clay, that we may conquer the enemy
of all righteousness, and rest our souls in the kingdom of God.
MORONI 9:6

How different the world would be if there were not those greatest and
most beloved of men, our prophets and apostles . . . who labor tire-
lessly and without ceasing in our behalf. Those glorious holders of the
priesthood have put behind themselves all personal agendas, . . . all
worldly titles and vestments, and have subjugated themselves totally
to the priesthood. They epitomize through their service the Savior's
admonition that the greatest shall be servant to the least.

(Beverly Campbell, *Eve and the Choice Made in Eden* [Salt
Lake City: Deseret Book, 2003], 144)

Daily Living

REGARDLESS OF THE RECEPTION OF THOSE YOU SEEK TO HELP, YOU MUST
BE DILIGENT IN YOUR LABORS. ONE NEVER KNOWS WHEN SOMEONE WILL
RETURN TO FULL FELLOWSHIP.

- ᖇ You shall be blessed when you labor with unwearyingness—
  Helaman 10:4–5

- ᖇ Pray for success to bring struggling souls to Christ—Alma
  31:34–35

- ᖇ Show your love for others by caring for the welfare of their
  souls—Mosiah 25:11; 28:3

- ᖇ When people struggle remind them of the goodness of God—
  1 Nephi 7:8–13

REMEMBER CHRIST AND HIS PROMISES

*My son, be faithful in Christ; and may not the things which I
have written grieve thee, to weigh thee down unto death; but
may Christ lift thee up, and may his sufferings and death . . .
and his mercy and long-suffering, and the hope of his glory and
of eternal life, rest in your mind forever.*
MORONI 9:25

Alma had this broad reach of the Atonement in mind when he wrote
that Christ would "go forth, suffering pains and afflictions and temptations of every kind; and this that the word might be fulfilled which saith
he will take upon him the pains and the sicknesses of his people. And
he will . . . take upon him their infirmities, that his bowels may be filled
with mercy, according to the flesh, that he may know according to the
flesh how to succor his people according to their infirmities" (Alma
7:11; Alma 7:11–12).

(Bruce C. Hafen and Marie K. Hafen, *The Belonging Heart:
The Atonement and Relationships with God and Family* [Salt
Lake City: Deseret Book, 1994], 151)

Daily Living

NEVER FORGET THE NURTURING POWER OF CHRIST IN YOUR LIVES, ESPECIALLY
IN YOUR TRIALS.

ↂ The Lord will nurture you and help through temptations—
1 Nephi 15:24; Helaman 3:29

ↂ The Lord suffered all things and knows how to nurture and
succor you—Alma 7:11–12

ↂ Have a good attitude during your trials receive strength from
the Lord—Alma 62:41

ↂ Remember you are given weaknesses that you might be humble—
Ether 12:27

PONDER THE POWER OF THE SCRIPTURES

*Behold, I would exhort you that when ye shall read these things,
if it be wisdom in God that ye should read them, that ye would
remember how merciful the Lord hath been unto the children of
men, from the creation of Adam even down until the time that
ye shall receive these things, and ponder it in your hearts.*
MORONI 10:3

When your testimony sags or appears to stumble along the way, why
not remember the goodness of the Lord? In the process of positive
recall, perhaps you can experience the spiritual healing that King
Lamoni and his father expressed. How exhilarating it is to ponder
the merciful nature of God, and how healing it is to remember the
eternal gifts of Christ!

(Carlos E. Asay, *Family Pecan Trees: Planting a Legacy of
Faith at Home* [Salt Lake City: Deseret Book, 1992], 90)

Daily Living

PONDERING THE WORD OF GOD, AND REMEMBERING THE GOODNESS AND
MERCY OF GOD IN YOUR LIFE, WILL FILL YOUR HEART WITH GRATITUDE—A
WONDERFUL CHRISTMAS PRESENT TO YOU FROM THE LORD.

- ಏ Delight in the scriptures and ponder them in your heart—2 Nephi
  4:15–16

- ಏ Ponder with a desire and belief that the Lord will make things
  known—1 Nephi 11:1

- ಏ The Lord encourages you to ponder His word that you may
  understand—3 Nephi 17:3

- ಏ Ponder the scriptures; your understanding will open—D&C
  138:1, 11

ASK GOD

If ye shall ask with a sincere heart, with real intent, having faith in Christ, he will manifest the truth of it unto you, by the power of the Holy Ghost.
And by the power of the Holy Ghost ye may know the truth of all things.
MORONI 10:4–5

As we sincerely pray to the Lord and rely upon his divine whisperings, that still, small voice will come to us. (See Hel. 5:30.) We will receive a peace, knowing that God has answered our prayers. Remember the peace that Oliver received. These spiritual embers can grow into a flame of testimony. (See Hel. 5:45.) . . .

Surely the Lord would not ask us to pray if he did not intend to answer our prayers. "He is a rewarder of them that diligently seek him" (Heb. 11:6).

(Robert K. Dellenbach, "Hour of Conversion," *Ensign,*
November 1990, 23–24)

Daily Living

PRAY WITH FAITH, SEEKING TO UNDERSTAND THE LORD'S WILL.

- ෨ Remember the Holy Ghost will show you all things to do—
  2 Nephi 32:5

- ෨ You can know that Jesus is the Christ by the power of the Holy Ghost—Moroni 10:7

- ෨ Fast and pray to know the things of God and the Holy Spirit will manifest them unto you—Alma 5:46

- ෨ When you fast and pray you can have the spirit of revelation and teach with the power and authority of God—Alma 17:2–3

GIFTS OF THE SPIRIT

*And I would exhort you, my beloved brethren, that ye remember
that every good gift cometh of Christ.
And I would exhort you, my beloved brethren, that ye remember
that he is the same yesterday, today, and forever, and that all
these gifts of which I have spoken, which are spiritual, never
will be done away, even as long as the world shall stand, only
according to the unbelief of the children of men.*
MORONI 10:18–19

Also, we need to use more fully the gifts of the Spirit, all of which
operate through faith. These gifts are available to us today. Even the
ultimate power—to raise the dead—is occasionally exercised by
those of great faith. The sick are healed, the blind see, the lame walk,
and evil spirits are cast out—from those possessed—all through
faith and priesthood power in combination. I feel we do not enjoy
enough spiritual gifts in our priesthood callings.

(John K. Carmack, "Faith Yields Priesthood Power,"
Ensign, May 1993, 43)

Daily Living

GOD IS NO RESPECTER OF PERSONS. HE SEEKS TO BLESS ALL HIS CHILDREN
ACCORDING TO THEIR FAITH.

- ༂ Remember to stir up the gift that is within you—2 Timothy 1:6
- ༂ There are many and diversified gifts of the Spirit—Moroni 10:9–17
- ༂ Remember that every gift comes by the Spirit of Christ—Moroni 10:17

SAVED THROUGH FAITH, HOPE, AND CHARITY

Wherefore, there must be faith; and if there must be faith there must also be hope; and if there must be hope there must also be charity.
And except ye have charity ye can in nowise be saved in the kingdom of God; neither can ye be saved in the kingdom of God if ye have not faith; neither can ye if ye have no hope.
MORONI 10:20–21

To be purified is to become literally a new creature in Christ, to die as to the old person that we were, literally to become of the heart and mind of our new father. The scriptures promise great rewards for those who qualify and take this step. The scriptural name for this new heart is "charity." Charity is to have a heart that loves with the pure love of Christ. Without that charity, we are literally nothing.

(Chauncey C. Riddle, "The New and Everlasting Covenant," in *Doctrines for Exaltation: The 1989 Sperry Symposium on the Doctrine and Covenants,* comp. Susan Easton Black [Salt Lake City: Deseret Book, 1989], 237)

Daily Living

WITHOUT FAITH, HOPE, AND CHARITY YOU CANNOT BE SAVED. WITHOUT HOPE YOU WILL BE IN DESPAIR BECAUSE OF YOUR INIQUITY.

   ⅚ With faith, hope and charity you can come to Christ—Ether 12:28

   ⅚ Remember the process of obtaining—2 Peter 1:3–10; D&C 4:6

   ⅚ Pray with all the energy of your heart that you may be filled with charity—Moroni 7:48

DO ALL THINGS

And Christ truly said unto our fathers: If ye have faith ye can do all things which are expedient unto me.
MORONI 10:23

How important it is that every individual member should through prayer and faith obtain an unfaltering testimony of the gospel and so conduct his life that faith may grow stronger day by day, doing nothing to displease the Lord, that his Spirit may not withdraw from him. If this were an accomplished fact, the knowledge of God would grow in the earth and the time of the Lord's second coming would be greatly hastened. As stated by Moroni, quoting the words of Christ, "If ye have faith, you can do all things which are expedient unto me."

(Joseph Anderson, *Prophets I Have Known* [Salt Lake City: Deseret Book, 1973], 240)

Daily Living

CULTIVATE A STRONG AND ABIDING FAITH IN THE SON OF GOD.

- ❧ If you believe, greater things will be made manifest unto you— 3 Nephi 26:9

- ❧ With faith, you shall have power to do whatsoever is expedient in Him—Moroni 7:33

- ❧ Exercising faith you can receive the Holy Ghost which can show you all things to do—1 Nephi 10:17; 2 Nephi 32:5

- ❧ When you become so righteous the Lord will give you whatever you ask—Helaman 10:5

PERFECTION

*Yea, come unto Christ, and be perfected in him, and deny
yourselves of all ungodliness; and if ye shall deny yourselves of
all ungodliness, and love God with all your might, mind and
strength, then is his grace sufficient for you, that by his grace ye
may be perfect in Christ; and if by the grace of God ye are perfect
in Christ, ye can in nowise deny the power of God.*

MORONI 10:32

The prophetic call through all ages has been, "Come unto Christ,
and be perfected in him" (Moroni 10:32; see also Matthew 5:48;
John 10:10; 14:6), that salvation is through the Only Begotten Son
of the Father (see John 1:14, 18; D&C 29:42). The call is universal
and applies to all of God's children, whether African, Asian,
European, or any other nationality. As the Apostle Paul declared to
the Athenians, all of us "are the offspring of God" (Acts 17:29).

(Merrill J. Bateman, "A Pattern for All," *Ensign,*
November 2005, 74)

Daily Living

YOU CAN BE PERFECTED IN CHRIST AS YOU DENY ALL UNGODLINESS.

- ଚ Just people live by faith and they are the ones that will be made
  perfect—D&C 76:69

- ଚ It is by grace that you are saved after all you can do—2 Nephi
  25:23

- ଚ To deny all ungodliness means to abhor all evil—John 14:15

- ଚ When you keep the commandments and hold out faithful to
  the end you are received into heaven and into a state of never
  ending happiness—Mosiah 2:41

GRACE OF GOD

And again, if ye by the grace of God are perfect in Christ, and deny not his power, then are ye sanctified in Christ by the grace of God, through the shedding of the blood of Christ, which is in the covenant of the Father unto the remission of your sins, that ye become holy, without spot.

MORONI 10:33

Indeed, one of the specific expressions of sanctifying grace in mortality is the spiritual endowment of "hope," which grants us a new inner sight that allows us to cope with our natural imperfections with a sense of serenity and optimism.

Other specific manifestations in mortality of the perfecting grace of Christ in the process of sanctification include the gift of charity, the overcoming of evil desires, and the blessings of peace and understanding.

(Bruce C. Hafen, *The Broken Heart: Applying the Atonement to Life's Experiences* [Salt Lake City: Deseret Book, 1989], 167–168)

Daily Living

BY THE GRACE OF GOD YOU MAY BECOME SANCTIFIED—CLEAN AND PURE.

- ෨ We return to presence of God only by His merits, mercy, and grace—2 Nephi 2:8

- ෨ There could be no resurrection save it be by the mercy and grace of God—2 Nephi 9:8

- ෨ Remember, it is by grace that you are saved after all you can do—2 Nephi 25:23

- ෨ Your meekness and humility can help you receive the grace of God—Ether 12:26–27

Index

About the Authors

ED J. PINEGAR

Ed J. Pinegar is a retired dentist and long-time teacher of early-morning seminary and religion classes at Brigham Young University. He taught at the Joseph Smith Academy and has served as a mission president in England and at the Missionary Training Center in Provo, Utah. He has been a bishop twice and a stake president and is a temple sealer. Ed and his wife, Patricia, are the parents of eight children. He and his wife are currently serving a full-time mission.

RICHARD J. ALLEN

Richard J. Allen is a husband, father, teacher, and writer. He has served on several high councils, in several stake presidencies, and as a bishop. Richard's teaching assignments in the Church have included service as a full-time missionary, instructor in various priesthood quorums, Gospel Doctrine teacher, and stake institute director. He has served as a faculty member at both Brigham Young University and the Johns Hopkins University. Richard has coauthored many articles, manuals, and books and has served on a number of national educational boards. He and his wife, Carol Lynn Hansen Allen, have four children and five grandchildren.